Lessons from Exceptional Language Learners Who Have Achieved Nativelike Proficiency

PSYCHOLOGY OF LANGUAGE LEARNING AND TEACHING

Series Editors: **Sarah Mercer**, *Universität Graz, Austria* and **Stephen Ryan**, *Waseda University, Japan*

This international, interdisciplinary book series explores the exciting, emerging field of Psychology of Language Learning and Teaching. It is a series that aims to bring together works which address a diverse range of psychological constructs from a multitude of empirical and theoretical perspectives, but always with a clear focus on their applications within the domain of language learning and teaching. The field is one that integrates various areas of research that have been traditionally discussed as distinct entities, such as motivation, identity, beliefs, strategies and self-regulation, and it also explores other less familiar concepts for a language education audience, such as emotions, the self and positive psychology approaches. In theoretical terms, the new field represents a dynamic interface between psychology and foreign language education and books in the series draw on work from diverse branches of psychology, while remaining determinedly focused on their pedagogic value. In methodological terms, sociocultural and complexity perspectives have drawn attention to the relationships between individuals and their social worlds, leading to a field now marked by methodological pluralism. In view of this, books encompassing quantitative, qualitative and mixed methods studies are all welcomed.

All books in this series are externally peer-reviewed.

Full details of all the books in this series and of all our other publications can be found on http://www.multilingual-matters.com, or by writing to Multilingual Matters, St Nicholas House, 31-34 High Street, Bristol, BS1 2AW, UK.

PSYCHOLOGY OF LANGUAGE LEARNING AND TEACHING: 18

Lessons from Exceptional Language Learners Who Have Achieved Nativelike Proficiency

Motivation, Cognition and Identity

Zoltán Dörnyei and
Katarina Mentzelopoulos

MULTILINGUAL MATTERS
Bristol • Jackson

DOI https://doi.org/10.21832/DORNYE2453
Library of Congress Cataloging in Publication Data
A catalog record for this book is available from the Library of Congress.
Names: Dörnyei, Zoltán, author. | Mentzelopoulos, Katarina, author.
Title: Lessons from Exceptional Language Learners Who Have Achieved
    Nativelike Proficiency: Motivation, Cognition and Identity/
    Zoltán Dörnyei and Katarina Mentzelopoulos.
Description: Bristol; Jackson: Multilingual Matters, [2022] |
    Series: Psychology of Language Learning and Teaching: 18 |
    Includes bibliographical references and index. | Summary: "This book
    opens a narrative window into the experiences of learners who achieve
    nativelike proficiency and offers insights into their pathways to success.
    Tying together themes of motivation, cognition and identity, the authors
    explore how these learners became so successful and whether their success
    can be repeated by others"—Provided by publisher.
Identifiers: LCCN 2022028458 (print) | LCCN 2022028459 (ebook) |
    ISBN 9781800412453 (hardback) | ISBN 9781800412446 (paperback) |
    ISBN 9781800412460 (pdf) | ISBN 9781800412477 (epub)
Subjects: LCSH: Second language acquisition—Psychological aspects. |
    Motivation in education. | Identity (Psychology)
Classification: LCC P118.2 .D59 2022 (print) | LCC P118.2 (ebook) |
    DDC 401/.93019—dc23/eng/20220705
LC record available at https://lccn.loc.gov/2022028458
LC ebook record available at https://lccn.loc.gov/2022028459

British Library Cataloguing in Publication Data
A catalogue entry for this book is available from the British Library.

ISBN-13: 978-1-80041-245-3 (hbk)
ISBN-13: 978-1-80041-244-6 (pbk)

Multilingual Matters
UK: St Nicholas House, 31-34 High Street, Bristol, BS1 2AW, UK.
USA: Ingram, Jackson, TN, USA.

Website: www.multilingual-matters.com
Twitter: Multi_Ling_Mat
Facebook: https://www.facebook.com/multilingualmatters
Blog: www.channelviewpublications.wordpress.com

Copyright © 2023 Zoltán Dörnyei and Katarina Mentzelopoulos.

All rights reserved. No part of this work may be reproduced in any form or by any means without permission in writing from the publisher.

The policy of Multilingual Matters/Channel View Publications is to use papers that are natural, renewable and recyclable products, made from wood grown in sustainable forests. In the manufacturing process of our books, and to further support our policy, preference is given to printers that have FSC and PEFC Chain of Custody certification. The FSC and/or PEFC logos will appear on those books where full certification has been granted to the printer concerned.

Typeset by Deanta Global Publishing Services, Chennai, India.

Contents

Acknowledgements	viii
In Memory	ix
Introduction	xi
A. Three Surprises and Two Warnings	xii
B. Our Selection Criteria: The Duck Test	xiv
C. A Matter of Interest	xv
D. This Book and Its Companion Volume	xvi
1 Theoretical Background	1
1.1 Past Studies Examining Exceptional Learners	2
1.2 Studies on Research Topics Related to Exceptional Learners	9
1.3 Summary	20
2 Methodology: Identifying Participants and Documenting Their Stories	21
2.1 Participants	21
2.2 Research Approach	27
2.3 Data Collection and Analysis	27
3 Defining Nativelikeness	30
3.1 The Native Speaker as a Concept	30
3.2 Native-Speakerism and Linguistic Discrimination	31
3.3 Nativelikeness as a Research Interest	33
3.4 Our Participants' Perceptions of 'Passing' as a Native Speaker	35
3.5 A Phenomenological Approach to Nativeness and Nativelikeness	39
3.6 Summary	41
4 A Favourable Set-Up	43
4.1 Resource Access and the 'New Global Generation'	44
4.2 Family Influences and the Impact of Early Childhood Experiences	46

	4.3	Social Expectations	49
	4.4	Favourable Conditions are Not Indispensable for Success	50
	4.5	Discussion and Some Lessons to Draw	52
5	A Unique Bond with the Chosen Language		55
	5.1	Rewarding Contact with the L2 Community	55
	5.2	Attraction towards the L2 Culture and Cultural Products	58
	5.3	Pragmatic Benefits of L2 Proficiency	60
	5.4	Attraction towards Specific Aspects of the L2	61
	5.5	Discussion and Some Lessons to Draw	64
6	Cognition and Other Facilitative Learner Characteristics		66
	6.1	Cognitive Endowment: Language Aptitude and Other Learning-Specific Factors	66
	6.2	Personality Factors	76
	6.3	Motivational Factors	81
	6.4	Discussion and Some Lessons to Draw	85
7	Attention to Pronunciation		91
	7.1	Triggers of Attention to Pronunciation	92
	7.2	Developing a Nativelike Accent	97
	7.3	The Flip Side of Good Pronunciation	100
	7.4	Discussion and Some Lessons to Draw	102
8	Intensive Effort and Strategic Learning		105
	8.1	Absorbing the Language Naturally	105
	8.2	Exerting Effort	107
	8.3	Strategic Learning	109
	8.4	Effort That Did Not Feel Like Effort	112
	8.5	Discussion and Some Lessons to Draw	113
9	Reinforcing Relationships and Social Expectations		115
	9.1	Family Members	117
	9.2	The Language Teacher	118
	9.3	Friendships	119
	9.4	Significant Others and Spouses	120
	9.5	Other Role Models	121
	9.6	The Workplace	122
	9.7	The L2 Community	124
	9.8	Discussion and Some Lessons to Draw	125
10	Sources of Persistence		127
	10.1	High-Octane Fuel: A Self-Concordant Vision	130
	10.2	Fuel Economy: Habitual Actions	131
	10.3	Fuel Regeneration: Progress Checks and Positive Feedback	133

	10.4 Additional Fuel: Positive Emotionality and Passion	136
	10.5 Breakdown Cover: Self-Control Skills and Capacity	138
	10.6 Discussion and Some Lessons to Draw	140
11	Second Language Confidence, Comfort and Ownership	142
	11.1 Confidence	143
	11.2 A Comfortable L2 Voice	146
	11.3 Ownership of the L2	148
	11.4 Discussion and Some Lessons to Draw	151
12	The Question of L2 Identities	154
	12.1 The Fusion of Language Expertise and Personal Identity	156
	12.2 A Separation of L1 and L2 Identities?	159
	12.3 Identity Erasure and Resistance to Mislabelling	162
	12.4 Family-Related and Professional Identities	165
	12.5 Discussion and Some Lessons to Draw	167
Conclusion		169
Appendix		175
References		177
Index		189

Acknowledgements

This book would not have been possible without the generous contribution of our 30 wonderful research participants. Thank you so much for your incredible enthusiasm for languages and cultures, as well as for your willingness to share with us and our readers so much of your learning history! You have been an inspiration to us, and we do hope that we have done your stories the justice they deserve. Special thanks are due to Capucine Trotignon, who was not only one of the 'Excellent Thirty', but who also helped us with processing our interview data, finalising the structure of this book and editing the stories that make up the companion volume, *Stories from Exceptional Learners Who Have Achieved Nativelike Proficiency* – you have been a fantastic asset to the team!

In Memory

Originally, I wanted to leave this book manuscript exactly as it was, exactly as Zoltán had last left it, without having to mar it with the memory that he is no longer here with us. Going back through the pages, I can hear his voice in every sentence, and it feels as though we are back in 2020/2021 having one of our hundreds of video chats about this project. But in the end, I would like to share some of my memories of him in the hopes that we continue to remember the incredible person behind the research.

I first met Zoltán while I was completing an MA in Applied Linguistics at the University of Nottingham in 2019. He convened the research methods module in the autumn with a fervour one does not usually find attached to that particular subject. As a result, our class soon developed a warm and lively group dynamic as Zoltán patiently held our hands through the struggles of SPSS and interview analysis. He was kind and passionate, and his enthusiasm was magnetic. He led his classes with an impressive amount of patience, but most of all he brought a youthful energy and curiosity to the table that left us all eager to come back the following week. Feeling encouraged, I visited Zoltán's office hours several times throughout the semester. Much like he did during class, he patiently listened to all of my questions, directing me here and there for extra reading, fomenting my own enthusiasm wherever he could. We soon developed a good rapport, and at the end of term, he asked rhetorically, 'You're taking my motivation module in the spring?' In fact, I was not; I had never really considered motivation as a research topic before. But Zoltán gave me this disapproving look, shook his head and said, 'You should take my motivation module.' Reflecting back on the excitement he brought to our research methods class, I decided that the convenor trumped the content and switched my enrolment. His question that day turned out to be the launching point of my interest and passion for research in language learner psychology, leading me to ask him to be my PhD supervisor in October 2020.

It was a few weeks after this that Zoltán first approached me with the idea for *Lessons* and *Stories*. Following that, we had meetings frequently and many more emails in between, and steadily we began to weave the threads of our project together. In our discussions, Zoltán's honesty was one of my favourites of his qualities, and it carried us through the genesis and development of this duology. He was kind as can be, but he was also very quick to interject with a frank, 'I disagree.' Conversely, it also meant that when he gave positive feedback, you knew that he meant it. Zoltán was like that: he was never afraid to tell you exactly what he thought about something, and he seldom beat around the bush. Yet right next to that honesty were also the respect he held for everyone and an openness to changing his mind. He might have been bluntly honest when he disagreed, but I found that if I did my research and persisted with more robust arguments, he would often change his mind. I came to enjoy our debates and discussions, knowing that it was our *joint* reasoning and knowledge that led us to a confluence. These are qualities not stereotypically associated with professionals as established and senior as Zoltán, and yet somehow there he was!

Still, even as the project grew, particularly in time consumption and stress inducement, Zoltán never forgot the person behind the researcher. Every meeting, he would ask how I was and genuinely want to know the answer. He was there, always training our eyes on the picture of how far we had come, even when all Capucine and I could see was how far we had to go. We talked about all manner of topics beyond this project, from Italian dialects to our respective immigrant identities and the best new pizza place in town. We laughed over our DNA ancestries, and he shook his head sympathetically at my lockdown complaints of north-facing windows. Together, we brought Multilingual Matters and 30 wonderful individuals on board with us, and a bit more than a year after we began, we had two finished manuscripts in hand.

Originally, this project was called *Attaining the Ultimate* as a play on words from the term 'ultimate attainment'. I was initially disappointed that my dad joke of a title did not make the cut, but thinking back on it now, it was the right decision. The 'ultimate' in ultimate attainment means 'final' or 'end state', but this project was always about the *process*: the process of exceptional language learning. It turns out that for me it was also about the process of the project itself – of getting to know Zoltán and to learn from him. He was kind and passionate, honest and open to new ideas, but most of all he was generous: generous with his time, with his thoughts, with his faith and encouragement. From the project's beginnings to its completion and onwards, Zoltán was the most steadfast and joyful research companion and mentor that one could ask for. So even though we are now at the 'end state' that we never envisioned and that we wish had never happened, I will always hold that process dear to me. May he rest in peace, and may his memory live on.

Katarina Mentzelopoulos
2022/09/10

Introduction

There are two exceptional achievements in the area of language learning: becoming a 'polyglot' (i.e. learning six or more languages) and mastering a foreign language at a 'nativelike' or 'near-native' level in ordinary circumstances (i.e. without any heritage background or extensive periods in a second language [L2] environment before adulthood). The former learners excel in maximising the number of languages they master, whereas the latter maximise their level of mastery in usually only one additional language. Becoming a polyglot is indeed admirable, and people tend to respect the zeal and enormous learning capacity of those extraordinary learners who do reach this unique status. However, this is primarily attractive only to a niche community because quite frankly, not many people are drawn to becoming multilingual to such an extensive degree, nor do they have much use for speaking that many languages. The other big L2 learning achievement – becoming 'nativelike' – is very different in this respect, as it involves a common goal that millions of people set for themselves every year upon beginning to learn a foreign language. It is thus rooted in a widespread human desire, and therefore what makes this achievement exceptional is not the unique nature of the motivation underlying it but rather the unfortunate fact that the vast majority of learners do not reach this initial target. This begs the question of how the few who arrive at this final destination manage to do so at all.

The idea for this book originated in a task Zoltán designed for his students at the University of Nottingham when he moved his course, the Psychology of Bilingualism and Language Learning, online due to the COVID-19 pandemic. He asked course participants to look for and share L2 learning success stories on an online bulletin board (Padlet), focusing on adult learners who managed to 'beat the odds', that is, who successfully achieved nativelike L2 proficiency in otherwise ordinary circumstances. To Zoltán's delight, not only did many of his students succeed in identifying such gifted learners among their family members and extended circle of friends, but it turned out that some students themselves qualified for membership in this elite, 'nativelike' group. Moreover, the stories they shared were fascinating, inspiring and ultimately irresistible, offering unique insights and quirky emphases that further sparked our curiosity. This gave us the idea for the current book, which summarises the lessons we can gain from the autobiographical life narratives of such gifted learners, and subsequently for its companion volume, *Stories from Exceptional Language Learners Who Have Achieved Nativelike Proficiency*, which presents a compendium of the actual success stories that we have gathered.

A. Three Surprises and Two Warnings

The 'fairy-tale-like' origin of this book does not, of course, tell the full story of how the present content came to fruition. During the process of planning and writing the material, we came across three surprises, which in turn warrant two preliminary warnings. The first surprise was that there have been virtually no systematic compilations and analyses of developmental life stories from this unique population of learners; as we will see in Chapter 1, existing investigations in this area have usually involved in-depth case studies or group-level performance analysis by means of statistical methods. Fortunately, we were delighted that the very recent publication of a theoretical summary of past research, *The Gifted Language Learner* by Alene Moyer (2021), became available in time for us to draw on it, indicating that attention to the subject appears to be surfacing. The success stories of the learners upon which our study has focused constitute a treasure trove that, when properly unearthed, has great potential to enrich this new research direction.

The second surprise was that even the limited existing scholarly research on exceptional learners has been *imbalanced*. It is true that there has been a solid body of investigation (usually focusing on some aspect of the Critical/Sensitive Period Hypothesis) showing that even highly advanced post-puberty learners are unlikely to ever achieve an L2 proficiency that cannot be differentiated from a first language (L1) proficiency in some form or another. However, precious little research has been carried out regarding understanding the psychology, strategies and learning history of those remarkable post-puberty and adult learners who do come to closely approximate nativelike L2 learning targets. A notable exception has been the Swedish research programme 'High-Level Proficiency in Second Language Use', conducted at Stockholm University under the direction of Kenneth Hyltenstam; however, as we will see in Chapter 1, this ambitious investigation focused primarily on linguistic rather than psychological or developmental aspects of the topic. That is, the Swedish research team concentrated primarily on analysing various grammatical and structural aspects of the attained L2 proficiency of nativelike speakers, often with a view on how those differed from their native speaker counterparts, in contrast to our interest in why and how some learners manage to attain such an exceptional proficiency level against all odds.

Reflecting on the curious paucity of relevant developmental studies, we have come to recognise some of the reasons why second language acquisition (SLA) researchers have tended to steer clear of this topic. On the one hand, it does indeed appear that the stories of learners who beat the odds and master nativelike L2 proficiency can offer many valuable theoretical and practical lessons concerning the steps they have taken to prepare for such an endeavour and the process of how they weathered their journey up the steep incline of the proverbial Mount Everest of language learning. On the other hand, as soon as one attempts to specify more rigorously the sample of learners who would qualify for an investigation in this area, one hits an obstacle: what seems to be a straightforward concept in everyday layman's terms – 'nativelike proficiency', that is, the degree of language competence that closely approximates that of a 'native speaker' – turns out to be a topic of controversy, heated debate and fluid interpretation in scholarly circles (see e.g. Canagarajah, 2013; Davies, 2003; Kunschak & Kono, 2020; Paikeday, 1985).

This being the case, the third big surprise for us has been that our seemingly forthright research agenda opened up Pandora's box and took us into what can be described as a theoretical and ideological minefield. We will address this topic further in Chapter 3, but a good illustration of the gravity of the matter is that many scholars firmly believe that 'the native speaker is dead', and in a recent review paper, some prominent scholars called the terms native speaker/non-native speaker (NS/NNS) outright 'toxic'. As such, we wish to address this issue directly to be clear about our operationalisation of the concept of nativelikeness. Our first warning is due at this point: the exceptionality of nativelike learners here is based on the fact that few learners *can* achieve nativelikeness – thereby making this cohort exceptional, as in 'atypical' – not because we think every language learner should strive for the same. We believe that highlighting the injustice of the native speaker as a linguistic standard is of grave importance, and as such have dedicated Chapter 3 to exploring our approach to the issue. This said, our primary aim is to draw theoretical and practical lessons from this select group of exceptionally successful L2 learners, and thus we are unable to enter the debate about the use of the term 'native speaker' itself in any meaningful way here.

Having said that, we have just hit our second obstacle by using the term 'L2'. This again raises concerns on several fronts, as it alludes to the 'monolingual bias' of SLA, by which it is often assumed that language learners are monolinguals learning their first L2, downplaying the multilingual experience. Our second warning concerns this matter: although multilingualism is a theme that we assign great importance to – and it is indeed Katarina's main research area – this book will have relatively little to say about it largely because the majority of our learners were indeed raised monolingually and have focused on only one target language in their lives. Even for those who studied some other language(s) at one point in their lives, their achievement in those was usually relatively unremarkable – that is, our investigated cohort were definitely not polyglots, and most of them did not even consider themselves multilingual speakers!

Now that we have issued two warnings about what we are *not* going to address in this book, it is time to specify what we *are* going to talk about. Accordingly, the rest of this introduction briefly addresses three questions: (a) How did we select the learners whose stories we will analyse? (b) Why do we think that such an analysis might be profitable? and (c) How will this book present our findings?

B. Our Selection Criteria: The Duck Test

For the current project, we selected 30 unique and in many ways exceptional language learners/users. Chapters 2 and 3 offer a more detailed description of them and of the selection process, but as a preliminary, it is useful to present here our primary selection criteria: a person qualified for our study if (a) they were recommended by people who knew them as someone who could be taken for a native speaker of the language by 'real' native speakers in a casual conversation for at least five minutes, provided the individual themselves (b) agreed with this evaluation and (c) could offer details of a variety of actual experiences of this happening in the past. Added to these conditions were the requirements mentioned earlier: the participants should not be in any way heritage language learners, and they should not have mastered their target L2 through an extended sojourn in the L2 environment before the age of 18. These criteria reflect Moyer's (2021: 1) definition of gifted language learning as 'mastering a language beyond the mother tongue(s), on par with native speakers according to external measures, despite commencing past the critical or "sensitive" age for language learning'. We are well aware of the fact that these requirements could sway under the test of scientific scrutiny as they contain several loopholes in their specifications. Yet, they turned out to be surprisingly robust in a phenomenological sense: when people recommended someone to us, they were quite confident in their recommendation, and most of the recommended individuals not only agreed with the evaluation but could also cite convincing evidence from their past about the fact that they had frequently passed for native speakers in the L2.

Undeniably, we had a few borderline candidates, and in those cases we preferred to err on the conservative side: if there was any doubt about the candidate's proficiency level or learning history, we did not invite the person to participate in our project. However, our simple selection criteria have turned out to constitute a remarkably strong benchmark, and both we and our participants were confident in the validity of our choices. The procedure we applied was, in effect, very much like the famous 'duck test': if it looks like a duck, swims like a duck and quacks like a duck, then it probably *is* a duck – even if we cannot prove that this is really so.

C. A Matter of Interest

What makes the experiences of a small cluster of unique language learners instructive and relevant with regard to achieving a better understanding of SLA? This is a critical question for our book, and we would like to begin answering it by stating something that might be unexpected: it was not really our participants' advanced level of proficiency that we were interested in. After all, as we will see in the following chapters, although they all excelled in certain language domains, they often had shortcomings in some others (e.g. L2 writing skills). Instead, the attraction for us lay in their attaining a fully comfortable and largely 'unmarked' L2 ability, which allowed them a great deal of social leeway and flexibility in developing their own authentic L2 voices, as well as a natural ownership of the L2 to which most other learners can only aspire. In other words, we were not particularly concerned about having iron-clad rigour in our selection criteria when it came to proficiency, because for us it did not make much difference whether someone could pass as a native speaker in a relatively easy task (i.e. a casual conversation) for five minutes or in a more probing activity for a longer period. What mattered was that they had reached the capacity to pass at all, which we assumed to reflect a qualitatively different proficiency state: 'ordinary' language learners must typically learn to live with their linguistic limitations and markedness, whereas our select few gained the luxury, if you will, to mould their L2 identities with dramatically fewer constraints. This makes them unique in a sense that, for example, we – Zoltán and Katarina – have never experienced: although Zoltán has been operating effectively in English for most of his adult life, never for a moment did he consider himself more than a high-functioning NNS of English, despite the fact that in many domains his L2 command exceeds not only that of some of our project participants but also his own L1 Hungarian language skills. And although Katarina is a reasonably multicultural person – with Greek/Indian heritage and an American/British upbringing – and can hold a conversation in three languages, she knows that she is a native speaker only of her L1 American English; in all the other languages she is still doing her best to circumvent her various non-native linguistic limitations.

Our point is that language learners who reach an advanced enough developmental level that allows them to sometimes pass as members of the target L2 speech community achieve a largely unprecedented degree of ease and fulfilment in L2 communication that none of us 'ordinary' learners ever experience. In many ways, then, they can be seen as the ultimately successful learners because they have more or less accomplished the furthest possible L2 learning goal. Of course, some caveats are due at this point, because we all know that virtually no one is ever fully satisfied with their achievements or feels that they have completely fulfilled their major life goals. However, as we will see, the language concerns and uncertainties of our participants are in an altogether different league from those of the average language learner. There is no other way of putting it: they are special – we know it, and they know it! And if they say, as some of our participants did, that they hardly ever think about such things, then this can be taken as the strongest piece of evidence for their special status, because ordinary language learners, and even L2 teachers, think about their linguistic limitations all the time.

Thus, we embarked on our project with genuine curiosity about how this special status comes about and what it entails, and we presume that you would not be reading this Introduction if you did not share this curiosity with us to some extent. Having now spent the last year on this exploratory applied linguistic enterprise immersed in the stories of our wonderful participants, we can assure you that they did not disappoint.

D. This Book and Its Companion Volume

To put it broadly, our book offers an analysis of how our 30-participant cohort achieved membership in the elite club of expertly successful language learners against a variety of odds. Our two guiding questions have been how they managed to do so and what aspects of their approaches are generalisable to other learners. In order to answer these questions, we applied a narrative research methodology: we elicited detailed learning life stories from each of our participants through in-depth interviews, and after transcribing nearly 50 hours of recordings, we obtained an overall corpus of over 460,000 words. This data set was then submitted to qualitative data analysis using NVivo, with a special interest in how participants overcame the kinds of obstacles and maturational constraints that so often impede similar L2 mastery for other learners. Furthermore, because a unique feature of our participants was that they had successfully reached the end of the journey many embark upon, we were also keen to find out what it meant for them to arrive at their destination: were they fully at ease with their L2 voice/identity, and how did they themselves evaluate their achievement of nativelikeness?

As part of the data analysis, we first crafted a condensed L2 learning history for each of the 30 participants, accompanied by a set of noteworthy interview excerpts. These stories turned out to be so engaging that we decided that they should also be shared intact – that is, without being segmented for the purpose of our theoretical analysis – with interested readers, hence the companion volume: *Stories from Exceptional Language Learners Who Have Achieved Nativelike Proficiency*. Similar work has been carried out in the past with researchers sharing a fraction of their participants' narratives within their reports – for example with visual or third-person narratives (see e.g. Benson *et al.*, 2013; Chik, 2018; Miyahara, 2015) – and we are delighted to be able to extend this undertaking to a full-length volume including all of our participants' stories for those interested in delving into the full complexity and diversity of experiences. In this book instead, we then further processed the material, aiming to distil theoretical and practical lessons. In presenting our findings, we begin with three overview chapters to set the scene: the first providing an overview of the relevant lines of inquiry in applied linguistics regarding exceptional language learners, the second summarising our methodology and the third providing a contextual background behind the topic of nativelikeness and how the concept is operationalised by the field more broadly and by our participants themselves.

The following nine chapters focus on our findings and the main themes that have emerged from our data. We have divided them into three clusters, roughly corresponding to the phase of learning to which they apply: (a) initial conditions (Chapters 4–6), (b) the learning process and sustaining the journey (Chapters 7–10) and (c) reaching the destination (Chapters 11 and 12). Readers can expect to find content relating to the subtitle of the present volume – 'Motivation, Cognition and Identity' – interspersed throughout these chapters as all three intertwined in a complex way in our participants' stories, with a broader focus on motivation throughout the volume and a particular focus on cognition in Chapter 6 and identity in Chapters 11 and 12. In these data analysis chapters, we endeavoured to approach the material with the kind of open mind that exploratory qualitative research requires, and we followed our agenda of foregrounding our participants' experiences by allowing them to speak for themselves as much as possible via generous interview extracts throughout the volume. Rather than performing our analysis as a theory-driven exercise, we allowed the range of topics to be driven primarily by our participants' experiences, and so while many topics may be familiar territory for some readers (e.g. some individual differences), many may not. We thus viewed our role largely as that of the librarian who offers relevant signposting and background information to facilitate the visitors' experience of the main focus: the participants' stories themselves.

In summary, the difference between the current book and its companion volume lies in the discourse's academic framing. The current '*Lessons…*' book is an extended qualitative research report, following academic conventions (although hopefully in an accessible and reader-friendly manner); the '*Stories…*' book is a compendium of life narratives rather than selected interview segments, and it can thus be seen as a storybook proper. We would like to stress that both books are self-contained, stand-alone volumes; that is, they do not require the other's support for conveying their full message. That said, we hope that curiosity will lead you to delve further into our participants' stories as it has for us; they are, after all, as exceptional as the learners to which they belong.

1 Theoretical Background

Let us first set the stage by providing a broad theoretical background into previous research on exceptional language learners. A review of the scholarly literature on the topic reveals a two-sided picture. On the one hand, as mentioned briefly in the Introduction, very little research has been conducted specifically on the primary topics of our interest, the psychological and experiential characteristics of these learners and the evolution of their second language (L2) proficiency towards nativelikeness. In a comprehensive overview of the subject, Biedroń and Pawlak (2016: 176) conclude, 'Gifted FL learners comprise a distinctive group of talented individuals that has thus far been poorly scrutinized and described', and Hyltenstam and colleagues confirm this assessment:

> The field of second language acquisition suffers from an empirical deficit when it comes to the most advanced levels of L2 proficiency. Research, and not least the debate among researchers, would profit from having a more detailed and exhaustive descriptive inventory of the most advanced stages. (Hyltenstam *et al.*, 2018: 10)

On the other hand, considerable work has been completed pursuing a number of topics that are tangentially connected to our research focus one way or another (typically related to issues concerning ultimate attainment and the Critical Period Hypothesis [CPH] – see below). As such, this chapter is divided into two parts: first, we explore previous research directly investigating exceptional language learners, and then we review an assortment of research topics indirectly related to the same population. Due to the dearth of psychology/development-focused research on this cohort of language learners, readers should expect this chapter to provide a broader overview into previous research without delving too deeply into issues that stray from our project's focus on gifted language learning. One issue in the literature – the question of the 'native speaker' and 'nativelikeness' – is central enough to the overall content of this book that we will address it separately in Chapter 3.

1.1 Past Studies Examining Exceptional Learners

According to Biedroń and Pawlak (2016), the main reason for the paucity of research on exceptional language learners has been the absence of an unambiguous definition of 'linguistic talent', which thus prevented the emergence of an established research strand in this area. This issue has already been touched upon in the Introduction and will be revisited periodically in this chapter. Biedroń and Pawlak also offer a second and more pragmatic reason that concerns the challenging nature of conducting research in this area:

> Researching exceptional talents is difficult because such talents are quite rare and it is difficult to assemble a group that would be large enough for statistical analysis. Besides, there exist idiosyncratic paths of development of gifted individuals that fall outside any classifications, the criteria adopted for the choice of such individuals are inconsistent, and the research methodology varies. (Biedroń & Pawlak, 2016: 156)

Indeed, since the 1970s there have been several decades of research into the more easily identifiable 'good' language learner (for reviews, see Griffiths, 2008, 2015; Norton & Toohey, 2001), but significantly less inquiry into their more extraordinary counterparts.

The difficulty of assembling a sizeable research sample has been reflected by the fact that the pioneering investigations into this set of language learners in the 1980s and 1990s invariably comprised case studies of unique individuals (e.g. Ioup et al., 1994; Novoa et al., 1988; Schneiderman & Desmarais, 1988). However, while these analyses served as intriguing eye-openers by offering captivating individual information, they did not tend towards generating any overarching theoretical themes (for reviews, see Biedroń & Pawlak, 2016; Moyer, 2021; Skehan, 1998). After the turn of the millennium, several group studies were also conducted, but rather than analysing the developmental process of reaching nativelike L2 competence, the dominant approach of these investigations involved either measuring static learner characteristics or comparing various aspects of nativelike proficiency to native speaker standards. In addition, they also tended to employ variable-based statistical designs that were not conducive to understanding the various trajectories through which language talent can manifest. Having said this, the existing literature does provide useful insights into several aspects of the two main types of exceptional learners: (a) polyglots and (b) otherwise 'ordinary' learners who acquire nativelike proficiency in contexts where this would not normally be expected. Let us consider the findings related to these two groups separately.

1.1.1 Polyglots

The term *polyglot* usually refers to a language learner who has successfully acquired a certain minimum number of languages, usually six or more (Hyltenstam, 2021). There can be no doubt that such learners are exceptional, but their language talent is rather different from that of the learners at the centre of the current book: while polyglots can function in a large number of languages, they do not usually reach a nativelike or even advanced command in them, and sometimes only have limited functional competence in some of them (e.g. being able to read but not speak the language). None of the 30 participants in our project were polyglots, and most of them did not even have advanced proficiency in a third language. To clarify, while polyglots maximise the number of languages mastered, our participants maximised their mastery of a *single language* (with only three of them reaching nativelike proficiency in a third language as well). For example, one of the most incredible L2 learners in our group, Uwe, succeeded in mastering nativelike British English in a purely instructed, institutional context in East Germany (still under communist rule), where by definition, very few and limited authentic resources were available. After this amazing feat, he settled in Hungary and married a Hungarian, but despite having spent over two decades living and working in Hungary since then, his Hungarian has yet to reach an advanced, let alone nativelike, level.

The difference between these two groups of exceptional learners does not mean, however, that they do not share some common features. Regarding polyglots, Hyltenstam and his colleagues have studied nearly 100 such gifted master learners over the past decade (see e.g. Hyltenstam, 2021; Hyltenstam *et al.*, 2018), and they conclude that polyglots' unique strength involves having an extreme fascination with language and a strong motivation to learn, often as a personal inclination or intrinsic passion rather than in order to satisfy some pragmatic necessity. As we will see in this book, most of our participants can also be characterised as having a passion for language learning per se, even though the pragmatic element usually plays a stronger part in their cases. While some polyglots have been documented as being able to pick up languages naturalistically – that is, largely by engaging in conversation with native speakers – the typical route to polyglotism involves exerting a great deal of time and effort pursuing an explicit learning approach with a particular interest in linguistic form, which has also been a standard feature of our participants. It thus comes as little surprise to find that polyglots' efforts are typically undergirded by a combination of above-average language aptitude and the utilisation of refined metalinguistic skills and strategies. This being the case, the outstanding aspect of their learning is not so much the unique way in which they go about it as the efficiency and vast capacity of their L2 study skills.

Several scholars have hypothesised that the unique learning ability of polyglots is linked to certain neural properties of their brains. This has been confirmed to some extent; for example, in his review of the relevant literature, Hyltenstam (2021) reports findings indicating that the polyglot brain displays different cell densities and cell types in regions that have traditionally been associated with language learning (e.g. Broca's area). Likewise, Jouravlev *et al.* (2021) present brain imagery results comparing polyglots and ordinary language learners, showing that the former recruit less extensive cortical areas within the neural language network of the left hemisphere, and activate these areas to a lesser degree. These findings suggest that polyglots utilise neural resources for language processing significantly more efficiently than ordinary bi-/multilingual speakers; however, at this stage it cannot be decided conclusively whether this is the outcome of experience (in a similar way as expert drivers use fewer cognitive resources for driving than their novice counterparts) or an inherent feature of their learning right from the beginning. It is certainly interesting in this respect that the processing efficiency of polyglots is not widespread in the brain: Jouravlev and colleagues explain that previous studies have not detected any significant differences between polyglots and their controls in other language-neutral brain networks.

1.1.2 Learners achieving nativelike or near-native L2 proficiency

The second type of exceptional language learners comprises individuals who succeed in mastering nativelike proficiency in an L2 without any heritage links or extensive early (i.e. pre-puberty) exposure to the language; Moyer (2021: 1) has defined such gifted language learners as individuals who master a language 'beyond the mother tongue(s), on par with native speakers according to external measures, despite commencing past the critical or "sensitive" age for language learning'. As pointed out in the Introduction, these learners are considered extraordinary because the vast majority of their peers with similar backgrounds, despite their best efforts, are unable to reach such an advanced stage. Research focusing on these super-talented learners has a history of three decades, but as Hyltenstam *et al.* (2018) summarise, the bulk of the investigations have focused largely on three areas:

(1) The extent to which these L2 learners confirm or refute the Critical/Sensitive Period Hypothesis (see below).
(2) The linguistic aspects (most notably, morphological, syntactic, lexical and pragmatic features) that characterise advanced L2 competence, and how this stage differs from native speaker proficiency.
(3) The sociolinguistic variation of advanced L2 proficiency, usually in multilingual contexts.

There has ultimately been a dominance of studies focusing on the linguistic aspects of this topic, with the prime example being the most extensive research programme to date, the 'High-Level Proficiency in Second Language Use' project at Stockholm University directed by Kenneth Hyltenstam (see e.g. Hyltenstam, 2016; Hyltenstam *et al.*, 2018). The limited existing research on the psychological and developmental aspects of reaching nativelike language proficiency offers relevant insights into three areas in particular: (a) learner characteristics, (b) some aspects of the learning process and (c) the limitations of nativelike L2 proficiency.

1.1.2.1 Learner characteristics

As mentioned earlier, a few intriguing case studies conducted before the turn of the millennium provided meticulous (and eye-opening) descriptions of some uniquely gifted learners, and while the nature of this research methodology does not allow for making generalisable claims, some recurring topics did emerge from these studies. For example, there is repeated mention in the literature of phonological abilities as a critical component, which draws attention to an important but lesser-known attribute of these learners, a 'good ear for languages'. This factor, which is of course closely linked to the capacity to sound nativelike, was also highlighted in Leaver and Campbell's (2014) review of highly advanced language learners, but it was, unsurprisingly, missing from the findings of the polyglot studies, because polyglots usually do not achieve nativelike proficiency in the multiple languages they learn. Because of the special significance of the phonological component, we will address the relevant research on it in a separate section below.

Phonological abilities temporarily aside, arguably the most common theme in the literature has been the attribution of the success of gifted learners to the *cognitive realm* (see Biedroń & Pawlak, 2016; Moyer, 2021), that is, to issues related to neurocognitive processing preferences and capabilities such as a high language aptitude involving outstanding verbal memory and effective linguistic self-monitoring and analytical skills (alongside advanced phonological abilities). We will expand on some of these topics below in more detail, as a variety of such cognitive factors have often been mentioned as potentially relevant. However, broadly speaking, few specifics have been offered regarding gifted learners beyond such rather generic statements as learners having an 'above-average' aptitude. One likely reason for this lack of clarity has been the fact that cognitive factors work in cooperation with motivational characteristics: nativelike learners have been typically described as having a *proactive mindset* that enables them to seek out L2 learning opportunities and to persevere (see e.g. Biedroń, 2011a; Nikolov, 2000).

Along similar lines, some researchers have investigated the overlap between nativelike language learning and certain personality features, with equally complex results. One of the few systematic studies in this area by Biedroń (2011b) identified one personality aspect where gifted learners differed from other L2 learners: *openness to experience* (or as it is often simply referred to, openness). This is one of the five primary components of Costa and McCrae's (1992, 2008) famous Big Five personality construct, concerning an openness to new experiences, thoughts and processes, with a high score representing an imaginative, curious, flexible, creative, novelty-seeking and artistic character. Interestingly, in an important study that examined the communicative competence and personality characteristics of teenage language learners in the Netherlands, Verhoeven and Vermeer (2002) also found that of the Big Five personality dimensions, only openness to experience correlated substantially with the children's linguistic abilities across three of the competencies underlying the children's overall communicative competence. In other words, it appears that openness may constitute the personality foundation of effective language learning at a broad level, from the lowest to the very highest; therefore, Moyer (2021: 52) is right to conclude that 'few would disagree that openness is a prerequisite for embracing new L2 experiences, and possibly expanding one's sense of self to incorporate the target language'.

On the other hand, while scholars regularly mention that this cohort of learners appears to be 'socially outgoing' (e.g. Moyer, 2021; Nikolov, 2000), the personality trait of extraversion has not emerged as a defining feature of gifted language learners. In fact, in Biedroń's (2011b) study, the personality trait that the non-gifted (control) sample scored the highest on was extraversion, and a language aptitude measure correlated *negatively* with extraversion. Also contrastingly, in their study on pronunciation talent, Hu and Reiterer (2009) did not find any significant correlations to extraversion either way (nor to openness). These inconsistencies are in line with Dörnyei and Ryan's (2015) summary that extraversion affects various aspects of L2 communicative competence differently, particularly at different stages of learning, and thus it remains difficult to make any generalisations. The current picture of exceptional language learner characteristics remains a tangled one, and it is understandably difficult to find consensus on the contributions of various factors, particularly due to the length and complexity of the language learning process. As Moyer expressively puts it:

> Gifted L2 learners do not awaken one day, surprised at their own accomplishment. Their abiding efforts have brought their goals to fruition. At the same time, some with a similar goal will not see its realization. A multitude of factors influences the outcome, and many changes will mark the process. (Moyer, 2021: 153)

Accordingly, she rightly concludes that the case studies of gifted learners reveal the intersection of cognitive, psychological and experiential influences in predicting exceptional outcomes and that there is no 'neuro-cognitive universal' (Moyer, 2021: 107) for gifted language learning.

1.1.2.2 The learning process

From the perspective of our project, some of the most relevant research findings are those that concern the evolution of nativelike L2 competence, that is, the various methods and procedures adopted by nativelike learners to attain their high-level proficiency. Unfortunately, when it comes to a survey of the strategies employed by gifted individuals, the available information is 'extremely scant' (Biedroń & Pawlak, 2016: 175). What emerges from the existing reviews (Biedroń & Pawlak, 2016; Hyltenstam *et al.*, 2018; Leaver & Campbell, 2014; Moyer, 2021) is that nativelike and near-native learners adopt highly personalised learning strategies and are, in fact, often largely self-taught. Given how much value they can add to any learning process themselves, they are usually able to adapt and take advantage of a wide variety of instructional situations without requiring any specific method. Such an autonomous approach is, in fact, usually not merely advantageous but also essential particularly in later learning stages, because, as Leaver and Shekhtman (2002: 3) rightly point out, very few L2 courses are aimed at bringing students to the superior level: 'There has been a tacit assumption among foreign language educators and administrators that language programs cannot be expected to bring students any further in the classroom than the Advanced High level'.

Finally, an important commonality among exceptional learners highlighted by Leaver and Campbell (2014) is that they tend to share a cognitive style ('intuitive sharpener') that allows them to recognise slight differences between their mother tongue and the target language and to identify subtle nuances between synonymous expressions. They also tend to pay a great deal of attention to linguistic form, recognise and appreciate patterns, discern rules without them being explicitly taught, make linguistic predictions and actively look for exceptions (Biedroń & Pawlak, 2016; Moyer, 2021). In terms of specific techniques, they utilise a wide range of creative procedures, from singing and visualising to shadowing native speakers, repeating aural input and inventing mnemonic devices. In other words, they are master learning strategy users, and as Moyer (2021) concludes, they also have the capability to shift strategies with changing learning conditions. As we will see in the following chapters, our own participants also display such creative and eclectic diversity in terms of the specific activities they have applied in promoting their own language development.

1.1.2.3 The limitations of nativelike L2 proficiency

A number of studies have examined highly advanced, nativelike L2 learners in order to check how closely their L2 competencies matched native speaker norms. The primary motivation behind such investigations has been to test the theoretical possibility of achieving such high L2 levels for learners who started the learning process later in life, beyond the closure of a critical or sensitive period (see below). Of course, many researchers such as Dewaele (2018) rightly point out that any native–non-native comparison becomes hugely complicated by the fact that native speakers themselves display considerable inter- and intrapersonal linguistic variation, which means that rather than representing a concrete threshold, native speaker proficiency should be seen as a broad range, which may also differ according to different areas of communicative competence (see also Andringa, 2014; Davies, 2003). In any case, in reviewing past studies, Hyltenstam *et al.* (2018) conclude that the results unambiguously show that even the most outstanding language learners never completely attain a level of L2 proficiency that is impossible to differentiate from native speaker proficiency. Dörnyei (2009b) also explains that even when standard measures identify someone as belonging within the native-speaking range of performance – usually within two standard deviations of the mean rating obtained for a native-speaking norm group – more elaborate assessments will still be able to detect subtle deviations from the native norm. Accordingly, two decades ago, Hyltenstam and Abrahamsson (2001: 157–158) stated that 'published studies have still not identified a single adult learner who is indistinguishable from a native speaker in all relevant aspects of the L2', and Abrahamsson *et al.* (2018) have recently confirmed that the situation has not changed over the years.

An interesting aspect of this line of inquiry is that sometimes the differences between the performance of nativelike learners and native speakers are so subtle – or as Hyltenstam *et al.* (2018: 9) put it, 'microscopic' – that even native speakers themselves often fail to notice them (which was in fact our criterion for participation in the present study). Abrahamsson and Hyltenstam (2008: 484) aptly refer to such cases as 'nonperceivable nonnativeness', which may characterise as high as 5–10% of post-pubertal learners in naturalistic learning environments (Birdsong, 2007). We should note that in the vast majority of such cases, someone will only pass as a native speaker temporarily and most often in certain cognitively less-demanding situations. Let us consider the nature of this act of passing briefly here, and we will return to examining the notion in more detail in Chapter 2.

Passing has been defined as 'the ability to be taken for a member of a social category (ethnic, racial, class, gender, etc.) other than one's own' (Cutler, 2014: 150), and for an L2 learner to achieve this is particularly noteworthy because native speakers are usually rather good at recognising other native speakers (Flege, 1984; Major, 2007). For a recent example, Hyltenstam *et al.* (2018) report on a highly controlled study in which a group of linguistically untrained native speakers of Swedish were asked to decide whether a range of recorded speech samples were produced by native speakers of Swedish or not, and it was found that the judges delivered their verdict with 99% accuracy.

Most research focusing on passing has concerned the complexity caused by the sociolinguistic variation of different language dialects (see e.g. Bijvoet & Fraurud, 2012, 2016; Bolton, 2016; Marx, 2002). For example, it has been found that non-native speakers may be more likely to pass for native speakers if they speak a version of the target language that is different from that of the judges (e.g. middle-class British judges evaluating the nativelikeness of an American English accent, especially if it includes the use of youth language features and slang) (Gnevsheva, 2017; Piller, 2002). The results of studies permutating the various parameters of communicative encounters indicate that even extralinguistic differences can lead to inaccurate speech perceptions (Lindemann & Campbell, 2017; Shintani *et al.*, 2019). Such findings carry a great deal of intriguing information about speech perception and group identity formation but are only tangentially relevant to our current project in terms of how our participants experienced this complexity towards the latter end of their journeys.

1.2 Studies on Research Topics Related to Exceptional Learners

Exceptional learners have been part of research projects whose aim did not specifically involve understanding their learning characteristics or why and how they achieved their outstanding language competence, but rather focused on related research questions and used high-level learners – along with other learners in control groups – as part of the research sample. The most frequently applied research theme in this connection has been the CPH, and age effects in language learning more generally, and nativelike learners have also been instrumental in exploring the nature of language aptitude. In addition, there has been a recent surge of studies on various aspects of pronunciation and accent, with a special focus on auditory processing and musical abilities. All these research directions offer useful findings regarding our specific area of interest, but at the same time their relevance is limited by the fact that their ultimate concern does not involve advancing our understanding of the *developmental* processes characterising the unique cohort of exceptional learners.

1.2.1 The Critical Period Hypothesis

One cannot explore the literature on exceptional language learners without constantly encountering references to the CPH. The reason for this seemingly inextricable link is that according to the strongest version of the hypothesis, learners who start the process of attaining an L2 after a certain age – usually after puberty – are thought to be biologically unable to reach native speaker proficiency. Therefore, the performance of adult learners with nativelike L2 competence is seen by scholars as crucial evidence for evaluating the hypothesis. As such, let us have a quick overview of what the CPH entails and how it is related to its weaker counterpart – the Sensitive Period Hypothesis – as well as to age effects in general.

The best-known prediction of the CPH is that nativelike L2 attainment is only possible for learners up to a certain age (Birdsong, 2004), a maxim that coincides with many laypeople's beliefs that the younger a learner is, the more likely they are to be successful in mastering an L2. Although the exact meaning of the CPH shows some variation from author to author, all the different conceptualisations specify a period in a child's life – that is, a 'critical period' (CP) – when L2 learning happens smoothly, naturally and almost inevitably, resulting in nativelike or near-nativelike proficiency. With regard to the actual time when the door closes on such a favoured period, the literature mentions just about every age between 5 and 13 and sometimes even later, up to 16–18, with the most common reference being made to puberty (which, of course, varies from person to person).

The concept of a *critical period* originates in biology, where it was observed that certain developmental events can only happen in a limited period that has a specific closure, after which the organism in question has 'missed its chance'. As Dörnyei (2009b) explains, the most popular illustration of the CP is the imprinting phenomenon observed by Austrian ethologist Konrad Lorenz in the first half of the 20th century. He demonstrated that incubator-hatched baby geese accept the first moving thing they perceive around them as their mother, and if during the brief critical bonding period (about 36 hours) it is a human who is around the goslings, this person will irreversibly be regarded as the mother goose. Further research discovered that such developmentally crucial periods may be found widely dispersed in animal and human neurobiology and behaviour, and the concept has been applied profitably in explaining developmental issues in a variety of fields.

Thus, the basic tenet of the CPH in language learning is that in naturalistic language learning environments there is a circumscribed developmental period – similar to imprinting in goslings – during which second language acquisition (SLA) is virtually guaranteed and after which nativelike mastery of an L2 is not achievable. However, SLA researchers soon realised that there are too many exceptions to such a rigid conceptualisation, and therefore they have started to increasingly use the term *sensitive period* instead (see e.g. Long & Granena, 2018). According to Knudsen (2004), a sensitive period is a broader category than the CP as it refers to any duration of time when the neural connections within the brain are particularly susceptible to environmental input; that is, when the brain displays a heightened sensitivity towards a particular type of stimulus whereby the stimulus occurring leads to learning with powerful and durable effects.

Some critics of the CPH have gone even further, claiming that any mention of a distinct period is misplaced, because the latter requires a relatively sharp discontinuity at the terminus of the period in question (e.g. Birdsong, 2005; Singleton & Ryan, 2004). They argue that what we find instead is a gradual decline that varies across the various components of L2 communicative competence, and therefore it may be more appropriate to talk about more general 'age effects' or maturational constraints, whereby a combination of multiple age-related factors causes a gradual decline in language attainment as one becomes older (Hyltenstam & Abrahamsson, 2003). To this complex picture we need to add at least one more element: that of *context*. We must recognise that both the critical and sensitive period tend to focus the discussion on language learning in *naturalistic* SLA contexts (e.g. immigrants learning the language of their new host country) rather than in *formal, institutional* learning contexts (e.g. studying a foreign language [FL] as a school subject). While in the former set of environments the younger language learner definitely seems to be better, in the latter it is exactly the other way round, because more mature language learners are much better suited to take advantage of the explicit learning opportunities that classroom instruction offers (for a detailed explanation, see Dörnyei, 2009b). The influence that formal language learning, or indeed a combination of formal and naturalistic learning, may have on ultimate attainment remains to be seen; as we will see later, the participants in our study often had the opportunity to take advantage of both.

The brief overview above offers only a taster of the interaction of the various considerations that make the question of the CPH so intricate, interesting and often frustratingly controversial. Despite the criticism, there is something irresistibly appealing about the notion of a CP and its explanatory power regarding the difficulties of adult language learning, and therefore it keeps re-emerging in the SLA research scene under different disguises and emphases (for insightful overviews, see Birdsong, 2014; Hartshorne *et al.*, 2018; Mayberry & Kluender, 2018). Nonetheless, for our current purpose there is little need to dig any deeper into this matter; although studies on the CPH can offer helpful information regarding the limits of adult language learning, our participant sample was purposely selected such that the CPH should not be relevant to it in any form: our interviewees either studied the L2 primarily in a classroom context or became exposed to it in a naturalistic environment only after the age of 18.

1.2.2 Language aptitude and linguistic giftedness

Most researchers and laypeople would agree that there exists a natural, innate ability to learn an L2 that varies significantly from individual to individual; yet as Doughty and Mackey (2021: 1) have recently put it, 'Aptitude is one of the most important, intriguing, messy, and often controversial topics in second language research'. Dörnyei and Ryan (2015) explain that this innate aptitude has traditionally been linked to intelligence and has been referred to under a variety of names, ranging from 'language aptitude' and a special 'propensity' or 'talent' for learning an L2 to more colloquial terms such as a 'flair', 'gift' or 'knack' for languages. However, we should note that despite the above consensus and the expressive labels, strictly speaking there is no such thing as 'language aptitude'; instead, what we have is a number of cognitive factors making up a composite measure that can be referred to as a learner's overall cognitive capacity to master a foreign language.

After a relative lull, research on language aptitude has recently increased dramatically (see e.g. Doughty & Mackey, 2021; Granena, 2019; Wen et al., 2017, 2019), although reviewing the new directions is beyond the scope of the current review. For our present purpose, the important aspect of language aptitude is that 'a high level of language aptitude is a requirement for the achievement of high-level, near-native, ultimate attainment in postpubescent L2 learners' (Hyltenstam, 2021: 59). In fact, language aptitude is the second most-examined factor in ultimate attainment studies and is said to account for 10–20% of variance in L2 ultimate attainment. Interestingly and contrary to much of the research on ultimate attainment, though, language aptitude measures have historically favoured skills in formal language learning contexts over naturalistic ones (Granena & Long, 2013). Nonetheless, no account of exceptional learners can ignore the existence of some superior cognitive component.

Given the multifaceted nature of the relevant aptitude constructs in the literature, it is rather difficult to pin down exactly what aspects are indispensable for reaching nativelike proficiency. For example, Hyltenstam (2021) attempts to distinguish the line between language aptitude and language awareness, the latter referring to a mixture of explicit knowledge about language combined with conscious perception and sensitivity in language learning. However, Hyltenstam (2021: 69) is the first to admit that the latter language analytic ability is tightly linked and partially overlaps with language aptitude, for example because both awareness and aptitude 'rely on, or include, what is often called metalinguistic awareness or metalinguistic knowledge (i.e. awareness or knowledge of rules that structure language in the broadest sense)'. As he concludes, available data on polyglots indicate that they tend to have an extremely high level of language learning aptitude and also a highly developed degree of language awareness – all the indications are that this is also true of most of the exceptional learners in our current study. Ultimately, as Kormos (2013: 132) puts it, language aptitude is not static but is rather 'a conglomerate of individual characteristics that interact dynamically with the situation'. Thus, while it is fair to conclude that a high language aptitude is a defining feature of language talent in general (see also Jilka, 2009), the exact ways this plays out in the language learning process need to be examined in more detail.

1.2.3 Pronunciation, accent and accent attitudes

Pronunciation appears to have a 'special status' in discussions on linguistic talent, particularly as there appear to be greater difficulties for adult learners to acquire pronunciation compared to other aspects of language (Jilka, 2009: 3). Yet, despite pronunciation's central position in the literature, it also tends to be one of the most overlooked aspects in language education, as we will see below. Most pertinent to our study, however, is the fact that in order to pass as a native speaker, a language learner needs to exhibit a very high level of phonetic talent in order to produce a sufficiently authentic and nativelike pronunciation. This can, in fact, be a stumbling block for even high-functioning L2 users; for example, both the Polish-born English language writer Joseph Conrad and the German-born US Foreign Secretary Henry Kissinger had a strong foreign accent even though other aspects of their English proficiency were not only nativelike but arguably exceeded average native speaker standards considerably. The issue of pronunciation/accent has been the subject of research from various vantage points, with scholars examining (a) the phonetic dimension of language aptitude, (b) speech accommodation and phonetic flexibility, (c) the relationship between auditory processing and foreign accent, (d) the relationship between pronunciation and musical ability, (e) the relationship between accent and language identity and (f) the teachability of pronunciation.

1.2.3.1 The phonetic dimension of language aptitude

We have seen above that the notion of language aptitude has been conceptualised as a composite measure of a number of language-related abilities, but regardless of the exact nature of the specific constructs proposed, one of the constituents of the aptitude complex has always been related to some aspect of phonetic coding. For example, the first and still best-known language aptitude test, Carroll and Sapon's (1959) Modern Language Aptitude Test (MLAT), includes a featured task called *phonetic script*, in which students hear a set of short nonsense words while following along with the printed phonetic script; after some practice, students are played one word at a time and are asked to identify it from four printed alternatives. Having analysed extensive empirical data obtained by the MLAT, Carroll (1973, 1981: 105) later proposed a general theoretical construct of language aptitude, identifying 'phonetic coding ability' as its most important component, defined as 'an ability to identify distinct sounds, to form associations between these sounds and symbols representing them, and to retain these associations'. Carroll (1973) argued that this component involves more than merely discriminating sounds, as it concerns identifying sounds or a string of sounds as unique entities and storing them in one's long-term memory – it therefore involves the coding, assimilation and recollection of phonetic material.

Another classic language aptitude test, the Pimsleur Language Aptitude Battery (PLAB), also conceptualised a component labelled 'auditory ability' as one of its three core factors, defined as 'the ability to receive and process information through the ear' (Pimsleur, 1966: 14). Following these two models of language aptitude, assigning the phonological dimension a special importance in theorising and measuring language talent persisted over the decades. Accordingly, in a factor analytic study of a number of different aptitude measures, Sparks *et al.* (2011) arrived at a factor solution which contained a central dimension labelled 'phonology/orthography', subsuming measures of phonetic coding and phonological processing represented by a number of phonological awareness skills such as decoding words and pseudowords, spelling, learning new sound–symbol correspondences and analysing sound or speech patterns.

These examples well illustrate that phonetic talent constitutes a distinct substrate of language aptitude, and a good neurological reflection of this relatively independent status is the intriguing condition called foreign accent syndrome (FAS). As Brendel and Ackermann (2009) summarise, FAS is a condition that sometimes follows brain damage whereby patients' first language (L1) begins to display a sound shift towards a different language system (i.e. they adopt a foreign-sounding accent in their native language use). The new accent may be related to an L2 that the person has been exposed to earlier in life, but in some cases monolingual learners' L1 displays the accent of a previously unlearnt language. Although this condition is not frequent, it does occur regularly and to date as many as 60 detailed case studies have been published. Because the FAS concerns individuals' mother tongues, it demonstrates clearly that an accent can constitute an independent layer added to one's otherwise native or nativelike speaker proficiency.

1.2.3.2 Speech accommodation and phonetic flexibility

Language aptitude research has demonstrated that learners vary greatly in their capability to develop nativelike pronunciation in an L2, and in a similar vein, we also find considerable variation in adult native speakers' ability to acquire different accents in their L1s (e.g. Hollien, 2002). One reflection of this capability is the process of *speech accommodation*, the phenomenon where speech interlocutors tend to minimise or maximise the social difference between each other through gesture or verbal communication (Giles, 2016). One form of speech accommodation is referred to as *phonetic convergence* or *phonetic adaptation*, by which two interlocutors in a conversational situation become more alike in their pronunciation over the course of the dialogue (Lewandowski, 2009) – that is, they start increasingly sounding like each other. It has been observed that some individuals are very good at displaying such a flexibility (consciously or unconsciously), and while most research on phonetic convergence has been conducted on L1 interactions, this ability appears to be transferrable to acquiring L2 accents. For example, Lewandowski and Jilka (2019) found that the phonetically talented L2 speakers in their study converged significantly better than their ordinary counterparts. Additionally, they cited evidence of the capacity for phonetic adaptation in an L2 being correlated with openness to experience, which we have seen earlier to be a personality hallmark of successful L2 learners. The study was part of a larger project on phonetic talent (see Dogil & Reiterer, 2009), which proposed and explored the existence of a generic 'phonetic talent', and as is evident, this proposal does not seem to be far-fetched. Our own findings follow a similar pattern, as indications of such a talent recur regularly in our participants' accounts, and we will see more of this in the following chapters.

1.2.3.3 Auditory processing and foreign accent

Both the existence of a phonetic substrate of language aptitude and the potential relevance of L1 phonetic flexibility to L2 pronunciation are connected to the more general research question of how individual differences in auditory processing can account for variability in SLA. Kachlicka *et al.* (2019) report on an investigation that examined a number of relevant psycholinguistic variables in this respect, such as psychoacoustic thresholds, auditory-motor temporal integration and auditory neural encoding. The study produced several meaningful correlations that, taken together, confirmed the researchers' hypothesis that individual differences in SLA success are connected to learners' domain-general capacities regarding auditory perception. This makes sense given that, as the authors rightly point out, the auditory channel is the primary source of L2 input for most learners – especially those in naturalistic contexts – and therefore how well they process this input (e.g. how accurately they can track patterns of timing and pitch) will affect their overall effectiveness as L2 learners and users. As Kachlicka *et al.* further emphasise, the role of auditory perception is paramount because there are links between auditory patterns and linguistic structure at every level, including phonetic, prosodic, lexical and grammatical features. Indeed, it may well be the case that auditory processing constitutes a bottleneck in SLA for many learners, and Kachlicka and colleagues have indeed found that auditory processing was a potent predictor of L2 learning success in their study. It appears that this area has further mileage in it for understanding exceptional L2 learners – and indeed, also for the whole field of SLA in general – but currently we agree with Moyer's (2021: 107) conclusion: 'There are intriguing indications that auditory acuity is crucial, but this requires more careful study'.

1.2.3.4 Pronunciation and musical ability

The intriguing question as to how closely musical ability and language learning skills are interrelated has floated around for a long time, with many people arguing that language and music share a great deal of common characteristics and therefore the human ability for each might be linked. Indeed, both music and language involve sound processing, message conveyance, learning by exposure and the sharing of features such as pitch, volume, prominence, stress, tone, rhythm and pauses (Nardo & Reiterer, 2009). The initial and largely anecdotal evidence supporting the link between the two has been increasingly followed up by rigorous research, and there has been a slow but steady flow of studies since the 1970s showing the influence of musical engagement on both L2 learning and linguistic acquisition and performance in general (see e.g. Besson *et al.*, 2017; Fonseca-Mora & Machancoses, 2016; Patel, 2007; Schön & Morillon, 2019). Cumulatively, the findings indicate that 'there is vast evidence of a significant relationship between music skills and second language (L2) acquisition' (Nardo & Reiterer, 2009: 233).

A particularly relevant aspect of this line of inquiry is how musical abilities and training correlate with a speaker's pronunciation. Intuitively, one would expect some significant association between the two, and Nardo and Reiterer's (2009) study supports this assumption: 'musicality, ideally in the form of a well-developed rhythm perception ability together with a good pitch perception ability and an enhanced ability and liking for singing, are the best ingredients for achieving talent and expertise in foreign language pronunciation' (Nardo & Reiterer, 2009: 238). Additionally, various aspects of musical ability can affect L2 acquisition and performance differently; for example, Christiner and Reiterer (2015) found that vocalists outperformed instrumentalists on foreign accent imitation (see also Slevc & Miyake, 2006). Of course, the terms *musicality* and *music aptitude* are as broad as the concept of language learning aptitude, and can sometimes refer to a sensitivity to, a knowledge of or a talent for producing music, while also overlapping with some aspects of the auditory processing skills discussed above. In order to test this potential connection, Zheng *et al.* (2020) examined the relationship between music aptitude, auditory perception and L2 pronunciation proficiency. They confirmed that music aptitude and auditory processing partially overlapped, but interestingly it was largely the latter that demonstrated significant associations with the various dimensions of L2 pronunciation proficiency in their study. Additionally, their measure of music aptitude was only secondarily related to prosodic aspects of L2 pronunciation proficiency, especially when the relative weights of auditory processing were partialled out. There is clearly further research potential in this fascinating topic, especially in light of our current project where, as we will see, musical abilities have repeatedly emerged in the participants' life stories.

1.2.3.5 Accent and identity

There has been a long-standing belief in SLA circles that the proximity of a person's L2 accent to native speaker norms is somehow related to the person's attitudes towards the L2 and the L2 community, or more generally, to aspects of the individual's language identity. Moyer (2021), for example, presents research linking accent and the comfort of assimilating culturally in the L2 community, and Baran-Łucarz (2012) concludes that pronunciation constitutes some sort of a psychological gateway to entering into L2 communication. At the heart of the association between accent and identity is the observation that pronunciation is a core area of linguistic self-representation. Therefore, the qualities of a speaker's pronunciation will depend on the nature of that person's identity; for example, cosmopolitan people on average might be expected to have more authentic L2 pronunciation than their ethnocentric counterparts (see also LeVelle & Levis, 2014). Such a close link between accent and identity is not restricted to an L2, and Kinzler offers a good summary of this matter in one's mother tongue:

> The way we speak shapes life in ways that we're only beginning to understand. It can make the difference between getting hired or being passed over for a job. It can be a tool for political oppression and a driver of social and economic marginalisation.... Simply having an accent considered more prestigious or higher in status can grease the wheels of interactions with individuals and with public and private institutions; having what people perceive as the 'wrong' kind of speech, conversely, can have the opposite effect. (Kinzler, 2020: 10–11)

One of the earlier and best-known psychological theories capturing the association between identity and L2 pronunciation has been Alexander Guiora's proposal of *language ego* and the permeability of *ego boundaries* (see e.g. Guiora, 1994; Guiora *et al.*, 1972). Although this theory is admittedly dated and even in its heyday had relatively little empirical support, it is appealing: it explains the common observation that one feels like a different person when speaking an L2, and it introduces the notion of permeable ego boundaries, that is, 'the ability to move back and forth between languages and the "personalities" that seem to come with them' (Guiora & Acton, 1979: 199). A permeable ego boundary is expected to facilitate better pronunciation, but this is a two-way impact because pronunciation can also delimit the boundaries of the language ego; as Guiora (1994: 88) puts it, 'the way we sound, marks us, defines us, in a singular fashion, not unlike our face or our fingerprints'. In other words, according to Guiora (1994: 90), pronunciation can be seen as a marker of identity and as 'the external self-representation expressed through language'.

Ehrman (1999) further explains that the notion of ego boundaries originates in psychoanalytic theory and is related to the fluidity of one's mental categories and the degree to which individuals tend to compartmentalise their experiences. Ehrman further emphasises the strong link between this fluidity and one's relationship with other people and alternative ways of perceiving the world: it affects receptivity to outside influences, such as new languages and cultures, and it defines a learner's proclivity to tolerate ambiguity and to develop a target language persona. However, Baran-Łucarz (2012) cautions against drawing the straightforward conclusion that thin ego boundaries facilitate L2 learning – including the development of authentic pronunciation – because the concept of ego boundaries is very broad and entails several personality dimensions and traits. Indeed, her empirical research did not find any systematic relationship between the thickness of ego boundaries and FL pronunciation attainment after a course in phonetics. Yet, Baran-Łucarz suggests that the process may be different in naturalistic rather than formal learning contexts, where pronunciation may be facilitated if learners thin their ego boundaries, in particular the boundaries connected with personal and group identity. While ego boundaries may thus represent an overly broad concept particularly in the face of the complexity of the L2 learning experience, it is clear that there is a relationship between accent and identity that warrants further investigation.

The close association between accent and identity can also result in some unexpected outcomes. In some FL contexts, for example, L2 learners with an authentic-sounding accent can be criticised as being pretentious or, even worse, traitors to their culture, and the pressure put on them can be so strong that they might deliberately increase the foreign sound of their pronunciation. Moreover, as McCrocklin and Link (2016) explain, some scholars even question whether teaching pronunciation in an L2 is altogether ethical, given the danger that this may threaten learners' L1 identity. On the contrary, however, they found strong evidence among English as a foreign language university students that the latter nonetheless desired a native accent and, in fact, did not fear any loss of identity due to the potential achievement of that accent (see also Derwing & Munro, 2009, for a similar point). In sum, accent and identity have been closely linked both in the literature and anecdotally, and we will see this relationship play out in a variety of ways in the following chapters.

1.2.3.6 The teachability of pronunciation

All of the above points lead to the question of whether L2 pronunciation is actually teachable in the first place. Of course it is to some extent, and plenty of tried and tested materials have been published to facilitate this process (e.g. Celce-Murcia *et al.*, 2010; Murphy, 2020; Pennington & Rogerson-Revell, 2019). The real question for the current discussion is how far this instruction is able to go (Thomson & Derwing, 2015). We should note that the stakes are high because there is evidence that improved pronunciation can initiate a powerful positive spiral of improved attitudes towards the L2, improved L2 motivation and improved linguistic confidence (see McCrocklin & Link, 2016; Moyer, 2007). The opposite can also be true, and Galmiche (2018) for example found in an interview study with French learners of English that their perceived poor accent was one of the most powerful sources of shame and subsequent demotivation; the following quotation from one of her students speaks volumes:

> The accent you have says a lot about you. It reveals who you are at the core, and I feel somehow that having a bad accent is tantamount to being stupid. Speaking badly displays a deficient and poor image of yourself, it betrays that you are lacking in something. You really feel bad and inferior, kind of isolated. (Galmiche, 2018: 114)

It is an undeniable fact that L2 instruction too often pays too little attention to improving learners' pronunciation (see e.g. Trofimovich *et al.*, 2016), and therefore the latter may fossilise before the learners know it. One reason for this neglect, as Derwing and Munro (2009) conclude, is that due to the widespread communicative focus of language teaching, instructors' views on pronunciation teaching have been rather pessimistic, resulting in the common misconception that teaching pronunciation is ineffective. This is further exacerbated by the lack of consensus regarding what linguistic models to use for teaching pronunciation and accent, and the absence of accent-related items in most language proficiency tests and exams has also helped to de-emphasise pronunciation. In contrast, Birdsong (2007) observed that the most successful late learners in his study of nativelike learners had received phonetic training and were also very highly motivated to improve their L2 pronunciation, a finding that, as he reports, has also emerged in other studies. The little data we have about effective pronunciation training suggests that it should go beyond merely practicing sounds and intonation, as instructional support and the motivation to sound like a native speaker also appear to be an indispensable source of 'input enhancement' (Bongaerts, 1999; Mayberry & Kluender, 2018), and as we have seen earlier, musical training has also been shown to improve pronunciation and oral performance (Nardo & Reiterer, 2009). Fortunately, pronunciation teaching is beginning to a see a gradual revival, although there remains much room for discussion regarding how this should take place (see e.g. Lee et al., 2015; Pennington, 2021).

1.3 Summary

This chapter has offered a broad overview of past scholarly work on exceptional learners. We began by stating that the literature shows a two-sided picture: on the one hand, very little research has been conducted on the evolution of nativelike L2 proficiency and the characteristics of these learners; on the other hand, considerable work has been completed on a number of related research topics such as the CPH and various aspects of pronunciation. We have tried to piece together the fragmented research findings into a coherent picture as much as possible, and our survey does highlight several important issues that will resurface in the analysis of our own data. The main lesson of this review exercise has been that the reason for the scarcity of relevant findings is that past research involving exceptional learners has largely pursued different research goals from our own. As the following chapters will show, we have no wish to either prove or discount any forms of the Critical/Sensitive Period Hypothesis, nor are we particularly interested in analysing the differences between near-native and native language proficiency. Instead, our focus will be on how our participants managed to beat the odds and turn their L2 learning histories into success stories, which is in stark contrast to the default perception of frustration and unfulfilled dreams in the area of adult L2 attainment.

Ultimately, of course, any study in SLA should align with the saying that the proof of the pudding is in the eating, and therefore our focus will be primarily on what aspects of our unique participants' approaches are transferrable for the purpose of improving ordinary learners' chances of turning their language learning into success. Moyer (2021: 5) addresses this issue head-on when she asks, 'Can we extrapolate the relevance of L2 talent, giftedness, or genius to long-term learning?' As we will see in the following chapters, the findings of our investigation suggest an affirmative answer: studying exceptional learners can offer many useful lessons even for their less-gifted peers.

2 Methodology: Identifying Participants and Documenting Their Stories

Our book offers a summary of the results of a large-scale exploratory study into the intriguing learning history of exceptional language learners who have managed to achieve nativelike proficiency against all odds. Chapter 1 provided an overview of the theoretical background of our research project, and in order to further set the scene for presenting our findings in the following chapters, we describe here the technical details of our investigation by explaining who the participants are, how we recruited them for the project, what kind of data we collected from them and how we processed and analysed this data.

2.1 Participants

Our total participant sample consists of 30 exceptional learners, who were recruited through a combination of our existing contacts and *snowball sampling*, that is, asking both our contacts and our participants to recommend additional potential candidates (Dörnyei, 2007). As described briefly in the Introduction, our recruitment criteria were fairly straightforward. Eligible participants were required to:

(1) be recommended by someone who recognised them as someone often taken for a native speaker in a second language (L2) by native speakers of that L2;
(2) confirm themselves that they are/were indeed nativelike in the particular L2; and
(3) be able to provide evidence of passing for a native speaker.

Furthermore, because we were interested in learners who had overcome common barriers to achieving nativelike proficiency, we only selected candidates who did not have any heritage links with their nativelike L2 and who had not been immersed in their L2 in any significant way (e.g. for more than a month) before the age of 18.

Cases that met these criteria on the borderline were discounted for the study.

Table 2.1 provides detailed demographic information about the final 30 participants who were included in the project. As can be seen, a few of them are nativelike in more than one L2, but some of these languages were not included in the full analyses because their learning experience did not pass all of our criteria. For example, Joy spoke Portuguese at a nativelike level as a child, but her immersion experience in Portuguese was before the age of 18. Similarly, Denny's English competence was also largely disregarded because she moved to England at the age of 16.

We did not perform any proficiency tests to gauge the actual level of proficiency of our candidates for two reasons. First, as explained in Chapter 1, realistically none of them would have been expected to produce scores that were on par with those of native speakers in every measurable area. Second, the important qualifying condition for us was the candidates' ability to pass for a native speaker because, measurable proficiency notwithstanding, having achieved such a remarkable level in an L2 was assumed to be associated with a unique language learning mindset. Additionally, it was not necessary for the participants to currently speak their L2 at a nativelike level, they merely needed to be nativelike at one point in their adult lives, because we assumed that they would be able to remember and reflect upon this experience regardless of any subsequent fluctuations in their L2 proficiency. Their achievement of such a language learning peak is not unlike qualifying for membership in an elite club, and our main research interest concerned finding out how they succeeded in this process and what exactly that membership meant for them.

To summarise, it was enough for us that our participants were recommended by a native speaker and could provide strong evidence for passing as native speakers themselves, a selection process that we characterised in the Introduction as the 'duck test': if they say they are a duck, can act like a duck and are accepted by other ducks as a duck, we accepted them as ducks. In fact, we aimed for a broad range of 'ducks' in our study in order to sample as wide a variety of experiences as possible. Therefore, as shown in Table 2.1, our participants' ages range from 16 to 67, their first languages (L1s) make up a total of 16 different languages and together they mastered nine target languages at a nativelike level. Some of them are students, others language specialists and, in fact, several work in professions that have absolutely nothing to do with linguistics. On the less positive side, our recruitment method resulted in participants with higher education levels than average, as well as a bias towards white European and female participants. Additionally, all participants were by necessity either L1 English speakers or nativelike in English, as our interviews were conducted in this language.

Table 2.1 Participant demographics

Name	Age	Gender	Status/ profession	L1(s)	Nativelike L2(s)	Other L2 experience	Age of starting to learn nativelike L2	Time spent in L2 environment	Country of origin	Country of residence	L1 of spouse/ long-term partner	Comments
Amelia	40s	F	Professor in foreign language teaching	English	German	French	13	20+ years	UK (England)	Austria	N/A	
Capucine	Early 20s	F	University student	French	English	Spanish	Primary school	3 years	France	UK	N/A	Lou's sister
Carl	16	M	Student	Swedish	English	German	Primary school	<1 year	Sweden	Sweden	N/A	
Colin	66	M	Retired language teacher	English	French, German	Italian, Spanish	11 (French); 13 (German)	7 months (France); 2 years (Germany)	UK (England)	UK	N/A	Sarah and Lisa's teacher
Denny	39	F	PhD student	Bulgarian	German	English	14	<1 year	Bulgaria	UK	English	Nativelike English with early exposure
Hanna	31	F	PhD student	Finnish	English	German, Spanish, Swedish	10	10 years	Finland	UK	English	
Heidrun	50s	F	University lecturer; secondary school English teacher	German	English	N/A	10	1–2 years	Austria	Austria	English	
Ira	20	F	Student	Dutch	English	French, German	10	2 years	Netherlands	UK	N/A	Rianne's cousin

(Continued)

24 Lessons from Exceptional Language Learners

Table 2.1 (Continued) Participant demographics

Name	Age	Gender	Status/profession	L1(s)	Nativelike L2(s)	Other L2 experience	Age of starting to learn nativelike L2	Time spent in L2 environment	Country of origin	Country of residence	L1 of spouse/long-term partner	Comments
Joy	Upper middle-aged	F	Language educator	English	Icelandic	French, Portuguese	Early 20s	10+ years	Canada	Canada	Icelandic	Nativelike Portuguese as child
Judith	67	F	Professor of Viking studies	English, Hungarian	Norwegian	French, German	21	2+ years	USA	UK	N/A	
Kerry	Middle-aged	F	University instructor	English	Italian	French	18	1–2 years	Canada	Canada	N/A	
Kristin	20	F	University student	Norwegian	English	Danish, Spanish, Swedish	7	2 years	Norway	UK	N/A	
Kristopher	41	M	Associate professor of Japanese literature	English	Mandarin, Japanese	N/A	High school (Mandarin); 22 (Japanese)	19 years	Canada	Japan	Japanese	
Lesley	50	F	Sales administrator; technical translator	English	German	French, Swedish	21	25+ years	UK (Scotland)	Germany	German	
Lisa	40	F	Government scientist	English	German	Spanish	12	15+ years	UK (England)	Germany	German	Colin's former pupil
Livia	34	F	Writer and lecturer in creative writing	Italian	English	French, Portuguese	8	12 years	Italy	UK	Italian	

Lou	24	NB	Feminist/ queer activist	French	English	Greek, Spanish	Primary school	<1 year	France	France	N/A	Capucine's sibling
Marjan	63	F	Retired physiotherapy lecturer	Dutch	English	French, German	12	40+ years	Netherlands	Netherlands	UK	English
Peng	36	M	Freelancer	Mandarin	English	French	10	1 year	China	China	N/A	
Ranko	Late 20s	M	College student	Kurdish	English	Persian	22	6 years	Iran	UK	N/A	
Rianne	32	F	Experimental physicist	Dutch	German, English	French	10	<1 year	Netherlands	Netherlands	German	Ira's cousin
Samuli	25	M	University student	Finnish	English	French, German, Spanish, Swedish	Primary school	<1 year	Finland	Finland	N/A	
Sara	26	F	English as a second language teacher	Slovenian	English	German, Serbian	5–6	<1 year	Slovenia	Slovenia	N/A	
Sarah	50s	F	Voluntary worker; former EFL teacher	English	Hungarian	French, German, Italian	22	10 years	UK (England)	UK	Hungarian	Zoltán's wife; Colin's former pupil

(Continued)

Table 2.1 (Continued) Participant demographics

Name	Age	Gender	Status/ profession	L1(s)	Nativelike L2(s)	Other L2 experience	Age of starting to learn nativelike L2	Time spent in L2 environment	Country of origin	Country of residence	L1 of spouse/ long-term partner	Comments
Shinhye	52	F	Professor in English education	Korean	English	N/A	13	4+ years	South Korea	South Korea	N/A	
Thamarasie	67	F	Retired office worker	Sinhalese	English	French, Italian	6	<1 year	Sri Lanka	Sri Lanka	N/A	
Theresa	Middle-aged	F	Research director	German	English	French, Spanish	10	20+ years	Germany	UK	English	
Timur	40	M	Linguistics training specialist	Russian	English	Burmese, Norwegian, Thai	10	5+ years	USSR (present-day Kazakhstan)	Thailand	English	
Uwe	60	M	Teacher trainer	German	English	French, Hungarian, Russian	14	1 year	East Germany	Hungary	Hungarian	
William	16	M	Student	Swedish	English	French	7	<1 year	Sweden	Sweden	N/A	6 years of English-medium schooling

2.2 Research Approach

As we have discussed previously, L2 nativelikeness is a complex phenomenon influenced by a variety of different factors including, at the very least, the learners' aptitude, personality, motivation, context and available opportunities. Because our investigation was by definition exploratory, adopting a qualitative methodology was the obvious choice, which was further informed by Ushioda's (2009) 'person-in-context' approach in order to capture the blend of our participants' unique, individual and contextually rooted experiences. Given also our interest in a developmental-temporal angle to explore the lived experiences of individuals who engage with language learning in specific socio-historical and cultural contexts, we selected narrative inquiry as our principal research method (see e.g. Barkhuizen, 2013; Pavlenko, 2007), and conducted in-depth interviews with our participants to document their language learning stories. Narrative interviews convey learners' experiences as an ongoing dialogue between their past actions, their identities and their social and contextual relationships; this interview style therefore created space for our participants to share both specific factors that they found relevant at particular points in their learning histories as well as recurring influences with more subtle but longitudinal effects.

We designed our interview protocol in three parts: first, we asked for a brief account of participants' experiences being taken as a native speaker in their L2. We then invited them to share with us their language learning history from its beginning to the present, guiding them through the telling in a temporal fashion with minimal interference (only asking clarification questions). Finally, we had a short checklist of specific points of interest that we inquired into if they had not naturally been mentioned earlier, for example musical training, role models and L1 maintenance, to name a few (see Appendix for the full interview schedule).

2.3 Data Collection and Analysis

Recommended candidates were initially contacted by email and were invited to a brief introductory meeting via an online video chat in which the project was explained, participation criteria were confirmed and participants' questions were answered. Following this initial meeting, they signed an agreement form regarding their participation in the study, involving research ethical and copyright matters, and they were given the choice as to whether they wanted to be identified or remain anonymous in the present work. The next step was the main data collection phase, consisting of an in-depth recorded interview whose length varied between 41 minutes and 3.5 hours, averaging 99 minutes and comprising a total of just under 50 recorded hours.

The recordings were uploaded to an online transcription software (Otter.ai) and the automatic transcriptions were then checked carefully against the recordings and amended as necessary. The resulting interview transcripts resulted in a corpus of over 460,000 words. Initial reflexive thematic analysis (Braun & Clarke, 2006) was conducted using NVivo 12, with a special focus on factors that facilitated the development of nativelikeness. We took an inductive, exploratory approach to our analyses as we wanted, first and foremost, to maintain the subjectivity of our participants' accounts while keeping in mind our own positionalities in our interpretation of the data (Braun & Clarke, 2021). Alongside the first rounds of analysis, an initial story summary accompanied by a selection of particularly noteworthy excerpts was synthesised from each participant's original transcript, resulting in a condensed corpus of about 280,000 words. Each participant's condensed version was then submitted to member checking (i.e. sent to the participants for verification) to ensure that our interpretation and writeup aligned with participants' experiences. Although member checking as a means of research validation is often discouraged in reflexive thematic analysis (Braun & Clarke, 2013), we deemed the practice necessary from an ethical perspective due to the personal nature of synthesising and subsequently sharing third-person narratives of our participants' stories (De Costa *et al.*, 2021).

The subsequent analysis involved several additional rounds of analysis, using primarily these summaries and interview extracts and referring back to the original transcripts as well as continued participant correspondence for elaboration wherever necessary. As co-authors, we took a collaborative, reflexive approach to exploring our individual interpretations of the data, and we invited one of our participants, Capucine, to join us in a limited capacity as a budding researcher herself. As such, the themes we generated were the combination of our participants' experiences through the data and our collective expertise and subjectivity. We then finalised the stories, which also included editing the inevitably rugged conversational transcripts into a more coherent style appropriate for written format. As such, the published interview excerpts have been 'smoothed over' by omitting any false starts, filler words, repetitions, etc., and passages have sometimes been condensed to clarify the interviewee's message. The finalised learning stories that were the result of this process, as well as the analytical excerpts present in the current volume, were subsequently returned to participants for a second round of member checking. The current book contains the scholarly analysis of this data in the form of an extended qualitative research report, whereas the companion volume (*Stories from Exceptional Language Learners...*) presents a compilation of participants' full learning stories.

As our methods largely involved participant-driven interviews and an inductive analytical approach, readers will find that the present volume includes a rather eclectic combination of topics, organised in a roughly temporal manner for easier access. While some topics in this volume relate to more commonly examined issues in language learning psychology – such as language aptitude and other individual differences (see e.g. Dörnyei & Ryan, 2015) – others will diverge according to our participants' emphases. We would thus be remiss if we did not stress that a report of this nature is necessarily the outcome of a collaborative experience between the participant and the researchers, and this applies especially so to the elicited learning stories here (De Costa *et al.*, 2021). Our own experiences and the way we condensed and compiled the raw data into narratives and analysis undoubtedly shaped the emergent meaning conveyed here. Therefore, to ensure that our positionality did not overshadow the voices of our participants, as well as to ensure that our participants were satisfied with how they have been represented in both volumes, we shared the story drafts with participants at least twice (as mentioned above), and the final product has been presented here only with their full input and authorisation.

3 Defining Nativelikeness

In the Introduction, it was briefly mentioned that the notions of 'nativelikeness' and the 'native speaker' have generated considerable debate in scholarly circles, some of it quite controversial, as we will see below. These terms will occur frequently both in participants' own accounts and in various discussions; therefore, there is a need to offer some more focused reflection on them. This chapter does so by addressing the native(like) speaker in both theory and practice, providing a brief overview on the debate surrounding the issue, outlining our own approach and finally exploring how nativelikeness was experienced by our participants. In an early interview we conducted, one of our participants, Uwe, questioned as to whether nativelikeness was indeed as big an achievement as we were so eager to assume, or if it was simply 'an outcome'. His remark went on to shape and underpin many of the considerations we took with our project over the following months. We repeatedly returned to the question of what it means to be nativelike in a second language (L2), both from an external, social perspective and in the eyes of our participants themselves in light of their experiences. Without intending to be conclusive, this chapter addresses this question, foregrounding a number of different emphases both from the literature and from our study.

3.1 The Native Speaker as a Concept

The concept of the *native speaker* has historically been – and continues to be – an elusive one. Used in everyday conversation, most people instinctively know what is meant by the term. Yet, when researchers have attempted to tease this definition apart over the last few decades, problems have presented themselves, particularly in the face of bi-/multilingual speakers and contexts (Canagarajah, 2013; Davies, 2003; Kunschak & Kono, 2020; Paikeday, 1985). To start with, the notion of the 'native speaker' appears to exist in dual dimensions:

(1) as a 'myth', whereby the native speaker is an idealised speaker of a language, representing the highest possible proficiency, and is

thus the ultimate guardian and protector of an immutable linguistic standard; and
(2) as a 'reality', whereby the native speaker is a speaker of a specific variety of a language with its range of cultural and grammatical nuances and permutations, displaying idiosyncratic variation in the different dimensions of communicative competence (Davies, 2003).

These two viewpoints come with paragraphs of fine print, exceptions and grey areas that are often ignored in the term's everyday use. Thus, when it comes to referring to and invoking the concept of the native speaker, it can be difficult to tell whether one or both dimensions are being summoned, and this has led to misuse, conflicting understandings and a world of hurt.

In his 1985 book *The Native Speaker is Dead!* Thomas Paikeday (1985: 21) collaborated with a range of colleagues in an attempt to define the concept and its uses, and one of his early questions aptly illustrates the tenor of his investigation: 'Is "native speaker" merely an ideal or a convenient linguistic fiction – myth, shibboleth, sacred cow – an etherlike concept with no objective reality to it, albeit embodied in a quasi-privileged class of speakers of each language?'. Paikeday's ruminations on privilege continued to endure and even grow through the following decades, but despite his and others' principled rejection of the term, the native speaker appears to be very much alive and kicking, as we will explore below.

3.2 Native-Speakerism and Linguistic Discrimination

While the native/non-native speaker distinction has been the subject of varied scrutiny since the 1960s, this discussion has been most recently fuelled by attention to discriminatory issues surrounding language teachers' native/non-nativeness, first coined *native-speakerism* by Adrian Holliday (2005) in his book on the struggles of teaching English as a lingua franca. Since its first use, the definition of native-speakerism has been expanded by Houghton and Rivers to the following:

> Prejudice, stereotyping, and/or discrimination, typically by or against foreign language teachers, on the basis of either being or not being perceived and categorised as a native speaker of a particular language, which can form part of a larger complex of interconnected prejudices including ethnocentrism, racism, and sexism. (Houghton & Rivers, 2013: 14)

Such prejudice and the discrimination that arises from it are based on the conception that L2 learners will never reach the same level of linguistic competence as the 'mythical' native speaker – an arguably impossible endeavour. What complicates this issue is that, as discussed in Chapter 1, there is indeed evidence to corroborate the view that most, if not all, L2 learners will never have the exact same linguistic competence in an L2 as a monolingual first language (L1) speaker of the same language. However, it was also shown that the differences are often so subtle and 'microscopic' – sometimes only a few milliseconds in a laboratory experiment – that they have very little to do with an individual's ability to operate in the language, including teaching it. Moreover, and without going into extensive detail here, effective teaching is certainly a function of a great deal more than linguistic competence, and thus a general consensus has been emerging within academic circles that nativeness should not matter in language teaching (Houghton & Bouchard, 2020). However, the view from the ground is often very different: many organisations continue to selectively hire those they deem native speakers for language teaching positions without a second thought, either to please their customers or because of their own contestable beliefs about language teacher qualifications. Such discriminatory hiring practices continue to be prevalent and most often occur, as Houghton and Rivers (2013) point out, at the intersection of other prejudices and systemic problems.

Beyond the education sector, additional criticism argues that the native/non-native dichotomy creates a two-tier system on a grander scale, in which L2 speakers are perpetually viewed as illegitimate or lesser language users compared to L1 speakers (e.g. Cook, 1999, 2016; Ortega, 2014). When unchecked, this bias can evolve into discrimination in a wide range of domains such as education, the workplace, housing and the legal system (Derwing *et al.*, 2014; Lippi-Green, 2012). Instead, Cook (2002, 2016) has proposed viewing bi-/multilinguals from a perspective of multicompetence, in which they are not set up against native speakers but rather are viewed as L2 speakers in their own right, with different – but not lesser – linguistic competencies. As a result, it is both unsurprising and understandable that some have called for the elimination of the native/non-native distinction altogether in favour of other alternatives such as 'L1/LX users' (Dewaele, 2018; Dewaele *et al.*, 2021; Hammarberg, 2010).

On the other hand, scholars such as Hyltenstam and colleagues object to the total abandonment of the terms 'native' and 'non-native speaker' as of yet. They acknowledge that the suggestion of alternative terminology is an example of 'the well-known process of substituting new terms for emotion-laden words that have become "impossible" to use' (Hyltenstam *et al.*, 2018: 6). The question they raise instead is whether the situation has reached the point at which the native/non-native dichotomy can indeed be successfully replaced, and their view is that 'we are not there yet' (Hyltenstam *et al.*, 2018: 6). They offer two arguments in favour of not rejecting the traditional terminology too swiftly:

First, they argue that alternative terminology alone does little to change the prevailing attitudes towards various groups that underlie any discriminatory tenor. This is, of course, an age-old and well-rehearsed dilemma regarding such terminological changes (e.g. concerning various ethnic groups), but this is especially the case with language. The way we speak any of our languages, L1 or L2, is a social indicator of group membership, perhaps even more so than physical appearance (Gluszek & Dovidio, 2010; Kinzler, 2020; Moyer, 2014). Research has shown that humans already begin demonstrating accent-based differential treatment of others fairly early on in childhood (Kinzler, 2021). A more principled use of terminology in the future can undoubtedly raise awareness and thereby contribute to a shift in our evaluation of nativeness and thus a reduction in discrimination, particularly in the workplace. Nonetheless, language will remain a social indicator that influences both the ways we connect interpersonally and how we define ourselves and are defined by others, and this cannot be erased by a terminological shift (Trudgill, 2000). While invocations of the mythical native speaker often only present more problems than they solve, the reality of the native speaker is an undeniable part of human existence, both in practice and within the field of second language acquisition (SLA). This is echoed by Hyltenstam and colleagues' second argument, that

> the native speaker as a benchmark is so deeply rooted and central to second language theory that the distinction between second language learners and native speakers can be discerned in almost all existing research in the area.... The use of this particular terminology is still the most common convention in second language research, and there is at present no widespread agreement on the substitute terms to use among the various suggested alternatives, should the prevailing terminology need to be abandoned. (Hyltenstam *et al.*, 2018: 6)

The prevalent use of the terms 'native' and 'non-native' is especially the case outside of academic circles, and indeed when asked, most of our participants themselves were unaware of any of the above-mentioned ideological issues. Ultimately, a hasty shift in terminology risks further alienating the very populations we aim to serve, particularly when the lack of public engagement in research is already being called into question (see e.g. Ushioda, 2020). Perhaps in more multilingual contexts, as Hyltenstam and colleagues suggest, a change in terminology might be appropriate, but in some contexts the terms' utility stands strong; the concept of nativeness, however constructed, also represents social groupings as they already exist – real, idiosyncratic, group-based nativeness – and we ourselves cannot see how we could have written the current volumes without the term 'nativelike'.

3.3 Nativelikeness as a Research Interest

In the light of Cook's (2002, 2016) theory of multicompetence and the burgeoning research into native-speakerism and linguistic discrimination (e.g. Houghton & Bouchard, 2020; Slavkov *et al.*, 2021;

Swan *et al.*, 2015), one may rightly wonder what would explain a research interest in nativelikeness? Moyer offers a good explanation:

> In the pedagogical realm, teachers commonly reinforce nativeness as a goal, even if an unspoken one, and learners may not see this as an unwelcome imposition; many consider it their target whether or not they are likely to reach it. (Moyer, 2013: 171)

Indeed, if we think about it, the L2 code that language learners study has been elicited by linguists from the performance of the natural users of this code – the community of L1 speakers – and mastering aspects of this L2 code is the objective of any language learning enterprise. In other words, ultimately, language learning can loosely be seen as a process of approximating nativelikeness in one way or another. Moreover, even when armed with an understanding of the fallacies of the native speaker as a linguistic standard, many learners continue to aspire to nativelikeness as a goal representing high learning merits and personal significance. There are a number of reasons for this, ranging from mere whim to a love for the target language's related culture, and many of these have little to do with the negative sides of the native/non-native dichotomy. By way of illustration, learners can want to be nativelike from a more positive perspective on group membership; for example, our participant Joy embraced the sense of community she found from being nativelike in her L2 Icelandic: 'Iceland was my home. Icelanders were my people – they were my husband's people, so they were my people'. There are, of course, downsides to nativelikeness, such as when it leads to misunderstandings about speakers' origins or causes them to be mislabelled, a topic we return to in Chapter 12. Yet for Joy, being recognised as nativelike in Icelandic was part of the bigger picture of her own demonstration of community participation and involvement. Whereas using the native speaker as a linguistic standard for *all* learners is problematic given the difficulty of achieving such a goal, on an individual level it can be a meaningful source of motivation.

We are not claiming that every learner needs to attain nativelike or near-native proficiency. However, given that for many this remains an objective, we believe it is an important research aim to pull back the curtain on the highest level of proficiency that learners might attain. Indeed, part of the reason why researchers in the past have dedicated so much time to measuring the differences between L1 and L2 speakers has been for the sake of determining the extent to which an additional language *can* be learned. In this sense, the learners of this project are 'exceptional' not because they have achieved the most desirable linguistic outcome, but because they have achieved what typical learners do not (sometimes despite their best efforts). Thus, by investigating the upper extremes of language learning, scholars hope to find themselves one step closer to being able to set reasonable standards and expectations for learners. To present an analogy: Mount Everest might be widely considered as the ultimate achievement in mountaineering. Many youths are initially motivated to become mountaineers after hearing stories about people who reach the summit, and they continually find inspiration from their dream of developing the skill set required for the ascent. Nonetheless, while some do go on to realise this dream, not every individual needs to climb Mount Everest in order to see themselves (and be seen by others) as a legitimate mountaineer; fulfilment can clearly be found from other peaks – or even hills – across the globe. We believe the same can be said for language learning: while nativelikeness is an achievement worth investigating and celebrating, learners can have all manner of legitimate goals for themselves that have little to do with nativelikeness. Yet, similar to the accounts of great explorers, those who have circumvented natural learning constraints and achieved the proverbial 'ultimate' of nativelikeness are likely to bring to the table something exciting: a unique experience full of lessons that many of us can learn from and apply in our own language learning endeavours.

We are aware of the fact that reflections such as those above can raise more questions than they answer, so let us begin pulling back the proverbial curtain of nativelikeness by turning to our participants themselves for insight. What does it mean for them to be nativelike, and what does it not mean?

3.4 Our Participants' Perceptions of 'Passing' as a Native Speaker

One of the key issues with the notion of nativelikeness is the elusive nature of the 'nativeness' that one approximates. As we discussed in Chapter 2, we have adopted the term *passing* to account for situations in which our participants qualified for being nativelike by being assumed to be native speakers by L1 speakers. The reason for the term 'passing' is that it is simply not enough to say that one is a native speaker of a language because, as we know, language is not a monolithic and unchanging entity, and a given language can have any number of dialectical variations. As Moyer (2013: 122) explains, 'In this age of societal multilingualism, who sounds foreign is ultimately defined locally and negotiated between individual interlocutors, one context at a time'. Being a nativelike speaker does not mean that one will be perceived as such according to every standard and by every interlocutor in every encounter. As such, factors such as the linguistic domain/context of an interaction and the interlocutor's own linguistic repertoire, among others, can influence whether or not a speaker is perceived as a native speaker (Lindemann & Campbell, 2017). Let us look at these factors more closely, in part as an illustration of the complexity of the matter.

3.4.1 Linguistic domain

In terms of instances in which our participants have passed for native speakers, they have a wide range of experience. Participants like Denny find themselves passing most often in casual, introductory conversations:

> I'd have to say I pass most often in everyday situations, everyday conversations, and it's usually with people who don't know me, people who meet me for the first time. And I suppose when you are in those sorts of situations, you have a few practiced phrases, and you kind of get used to saying those initial introductory things.

The domain and topic of participants' conversations do indeed appear to be a critical factor affecting the ability to pass in the whole of our sample, as illustrated by Judith and Marjan:

> I think in ordinary, everyday situations I could carry on a perfectly normal conversation, and people would not think I was not a native speaker, but what I probably couldn't do is carry on, for example, an academic conversation or something like that. That would be more difficult. (Judith)

> You can definitely hear it [my non-nativeness] if I'm in front of 300 students at a university doing a lead lecture, or if I'm in a conference and I find it stressful; you can definitely hear it. But on a day-to-day basis, not many people can hear it now. (Marjan)

Both Piller (2002) and Gnevsheva (2017) found that there was a fair amount of contextual variation in passing for a native speaker in their research; casual, transitory conversations are most conducive to passing perhaps because the interlocutors' identities and origins are ambiguous and often irrelevant to the communication at hand. Additionally, while we did not specify any distinction between speaking and writing in our interview questions, all responses focused on learners' experiences with speaking rather than written discourse, with Samuli being an exception:

> Well, in a written conversation, I don't really see what would give away the fact that I am not a native English speaker. I consider myself perfectly at a nativelike level in English, and possible mistakes or spelling errors would be seen as typos, on par with those that any native speaker could make just as well.

Interestingly, our sample does contain particularly exceptional participants such as Kristopher and Livia who felt they could pass indefinitely in most encounters:

I don't know how long [I could pass]. As long as I wanted, I guess. (Kristopher)

I'd say probably what tends to happen is people won't be able to figure out that I'm not a native speaker unless I reveal myself. (Livia)

3.4.2 Interlocutor-specific factors

Hanna's account below is a good illustration of the fact that the ability to pass as a native speaker is also dependent on the speech variety and linguistic experience of the interlocutor:

In England, I think I could pass for maybe the first half hour, but sometimes, particularly if it's people who are not from the UK – for example, when I met Americans – they just assume that I'm South African or something. Actually, it's never really come to the point that they actually found out that I wasn't, until I told them, 'Hold on. Wait, I'm actually Finnish', [to which they respond] 'What?!'

Thus, while listeners tend to be quite good at distinguishing non-native accents from native accents (e.g. Flege, 1984; Major, 2007; Munro *et al.*, 2010), sometimes variations in speech can be misattributed to a different dialect of the same language. Indeed, Gnevsheva (2017) investigated the dialectical variation in passing for a native speaker and suggested that passing for a different dialect might be an intermediate step before passing for a speaker of the same dialect. Another example of this phenomenon would be Colin's account of being taken for a Belgian in France, and the following recollection by Heidrun is typical among our project participants:

I suppose [British-]English-speaking people wouldn't think that I'm British. No, because they can hear my accent. But in America, it happens regularly that they ask me if I am British. And it happened very early on because they think that I'm British because they can't quite place a British accent. But in England, I don't think it's ever happened.

The main lesson of these considerations for the current discussion is that listeners' own linguistic repertoire and training can factor into whether or not an L2 speaker passes for a native speaker in a given situation.

3.4.3 Other factors

While some obvious criteria of passing for a native speaker include a strong command of grammar, vocabulary and accent/pronunciation, other aspects of one's communicative competence such as sociocultural knowledge can also have an effect on passing for group membership. Shinhye, for example, recounts:

> Over time I realised that pronunciation is not really a big problem. It's more about how you want to participate and how you want to relate with each other. And how you want to be in this group, and acting similarly so that you can be in this group. That's more important [for nativelikeness].

To be recognised as a member of an ethnolinguistic group, it is thus also important to act as part of the group. This poses definite limitations, but luckily many situations are quite forgiving in this respect; for example, Kristopher is often taken as 'boorish' or 'kind of rude' rather than non-native when he uses *keigo*, Japanese honorific speech, in a somewhat imperfect manner. A less forgiving factor that contributes to passing is one's physical appearance, illustrated by Joy's experience in two different countries:

> Although when I was a kid in Brazil I could pass too, I didn't look the part. And because I didn't look the part [as she is blonde] where we lived in the northwest of Brazil, people don't expect you to pass. They don't expect you to sound like them, and so if people don't see you, it's one thing, but when they see you, it just kind of messes them up for some reason. Whereas in Iceland, I guess I looked the part and so it seemed that I passed fairly well.

Other participants, like Kerry in Italy and Kristopher in Japan, had similar experiences and were usually only taken for native speakers when they were not seen by their interlocutor (most often over the phone, or in one instance, by an elderly hotelier with poor eyesight). Conversely, there is even consistent (and often funny) anecdotal evidence about native speakers with foreign-sounding names talking on the phone with fellow native speakers for several minutes without the slightest problem, but upon introducing themselves, their interlocutor immediately started speaking slowly and more loudly! On the other hand, Joy's experience in Iceland shows that appearance and other listener perceptions can also function in the opposite direction, when the interlocutors assume that a nativelike speaker's background matches theirs. For example, although Shinhye (who is Korean) considers herself only at an A2 level in Mandarin, she found herself passing for a native speaker for very short periods when she visited China:

> When I actually went to China and used the very limited, formulaic expressions a little bit, they started talking to me in Chinese. And they asked me for directions in Chinese. So I can fool them for some seconds!

3.4.4 The fallacy of unmarkedness

One of the most desirable aspects of nativelikeness is the idea that one's language use might become 'unmarked', that is, it becomes something that simply exists without anyone noticing it. This is related to the broader issue that, as Liddicoat (2016) explains, one problematic aspect of idolising the mythical native speaker as the guardian of language is that it can translate to an asymmetry of power, where native speakers can turn the focus of any interaction to an L2 speaker's language. Kramsch and Zhang (2018: 23) further add, 'The issue is not the symbolic power game itself: people will always seek ways to distinguish themselves from others through the way they talk, dress, or behave'. As society continues to operate on such a system of distinction, one might then assume that a perk of becoming nativelike is to avoid this power asymmetry by having an unmarked accent, unattached to any ethnolinguistic group in particular. As Timur says:

> In a group of people who all speak English, I just want to be sort of unmarked. Yeah, and also maybe a little bit of a fly on the wall, like no one is like, 'Oh, tell me about your background', you know?

Therefore, in theory at least, by becoming unmarked, an L2 speaker might hope to function as a native speaker from a practical perspective without needing to linguistically identify with any specific region or group.

In practice, however, being unmarked may not be quite so simple, and Uwe's experience with his L2 English reflects well the potential complication: his pronunciation was developed from listening to different varieties of British English, resulting in what he calls a 'mongrel' accent that does not mark him as belonging to any specific place in the UK. However, as he laments, this so-called unmarkedness led to many a conversation in which the listener tried to place his accent to somewhere within England, which in fact made him feel more 'subconscious' than any earlier commentary he might have received about his previous L1 German accent. From this perspective, nativelikeness might be considered an undesirable outcome for some, a negative framing we return to in Chapter 12. Uwe's experience is thus a good reminder that becoming nativelike in an L2, although perhaps desirable for a variety of other reasons, may not act as an invincible shield against human curiosity or group-based appraisal.

3.5 A Phenomenological Approach to Nativeness and Nativelikeness

We have seen earlier that several scholars have suggested abandoning the term 'native speaker' because of its discriminatory connotations, and we have also cited Hyltenstam *et al.*'s (2018) caution about doing so because of the centrality of the term on the ground and in most SLA theories. We would like to finish this chapter by raising yet another aspect of the issue, the *phenomenological reality* of the terms. Having spent a lifetime functioning as an L2 speaker of English in an L1 English environment – with even his family life largely in English – Zoltán still considers himself a high-functioning *non-native* speaker of English, both practically and psychologically. One may argue that in several linguistic domains, he operates at a higher level in English than in his L1 Hungarian (or even compared to many L1 English speakers), but while this is certainly true, he still describes this comparison as his advanced non-native language skills exceeding his rusty or less-developed native language skills. The point is that, linguistic expertise aside, he senses a distinct phenomenological quality of ease and naturalness of native language use (even if it does not go well) in contrast to the cognitive demand of non-native language use (even when it goes exceptionally well). More generally, one may argue that most language learners, even high-functioning ones, know perfectly well when they are speaking an L2 that is different from using their L1, which indirectly validates the two categories, regardless of the terminology we use to refer to them.

We believe that such a phenomenological approach is a legitimate one and should be seen as part of the wider discussion on the subject, but we should also note that it raises some questions about the notion of nativelikeness that is at the heart of this book. Most importantly, from a phenomenological vantage point, which category do our project participants belong to: native or non-native? The easy answer would be the former since the idea of nativelikeness, historically perceived as the highest reachable language learning goal, goes hand in hand with an unquestionable confidence in one's L2. In all honesty, however, most of our participants did not find this degree of ultimate confidence, even though they clearly went beyond the phenomenological level of 'non-native performance', and, as we summarised in the Introduction, their language concerns and uncertainties were in an altogether different category from that of the average language learner. This, then, places them somewhere in between the two categories. We explore this theme further in Chapter 11, but let us here briefly illustrate the issue with two excerpts, from Capucine and Colin. Capucine categorised herself as a simultaneous learner *and* speaker of her nativelike L2 English:

> [I feel like I'm still learning] every day of my life. I don't think you'll ever stop learning English. I think it's an endless process… there's always going to be words, sentence structures that you wouldn't have thought about. Always. It's the same thing with your first language. You just can't reach that point where you know everything about the language. It's just humanly impossible.

The key phrase in Capucine's account is 'It's the same thing with your first language', and Capucine was not alone among our participants in categorising her L2 experience on a similar level to that of her L1. This non-distinction speaks volumes, because virtually no ordinary language learner would make such a comparison. Thus, while nativelike language learners may not find an unquestionable L2 confidence, what they do acquire is something almost as valuable: a sense of *comfort*. When Capucine describes how she feels about her nativelike L2 English, she finds that it feels 'safer' and that she 'could express [herself] with absolutely no pressure and also no boundaries'. Similarly, one of the most experienced L2 speakers in our sample, Colin – a retired language teacher who has mastered both German and French at a nativelike level – further clarifies how the difference between the L2 and the L1 can gradually fade away:

> When you're learning a language, there's this big barrier. And then the better you get in a language, that becomes maybe a glass barrier: you can see through, and people see you, and it's getting better. But when there's no barrier there at all, you can just walk through and you can become part of that. And I think that's what I felt with German… you just felt completely at home.

In many ways, therefore, the exceptional language learners of our investigation tend to straddle simultaneously two distinct phenomenological categories, native and non-native, which makes their insights genuinely precious: they can glimpse beyond certain screens that would otherwise, as it does for most of us, block the view.

3.6 Summary

This chapter has offered a look into the complexity surrounding the concept of nativeness both within the existing literature and with regard to our participants themselves. We opened the chapter with a brief overview of the challenges of defining and labelling the notion of the native speaker, and how the term has been used and abused. The complicated nature of the topic was further illustrated by describing various aspects of the notion of passing for a native speaker. The purpose of this chapter was thus to provide a contextual background regarding the way we operationalised the concept of nativelikeness in our study, from both a theoretical and a practical perspective. Although brief, this will hopefully provide a sociolinguistic backdrop against which we will frame our primary research interest of investigating the developmental processes of exceptional language learners.

The native/non-native speaker dichotomy, and unfounded assumptions of what it means to be either, have long been used as a quick and easy excuse for blatant discrimination, particularly in the world of language teaching. However, for many learners, aspiring to nativelikeness is a very positive and energising goal that motivates them to reach for the stars. Some see it as a symbol of community contribution, belonging and group membership, while others see it as a source of confidence, comfort and expression (and many see it as both). Our own conviction is that one of the most important goals for researchers is to empower language learners to set reasonable and attainable goals for themselves. Since reaching nativelikeness is a common objective for many, in this book we strive to illuminate both the journey towards this goal as well as what learners can expect at the end of the journey, while maintaining a sense of reality about the fact that climbing this linguistic Mount Everest is not an option for most learners. Although we ordinary learners cannot emulate our participants' exact experiences, we *can* learn from the stories of these great mountaineers and draw lessons from how they have achieved nativelikeness, as well as from the comfort that comes with it. To this latter end, we further explore the topic of comfort in Chapter 11, and then in the final chapter (Chapter 12) we analyse how our participants' journeys changed their understanding of their various linguistic and personal identities. This, however, is quite a jump ahead. In order to fully understand and appreciate our participants' post-summit experience of nativelikeness, let us first follow them through the journey up the mountain, starting from the beginning as explored in Chapter 4.

4 A Favourable Set-Up

We have thus far provided some much-needed contextualisation for this exploratory endeavour, so let us now begin detailing our findings in this and the following chapters. Exceptional learning achievements are energised by exceptional levels of motivation, and it is reasonable to assume that at least some of this motivation is rooted in the favourable characteristics of the set-up into which a person is born and brought up. Three main dimensions of this contextual foundation emerged in our study: (a) the availability of second language (L2)-related resources in the learning context, (b) family influences and the impact of early childhood experiences and (c) L2-specific social expectations and norms prevalent in the learner's social environment. However, while the motivational power that each of these three areas can exert is formidable – and we do find many cases in our sample where such early influences played a decisive role in shaping the participant's subsequent learning history – none of them are indispensable for success, as we will see in the following discussion. There are, indeed, several learners in our sample whose extraordinary achievement emerged from a rather unexceptional background. On the whole, our findings suggest that an L2 learner is placed on a language learning fast track by an *optimal combination* of a number of dynamically interacting and idiosyncratic conditions, faculties, pushes and pulls that they encounter or possess.

We should note that the absence of a single key to excellence – that is, a 'silver bullet' – is not restricted to the topic of this chapter but will also apply to all other aspects of exceptional L2 learning explored in the following chapters; as Moyer (2021: 138) concludes, 'there is no single, magic needle in the proverbial haystack'. This is, in fact, encouraging news for ordinary language learners: the fact that we cannot identify an indispensable prerequisite for high achievement presents a picture with multiple possible and accessible pathways to success. Indeed, if we consider the 30 participants in our project, they display diverse capabilities and trajectories, with the only common feature among them being that one way or another they have reached nativelike proficiency in at least one L2.

4.1 Resource Access and the 'New Global Generation'

Arguably, one of the most significant and favourable types of set-ups we encountered in our data set involved some of our learners' unprecedented access to L2 resources, something that has only become available in the last two decades or so. Traditionally, one could distinguish two distinct ways of learning an additional language. The first involves being immersed in the L2 environment and picking up the language naturalistically, a process sometimes referred to in the scholarly literature as *second language acquisition*. Conversely, the second, often referred to as *foreign language learning*, involves acquisition through conscious learning, often through self-study and educational classes with limited authentic contact with L2 speakers. Recently, however, this distinction has become blurred in some contexts due to globalisation and the internet, which have created widespread access to some languages (especially English) through channels such as social media, YouTube, video games and access to subtitled international television. As a result, in some countries (e.g. Sweden and the Netherlands) a new generation of learners has emerged who are able to pick up a great deal of L2 knowledge naturalistically, almost as if they had been immersed in the host environment. Our sample includes representatives of this 'New Global Generation', and Kristin's case offers a good illustration:

KRISTIN: 'READING AND WATCHING FILMS MADE ENGLISH NATURAL TO ME'

Kristin's initial L2 foundation, from both a linguistic and a motivational perspective, was set by her consumption of English language cartoons and films:

> I loved watching TV. I know that's bad as a child, but I loved it, like the Disney channel. In Norway the Disney channel is dubbed into Norwegian, but if you watch it after 6pm, it's all in English. And because I had an older sister who was three years older than me, she preferred watching it in English, so we just spent a lot of time watching movies and shows.

When Kristin reached her teens, she also began searching for more shows online. Slightly before the age of Netflix, she watched whatever she could find on YouTube or similar sites, which were never dubbed or subtitled into Norwegian. She nonetheless found she could understand them, and as she got older, she found the subtitles on television 'became sort of annoying, because I didn't need them anymore'.

Consequently, when she took an interest in reading in English as a teenager, she did not experience traditionally expected language constraints:

> When I started reading and really fell in love with the language, by that point I had the vocabulary down because of the movies and TV shows that I was watching. And so I never really had to think, 'I need to learn this and that'. I never really experienced that. I was motivated to use the language, but I never had to motivate myself to learn it because I already felt like I knew it.

Television and films thus gave Kristin a huge leg up, but they were only a part of the picture. In Chapter 5, we will see how much reading and writing in English helped Kristin to develop her nativelike English proficiency.

Kristin's account is not unique. Some of Carl's earliest memories also include him watching English language films with his father (in Sweden), who would translate for him because he was too young to read the subtitles. He also watched YouTube, but for him it was his avid interest in video games that played the primary role:

> I played a lot of Swedish [console] games, but then when I moved from console to PC, I started playing [online] games like Minecraft, which forced me to use English, as I was playing online with English people. So I had to speak the language, basically.

Carl summarises the common theme of the L2 learning of the New Global Generation: 'I kind of passively picked up on English and it formed as an interest over time'. Now as a teenager, he still spends most of his time outside of school on the internet, either browsing around YouTube or discussion boards, or gaming with others internationally through Discord. William, another Swedish teenager in our sample of exceptional learners, concurs: 'I don't think I've ever watched Swedish YouTube. I just find American stuff more amusing, and some British stuff too'. The power of such passive L2 acquisition should not be underestimated. Zoltán, for example, was stunned to hear a first-hand account of his teenage nephews successfully 'chatting up' two girls on the beach in German, without their parents having any knowledge of them being able to speak German. Although the boys grew up in Norway, it turned out that they used to watch German language children's television!

The circle of countries where learners can have such vast and almost effortless access to an L2 is gradually increasing with globalisation. Sara, for example, is Slovenian, and her account is not too different from that of her younger Scandinavian peers:

> Even back when I was growing up, we had Disney Channel, Nickelodeon, Cartoon Network. All of those were in English – they weren't dubbed or

anything. So we just watched, and what we could get was great. I would say that's another layer that contributed to the success of my English proficiency.

It should be noted that while television may be a more traditionally effortless mode of accessing the L2, particularly for young children, an increasingly wide and more diverse range of resources can be found on the internet, as witnessed by William and Carl. This is good news for the ordinary foreign language learner: no matter one's country of birth and its corresponding national television (or radio!), it is increasingly possible nowadays to access a favourable set-up.

4.2 Family Influences and the Impact of Early Childhood Experiences

Although as stated above, a favourable initial set-up is not indispensable for learners' future success, it still provides a considerable leg up. Our older participants may not have had access to YouTube or international television during their early learning days, but it was still possible to benefit from a favourable set-up through the influence of their families and early language-related childhood experiences. The best illustration of the positive role one's family background and upbringing can play is perhaps Rianne's story. Rianne's journey to nativelikeness is especially unique because her lifelong passion is physics, and L2 learning was never a particular point of interest for her. As she recalls:

> I never had a really big affinity with German in high school. Actually, it was one of my worst grades because I really didn't like it. I'm more orientated towards physics and those kinds of things, so languages were bad anyway…

Despite her otherwise muted language learning motivation, Rianne went on to become nativelike in not only one but two languages: English and German. Her outstanding accomplishment is due in large part to her childhood experiences, as we will see below:

RIANNE: SET UP TO SUCCEED IN LANGUAGE LEARNING

Rianne's childhood experiences are aptly characterised by her statement, 'There was always this international thing in my family'. Indeed, a Dutch native, she was born in the United States (still qualifying for our project because her only input at the time was Dutch, she did not attend day care or have a nanny, and her family returned to the Netherlands when she was less than two years old). When she was seven, her family moved again, this time to France for three years. Even though French did not become a language that she mastered at a nativelike level, this experience turned out to be decisive for her future language learning, giving her the confidence to later acquire both English and German to an unmarked and nativelike extent:

> I was just dropped in a French class as a Dutch person who didn't know anything about the language! And for a kid, this worked amazingly. So I had this idea already that even if I'm being dropped in a country where I don't speak the language, somehow you'll manage: because I managed as a kid, so I will probably do it as an adult as well.... I think I gained the feeling that a new language can be mastered, that somehow you are able to go to a completely different country and learn it as long as you're open for it.

The 'international thing' carried on after her family returned to the Netherlands:

> My parents had international friends that they kept in touch with, and an atmosphere of internationality came along with this: if you want to communicate with people, you're going to have to learn the language.... And it's not because of language per se, but because you want to be part of the community. I think that's what I really got taught from my family: that if you want to be internationally orientated, and if you want to live in other people's countries, then make sure you have the tools you need for it, and language is one of the tools.

Rianne's international orientation was further strengthened by the supportive milieu in the Netherlands:

> In the Netherlands there's a kind of international-looking perspective, or at least I had that feeling.... You start to realise, I think already in high school a little bit, that for certain topics Dutch is just too small to be having the books in Dutch, or to have the ideas in Dutch.

In sum, in her formative years, Rianne was thoroughly socialised into having an international mindset, and as we will see in Chapter 5, when she needed English and German for professional purposes, this foundation created sufficient impetus for her to go beyond the level that most L2 learners would have reached in a similar situation. The power of her family background is also reflected by the fact that her cousin, Ira (incidentally another of our project participants), also mentions that her aunt's family (i.e. Rianne's family) being 'internationally oriented' was one of her major childhood influences.

Rianne's childhood experiences provided her with a sense of self-efficacy that eclipsed her language learning indifference and spurred her on to exceptional success. Her story is inspiring, but we need to remember that this vignette describes only part of the picture, because not everybody would have responded to her experiences (e.g. being dropped in a French school with zero French experience) in such a constructive way – as mentioned above, every language learning trajectory is guided by a combination of factors. Keeping this in mind, there are similar stories in our sample that indicate that positive childhood experiences can be particularly instrumental to L2 learning. Let us look at a few typical examples:

- As the daughter of missionaries, Joy spent her childhood in Brazil and recalls that her parents

   had a great love and respect for the people that we interacted with. And my dad would never let us speak English in front of people who were Portuguese speakers if they couldn't speak English. This was instilled in me and became a natural part of my experiences: you respect people by respecting their language.

- Similarly, Marjan recounts that her parents 'always encouraged me as a child to be abroad, to connect with other children', taking her on holidays throughout Europe and instilling in her a love for foreign cultures, customs and people, as well as a willingness to communicate in other languages although 'they weren't very good at it'. Marjan attributes her learning success to this communicative outlook, which gave her 'the sort of edge to think that's what [language learning] is about'.
- Judith, now nativelike in Norwegian, was born in Hungary, and her parents moved to the United States when she was three. Consequently, she believes that 'becoming bilingual at the age of three is the real difference in my life, compared to other people. It made it easy to learn languages', adding, 'it just taught me that different languages work in different ways'.

Other participants also recalled a variety of forms of positive parental influences, from explicit encouragement to learn languages to role modelling L2 learning themselves:

- Lesley remembers her parents telling her, 'There's a big wide world out there; get out there and explore it', and this cosmopolitan ethos was further strengthened by her brother living in Brazil and her uncle and cousin speaking Japanese and Chinese, respectively.
- Our sample includes two French siblings, Lou and Capucine, who both managed to acquire nativelike English proficiency, even

though – unlike the Netherlands in Rianne's case – France has not traditionally been a particularly favourable context for facilitating foreign language learning. This would suggest the existence of some shared family underpinning. Indeed, their mother had been an au pair in London and emphasised to them that it was 'very important that French people could learn to speak English' (and became angry when she encountered French people who fulfilled the stereotype of a disinterested L2 attitude). Furthermore, their family was very 'cultural and artistic', involved in the film industry; as Capucine recalls, 'My family was obsessed with watching movies in the original language... And once you start doing this, then you just can't stand the French dubbing. You can't go back'.

- Kristin remembers fondly her time spent doing her English homework with her sister and father, who was 'quite good at English', and reflects on it now as 'a bonding experience'.
- Lisa recalls that they had a bookshelf of *Teach Yourself German* and *French* courses at home, as well as lots of dictionaries and foreign language books. Language learning was a normal part of life in both her nuclear and extended family.

Ultimately, parental influences can facilitate a lifelong interest in foreign cultures and language learning, and similarly, early language-related experiences can provide learners with a sense of self-efficacy that follows them throughout the lifespan, both of which contribute to a favourable learning set-up.

4.3 Social Expectations

While the factors above tend to be more explicit forms of positive stimuli, social expectations on a broader scale, while less obvious, can set learners up for success just as well. We have seen earlier from Rianne's story that she partly attributed her international mindset to the prevailing expectation in the Netherlands for everyone to learn foreign languages. As her cousin, Ira, explains:

> Dutch people study many languages in school: Dutch, English, French and German, and all of these for at least two years. From a very young age, we are taught the importance of multilingualism, as our economy is greatly dependent on exports, and Dutch isn't very widespread either.... The Netherlands is a tiny, tiny country, so they basically say, 'Well, you need to speak these other languages, because otherwise you're not going to be able to function'.

Several smaller (and even some larger) countries share this mentality, particular with the rise of English as a lingua franca. For example, Hanna tells us that in her home country of Finland, 'they refer to [English] as the third national language... it's not a foreign language, it's just the third national language'. As she further explains, 'learning English is very neutral... similar to how you know that you will need to learn some basic maths because you will need to manage your own finances one day. It's that sort of thing'. This is a relatively new and powerful social expectation that is emerging in more and more contexts in the globalised world: some knowledge of the lingua franca, Global English, is simply taken for granted – in Hanna's words, 'it's part of your everyday life as teenagers... it's just there'. Quite tellingly, when Hanna was due to start learning her first foreign language at school at the age of nine, her parents chose German for her rather than English, following the rationale, 'You will learn English regardless. So just as well you'll get at least the basics in another language first'.

Thamarasie's case offers an interesting twist to the case of Global English, because in her home country, Sri Lanka, the significance attached to English was both strengthened and weakened by the country's colonial heritage. Thamarasie qualified for our study because during her childhood, the Sri Lankan government suppressed English, banning it in schools and universities and discouraging the consumption of English media – meaning that she did not grow up speaking English with her family, and her exposure to English in the Sri Lankan countryside was very limited. In her case, the national sentiment of the time towards Global English prevented her from having the naturalistic learning process that often occurs in Sri Lanka today. Even so, English was too deeply embedded, and Global English as a necessity prevailed: Thamarasie reflects, 'you couldn't do higher studies, you couldn't go abroad without English... I kind of took English for granted' – a nonetheless favourable set-up. Although she learned the language in the classroom and not naturalistically, when she transferred to the more urban Colombo and was expected to communicate fluently in English, she found herself well prepared to smoothly slip into the role of an English speaker.

4.4 Favourable Conditions are Not Indispensable for Success

We thus find that project participants like those above had a good start in life in terms of a facilitative language learning environment and an internationally oriented mindset, giving them an advantage over many of their peers. This finding was not unexpected, but what is perhaps the more important lesson of our investigation is that

(1) a privileged L2 background does not *automatically* predestine someone to become an exceptional language learner, and
(2) the lack of a privileged L2 background does not *prevent* someone from becoming an exceptional language learner.

Regarding the first aspect, we saw earlier that Capucine, Lou and their younger brother were pressed to watch films in their original language, which Capucine and Lou believe contributed considerably to their own L2 development. At the same time, their brother never reached a similarly high level of English proficiency, perhaps because 'while he likes English, he isn't as interested in learning the language'. Likewise, Kristin's older sister positively influenced her to master English, yet she herself has not achieved a nativelike level. Kristin puts this down to insufficient exposure and practice in the language to seal the deal in her case. A favourable set-up, although helpful, is thus not a one-way ticket to learning a language – and certainly not to nativelike L2 mastery.

Regarding the second aspect, other participants came from backgrounds that were less facilitative than one might expect. In certain cases, it was largely external circumstances that acted against the L2. For example, in Denny's case, her appreciation of her L2 German was initially smothered not only by her love for her first foreign language, English, but also particularly by the fact that she was forced to learn German without any choice in the matter: 'Then four years later [after I started learning English], German was introduced at secondary school. It wasn't a choice, and I absolutely hated it. I detested not being given the choice… I felt so indignant'. The beginning of Denny's German learning journey was thus particularly non-facilitative, and so it comes as a surprise that she ultimately went on to develop a passion for the language and eventual nativelikeness.

While with cases like Denny's, the wider education system contributed to her lack of initial motivation to learn German, the root of other participants' non-facilitative set-ups can be found closer to home. Unlike examples such as Capucine and Lou's early positive influences from their family, other participants come from what could be characterised as 'ordinary' or particularly 'non-international' families in terms of language interest, with nothing predicting participants' own emergent passion for an L2. A case in point is Colin. His identical twin brother does not speak any foreign languages and has not been hugely interested in languages, thereby following what appears to be a family tradition; as Colin recalls, 'my twin brother was so bad at languages… I got the languages gene, because he is hopeless'. Kristopher similarly comes from a background bearing no inherent connection to his language learning, with his family approaching his early interest in Mandarin with a sense of bewilderment:

> [My grandfather] couldn't make heads or tails of it. And my grandmother said too, 'He's weird. He's not from this planet'. And my mother, I don't think she minded much either way… so they all just thought, 'Well, he's weird! Let him do what he's gonna do'. But I was certainly never discouraged…

Although Colin and Kristopher were never actively discouraged, they certainly did not have the energising encouragement present in many of our other participants' backgrounds. In effect, they must have therefore brought something unique into their respective set-ups to overcome their families' relative apathy towards language learning.

Such a personal contribution is even more prominent in participants who not only lacked a facilitative background but who were also in fact directly dissuaded by their families from learning an L2. Like with Kristopher, 'weird' was also the way Kerry and her passion for Italian were described by her family, but with more negative undertones:

> [My family] thought I was weird. They still do – well, that's the impression I get. Language learning was always kind of 'What do you want to do that for? What's the point of that?' My dad had never been taught any foreign languages; his brain functioned in English. He didn't get it; he was like, 'Why do you want to do this? English is the language everybody uses. Isn't it good enough for you?' He never actually said that, but that's the impression that I got. Like, 'What's the point of this? … English is the language everybody uses, so what's the point of learning another language?'

Kerry's response was nonetheless determined: 'It was just in me… it really felt like this is what I have to do. This is my path'. Kerry's and the above examples underline the fact that language learning needs no silver bullet: even exceptional L2 achievement can emerge from an unfavourable set of learning circumstances.

4.5 Discussion and Some Lessons to Draw

It is a well-known fact in L2 motivation research that environmental factors and especially external encouragement can shape a learner's motivation considerably (see e.g. Dörnyei & Ushioda, 2021; Gardner, 2019). Therefore, we expected to find some salient facilitative influences in our participants' life stories, and we were indeed able to identify such assisting supporting factors. One set of contextual characteristics in particular appeared to have an especially potent effect: access to an L2 – especially Global English – in the learners' childhood environment, creating what we have called the New Global Generation. The participants we identified as being from this subset of learners had the opportunity to have enhanced L2 input from early on in childhood, most often via target language television, films and vlogs. While media consumption is not the equivalent of being immersed in an L2 environment, many studies have shown that it can indeed be beneficial for language learning (e.g. Kuppens, 2010; Muñoz *et al.*, 2021). An extension of such naturalistic L2 input is social media, as well as the flourishing genre of online cooperative video games, which typically use English but can often provide access to other major languages. Media such as these have been found to be even more beneficial to L2 learning than traditional modes, perhaps because they provide not only authentic L2 input, but also a space for L2 production (De Wilde *et al.*, 2020). Ultimately, in the last few decades, media availability and exposure has expanded tremendously, and the effects of this have been undeniably positive for our younger participants.

Of course, it should be noted that the expanded access to L2 input through mass media that we have seen in this chapter has been facilitated at least in part by the rise of Global English. Many traditionally non-English contexts, such as the Netherlands and some of the Nordic countries, have incorporated English language media into not only their education but also their news, television and even government communications. Furthermore, learning English in many places such as these is often both expected and taken 'for granted', as astutely pointed out by Hanna and echoed in the literature (see e.g. Graddol, 2006; Ushioda & Dörnyei, 2017). Truthfully, this kind of context in which a foreign language robustly infiltrates learners' lives outside the classroom is unlikely to occur for the majority of languages other than English. Luckily, however, the modern-day internet provides an unprecedented opportunity for virtually unlimited linguistic input in a growing variety of languages. Therefore, while our sample did not include learners from the New Global Generation who were nativelike in a language other than English, moving forward it would not be surprising to see such cases emerging as access to other languages inevitably increases.

Besides indirect childhood L2 exposure, it was also easy to identify other kinds of early foreign language experiences that positively influenced learners. For example, with cases such as Rianne's French experience and Judith's early bilingualism, participants attributed the self-efficacy that facilitated their nativelike L2 mastery to early experiences with language learning in general. Indeed, positive experiences abroad or with foreign language speakers often create a sense of self-efficacy in language learning, which can bolster motivation and ultimately lead to better learning outcomes (for a recent review, see Ahn & Bong, 2019). As we saw with participants such as Lesley and Lisa, positive self-knowledge and language learning motivation in young learners can also be more explicitly fostered by parents and close relations (see e.g. Zentner & Renaud, 2007). Finally, on a subtler level, social expectations (such as those regarding Global English) can contribute to learner motivation and ultimate success on a grander scale, although it is also possible for this to have negative effects on learner motivation for other languages (Busse, 2017; Lanvers & Chambers, 2019).

Ultimately, a great many factors can intertwine to provide learners with a supportive environment that facilitates language learning. Yet, it turns out that such a favourable set-up is, in fact, not strictly necessary in language learning, even for the upper echelons of L2 mastery. Although there were indeed some particularly strong sources of encouragement mentioned in our participants' stories, our overwhelming impression when we took stock of these stimuli was that the beneficial influences did not often exceed similar ones found in more 'ordinary' students' learning histories, and in participant cases like that of Kerry, set-ups were in fact negative and played a detrimental role. This is a clear indication of a dynamic systems set-up: the positive influences in our participants' lives interacted with a variety of other components to augment the overall impact, and the unexceptional or outright negative influences were overridden by other factors to result in positive outcomes.

Thus, the primary lesson to draw from this chapter is that providing learners with an environment that contains rich L2 input can trigger a deep personal interest in foreign languages and may place them on an L2-learning fast track. However, it will not do this automatically; therefore, we are in agreement with Moyer's (2021: 48) conclusion that exceptional learners 'make the most of the resources at hand'. This was particularly clear in the cases when participants who did not come from exceptional backgrounds still managed to take more advantage of the existing favourable factors that surrounded them than their peers.

5 A Unique Bond with the Chosen Language

This chapter describes what we have come to regard as one of the most important productive features among our participants: their forming a *unique bond* with their chosen language. The best way to describe this kind of relationship with the second language (L2) is that the participant *fell in love* with it at some point in their lives, sometimes in an instant, dramatic manner and sometimes in a less vivid way as something that happened to sneak up on their lives, defining them before they even realised it.

Developing a unique bond with a language inevitably involves a holistic appreciation of every aspect of the L2, ranging from one's attitudes towards the L2 community to the appreciation of various properties of the L2 and its acquisition; however, we have found in our data that there are a number of distinct inroads into generating this overall positive disposition. Four channels in particular were mentioned by participants as having salient bonding power: (a) rewarding contact with the L2 community, (b) attraction towards certain cultural aspects or products associated with the L2, (c) appreciation of the pragmatic benefits of their L2 proficiency and (d) attraction towards specific aspects of the L2 itself. All four of these components are well-known ingredients of L2 motivation (for an overview, see Lamb *et al.*, 2019), but as we will illustrate in more detail below, they impacted our participants' lives with unusual intensity, so much so that participants could often recall unique and specific events in one or more of the four channels that played a special role in triggering their lifelong connection.

5.1 Rewarding Contact with the L2 Community

Perhaps the most obvious way of falling in love with a language is through visiting a country where the L2 is spoken. Anecdotal evidence abounds regarding the huge impact that a foreign holiday or a study abroad can have on language learners, and we also find several examples of this among our participants. Kerry's case represents the epitome of this experience.

KERRY: FALLING IN LOVE WITH ITALY AND ITALIAN

Kerry was born in Canada and studied French at school, as most Canadian kids do, without particularly enjoying or excelling in it. She recalls that although she loved the sound of French, she did not relate to the way it was taught ('not very well… it was learned by rote, memorising dialogues and verb tenses'). After graduating from high school she went on a four-month tour of Europe with a friend, and as part of this trip she visited Italy and encountered the Italian language, which she had known very little about before. She experienced love at first sight:

> I felt strangely at home there… it was that immediate connection! I felt so comfortable with Italians that I sometimes wondered whether I had been Italian in a past life. It was that kind of thing, you know, that this language feels like it belongs to me. It's almost like it's rooted inside me in some way. People would speak to me and often I found that I could understand what they were saying even when I didn't understand the words. I would get the gist. Even with little knowledge of the grammar and a minimal vocabulary, I instinctively understood and responded to the rhythm of the language and shaped my own speech in imitation of its seductive melody. Italian is such a beautiful language. Like when you hear some people who speak and it sounds like water, a stream rippling over rocks, the way they speak. It's like, I wish I spoke that way. It was like this affinity that's like, 'Oh, I really want to do this'.

And she did indeed start to speak that way! Although her knowledge of the language code was still rather limited and her mastering Italian was to be a gradual development over time, she reckons that she first began to sound nativelike after her first month-long study abroad in Italy three years later:

> I think [sounding native] really started to happen at the end of that first summer, that one-month summer, because I had just said, 'I'm going to open myself, I'm going to soak up everything, I'm gonna connect with as many people as I can'.

The unique nature of this connection with Italian comes out clearly when she compares it to her relationship with French:

> I've had some really nice interactions with people when I was using French, but not in the way as with Italian; from day one, no matter how bad my Italian was, how simple, they would still gasp, 'You speak Italian!' They would be so warm and so welcoming, and so encouraging and so interested. Like 'How did you learn it? Why did

you learn it?' And I'd often tell them I learned because of *amore* [love] and they were just all over that, 'Tell us this love story!' So then it was 'Oh no, *l'amore della lingua* [love of the language]'. They just loved that... there was a connection somehow that just has never been there through French.

This love affair turned out to be an unbreakable bond that carried Kerry through years of Italian classes as she perfected her command of the language: 'From my first visit to Italy, I wanted to study Italian and to master the language'.

Kerry's bond with Italian was more or less instantly forged during her first visit to Italy, and this bond would spur her on to relentlessly pursue Italian language and culture for several years to follow. It is noteworthy that the attraction of a place/community can reach such a powerful level that it can even override previously negative attitudes towards the L2 in question, as Theresa's case illustrates below.

THERESA: FROM HATING TO LOVING ENGLISH

Theresa was born in Germany and her schooling experience of English as a foreign language was not a positive one (to say the least): 'I hated English. I absolutely hated it', so much so that she even refused to pronounce the names of her textbook's characters as English names, insisting on their German variants. Although later in her studies she began seeing English in a more positive light due to the richness of the English media she encountered (in books and magazines especially), she was not particularly enamoured with the language and only chose it for her final secondary school examinations because the alternative subject's teacher was 'just horrible'.

The turning point for Theresa, however, came when, after graduating from secondary school, she travelled to Scotland as an au pair. Why Scotland? Today, she is not quite sure except for the existence of 'this weird connection between the German psyche and Scotland'. Theresa's bond formed soon after she arrived there:

> Somehow, I just loved Scotland. I loved the countryside. I loved the people. I loved the weird weather. I loved the architecture... and it was a language I thought I was quite comfortable in. I loved Edinburgh, in particular.

Although she did not particularly appreciate the au pair experience, she immersed herself in English, met 'a nice Irish bloke', signed up for

> activities such as Scottish dancing classes and Gaelic language classes, and quickly found a cohort of like-minded friends. The rest is history – she has now been living in the UK for over 20 years.

The potential power of encountering or visiting the L2 community has been consciously utilised by Colin throughout his language teaching practice by organising student exchanges year after year:

> One of the main things that led me to run an exchange for 35 years at schools every single year is because there's no point in learning a language just in school. You're never going to get that good unless you have contact with native speakers.

His efforts bore ample fruit, and his former student, Lisa, specifically recalls that the most important contributor to her language learning experience was participating in the school exchanges. Around year eight – and every year following – she had the opportunity to go on a German school exchange for a week and a half at a time, and the bond forged there with the German language and culture (as well as with specific individuals, as we will see in Chapter 9) was strong enough to sustain her learning until she reached nativelike proficiency in the language.

5.2 Attraction towards the L2 Culture and Cultural Products

When one thinks of the process of learning another language, usually communication and the more practical aspects of language learning come to mind. However, language does not merely involve stringing some words together to convey a message; rather, it fulfils a unique niche in human society through which culture is almost always intricately intertwined. It thus comes as no surprise that another common inroad into developing a unique bond with the L2 involves forging a connection with the culture associated with the language. Judith's mastery of Norwegian offers a good example. As part of her undergraduate degree in English and medieval literature, Judith studied Old Norse and read some Norwegian literature, which changed her life:

> I read Bjørnstjerne Bjørnson's *Synnøve Solbakken* – this is a 19th-century novel that is not very well known nowadays but was extremely popular in its own day and was translated into English. It was what they call national romanticism in Norway, life in a small place in the countryside, in a farming community, and it was just so different from my own experience of life that I really fell for it, and I really wanted to see this place that it described, because the landscape of Norway is also very distinctive.

She visited the country on holiday soon after and fell in love with it. Following her degree, Judith found a family through the grapevine who needed an au pair and decided to move to Norway for a year – ultimately leading her to become professor of Viking Studies years later.

Judith's route is not unique in the sense that a draw to various kinds of cultural products also constituted a significant stepping stone for other project participants. For example, Kristin and Ira formed a bond with the language through extensive *reading*: Ira loved science fiction and fantasy novels, many of which were not yet translated into her native Dutch, while Kristin and her best friend found literal refuge in online fiction communities like Wattpad, where you can read amateur writers' creations and contribute your own, predominantly in English. Kristin soon added published novels to her reading repertoire in English and recalls: 'I fell in love with reading. And I knew at that point that I wanted to use the English language in my everyday life'.

Another significant cultural product that helped forge a unique bond with the L2 was *music*. For example, Uwe recalls himself as a teenager in East Germany recording English language songs from the radio onto his magnetic tape recorder, listening to them 'over and over and over to get the lyrics and write [them] down verbatim' because he wanted to play them on his guitar. Similarly, as a schoolgirl, Livia would 'obsessively' listen to English music artists, pouring over lyric translations in her free time. She even began helping her friends who were in bands translate their own Italian lyrics into English; this, she recalls, was the 'starting point' for her English. It is appropriate to conclude this section with Heidrun's story, which exemplifies how a cultural bond can even override language learning mediocrity.

HEIDRUN: HOW HER CULTURAL 'CRAVING' CATAPULTED HER OUT OF L2 MEDIOCRITY

Heidrun, born and raised in Austria, was a chronically good student and literature lover from a young age at school. She began learning English as a compulsory subject at the age of 10, but she 'didn't really feel connected to it' and 'found it confusing'. Needless to say, she did not do particularly well in it. When she was 16, her mother recommended she do an exchange with an English girl. At the time, her English was fairly average and 'not communicative' at all, but in just two weeks her life was turned around. She excitedly observed all the positive differences she saw in England, from the everyday kindnesses to the way women were treated on a grander scale at the time. Her host family took her on trips to Cambridge and London, where she was able to see a Shakespeare play. She fell in love with the culture and thought, 'Language learning has become really meaningful'. As she recalls:

> When I first went to England at 16, I wasn't very good at English – I really wasn't. I could say a few things, but it was very bad. But language learning has something to do with liking the culture, and this is a huge motivation. My stay in England blew my mind, on so many levels… especially the language, which I realised I really needed to improve. But also in the way of how people lived, how people behaved towards each other… so it was also a cultural blowing of my mind. And I knew I needed to learn more about this country, because this was the way I wanted to live. Don't forget, I was 16 years old, which is the age when you actually want to find your way in life.

Heidrun is now a teacher of English in Austria and married to an Englishman, and she reflects on her initial experience abroad as a kind of gateway:

> I don't know whether you can have a passion for language teaching unless you have some emotional bonds with one of the countries…. If I hadn't gone to England, I don't think I would have been that much into learning the language. I would have learned it as my sister did, but I think if I hadn't had the emotional bond, and this sort of craving for this fantastic culture that I craved, I don't think I would have learnt so much.

5.3 Pragmatic Benefits of L2 Proficiency

Although the practical benefits of knowing a foreign language alone rarely offer a strong enough incentive to create a unique bond with a language, such a utilitarian dimension can serve as a powerful reinforcing factor. Often, these benefits function alongside other motives, not acting as the sole driver but nonetheless contributing to participants' bonds with the L2. Indeed, participants whose nativelike L2 is English commented on the well-known pragmatic benefits of this global language. Because this sense of pragmatism, sometimes termed *instrumental motivation*, is a fairly familiar component of L2 motivation (see e.g. Gardner & MacIntyre, 1991), let us offer just four brief examples:

- Carl, a Swedish teenager, summarised the essence of the issue succinctly:

> Well, the world is very globalised now. It's far more globalised than it has ever been, and that has, of course, put a lot of pressure on English[-learning] students to actually learn the language. Since it's become a part of everyday life, basically.

- Livia's first positive experience with English was related to its capacity to enable international friendships. Around the age of 9 or 10, she went on holiday to Portugal with her family and recalls the following triggering event:

   And there were a bunch of Dutch kids, and Dutch people generally have much better English than Southern Europeans [like myself] on average, and they're all speaking English. And I remember my dad says that I came back and said to him, 'When we go back, can I take lessons? Because I really want to be able to make friends'.

- Interestingly, Rianne, who is one of the most successful language learners in our sample for having mastered both English and German at a nativelike level, viewed language learning as merely a 'side track' in her pursuit of her main passion, physics. Her younger self's thought process was as such:

   I want to be able to get my physics degree, to understand the physics behind it. And I will do what is needed in order to get there. And if this means I have to improve my English, then so be it. I'll just do that alongside.

- Ira, around the age of 16, began nurturing an interest in creative writing, and came to the following conclusion, which is the closest in our data set for a pragmatic motive to play a genuine triggering role:

   Realising how small the number of people is that actually speak [my L1] Dutch, I thought, 'Do you know what, if I want to be a writer and actually sell loads of books, then it would be a lot easier to just write in English'. Because there's loads of people even in my country that translate their own works into English so they can be sold in like, Germany and France or somewhere else. So I guess that's how it got started.

5.4 Attraction towards Specific Aspects of the L2

While participants such as Kerry and Judith recount bonding with the L2 through interpersonal or intercultural relationships, another finding of our interviews was that participants could fall in love with certain linguistic properties of the L2 itself. The most extreme case of this is Kristopher, who discovered an unexplainable attraction towards *Chinese characters*, which set him on a trajectory of mastering not one but two languages, Mandarin and Japanese, at a nativelike level. This is all the more remarkable because as described in the following vignette, he was originally completely dismissive of ever learning another language.

KRISTOPHER: AN INEXPLICABLE CONNECTION WITH CHINESE CHARACTERS

Born in Canada, Kristopher's first experience with learning French in school was very negative:

> It really put me off of language learning. And so all throughout my youth I just thought I was never going to learn another language. I thought it was awful, so I was not intending on learning languages. I didn't know that I *could* learn languages. I had no idea.

However, around the latter half of high school, Kristopher had his first encounter with Mandarin. Having recently read a book on ancient Chinese philosophy he found in the school library, he happened to notice a Mandarin language textbook while visiting his friend Sean's home. Despite not recalling having laid eyes on Chinese characters before, he felt a strong sense of nostalgia. As he explains:

> I remember saying to Sean, 'I feel like I've seen this before'. You know, a strange feeling like that? I said, 'I've seen these characters before, this writing…'. Something happened there when I went to my friend's room… it was weird; I just connected with it immediately.

Kristopher borrowed the textbook soon after, and his inexplicable attraction to Chinese characters fuelled his subsequent learning interest:

> I used to write them all the time. In the back of books and on my grandmother's leftover baking paper. And because we didn't have much paper, I used to use first pencil and write in pencil, and then blue pen over that. And then black pen. So I could use the same piece of baking paper three times.

He found he was able to pick up all the Chinese characters very quickly: 'And still now when I read new Chinese characters, I don't forget them. It's wonderful. It's strange, but I don't forget them'. This unique attraction was also a major driving force in his Japanese learning:

> I do have a number of other curious tales I could tell regarding my own language learning process – like the several times I fell asleep in a graveyard in Ogawa (Kumamoto, Japan) tracing the Chinese characters engraved on Meiji-period tombstones with my finger – but I fear that would take up too much space!

On a broader scale among our participants, falling in love with a specific aspect of the L2 tended to occur in one of two forms: those who fell in love with some essence of the language's structure, or those who fell in love with some phonological property of the L2. Some examples of the former include:

- Kristin found English appealing particularly because of its *rich vocabulary*, especially when it came to reading and writing literature.
- Lou was attracted to the *ungendered character* of English in contrast to the more strictly gendered nature of their first language (L1) French, as they found they could explore their non-binary nature more explicitly in English.
- William was captivated by the *dialectical variation* he encountered with English, both online and in the classroom.
- Colin found that placing the words correctly in an L2 was like a wonderful puzzle, and associated language learning with his love of mathematics:

  Knowing language is nearly always about patterns, and learning the repetition of patterns and different endings. I equated that with maths and learning formulae. So that was the abstract side of language learning, which I really liked.... And I used to love the fact that there were lots of German words which had a different meaning, depending on whether it was a *der* or *die* or *das*.

- Amelia's case was particularly intriguing in that initially she was actually better at learning French than German (the language in which she eventually became nativelike), and yet she particularly appreciated what she calls the '*mathematical structuring*' of German compared to French with its myriad exceptions:

  I could see how you could build words. There were rules, and when you learn the rule, that was it. It was done. You'd learnt the rule; that's how it works. There was a lot of structure to the language. And that just appealed to me more than French... French just never sat with me the same way that German did.... I loved German as a language – my motivation was the language as a subject and structure to be mastered!

Other participants had a more aesthetic appraisal and subsequent bond with the L2, which we will explore further in Chapter 7:

- Denny found German *poetic* and *melodic* and is quick to defend the language's softer aspects in the face of contrary popular perceptions.

- Uwe also had a strong 'harmonious' attraction towards the *musicality* of his preferred L2, which was English, especially compared to some of his other L2s like Hungarian.
- Peng found English's 'rhythmic beauty enriched [his] aesthetics' in a way that his L1 Mandarin, though visually beautiful, did not.
- Kerry (as we saw above) was drawn to the beautiful *melody* of Italian.

Kerry's story is particularly noteworthy for two reasons: first, it is a prime example of more than one channel contributing to forging an L2 bond (her love for both Italy and the sound of Italian), and second, because it also demonstrates the facilitative role of previous language learning experience: Kerry's encounter with French developed her metalinguistic awareness and increased her sensitivity to particular aspects of Italian, thereby enabling her to form a bond with the language. In fact, this trajectory is echoed by other participants such as Amelia, Hanna and Denny, who initially began learning other languages before going on to encounter and establish strong connections with specific aspects of their now-nativelike L2s, and their enhanced metalinguistic awareness perfectly placed them to be able to notice and internalise specific aspects of the L2. While this was not the case for every participant who bonded with specific linguistic aspects of the L2, this was a clear subchannel, especially for learners of languages other than English.

5.5 Discussion and Some Lessons to Draw

The main lesson offered by this chapter is that it is possible to form a special relationship with an L2, and if such a unique bond has been established, it can supply formidable fuel to energise the L2 learning process. From a theoretical point of view, this was probably one of the biggest discoveries of our project, offering a wide range of implications. The learner's relationship with the L2 has traditionally been treated in L2 motivation circles as the 'attitude towards the L2/L2 community' (see e.g. Dörnyei, 2020; Dörnyei & Ushioda, 2021; Gardner, 1985); however, the vivid cases in this chapter demonstrate that the notion of 'attitude' does not do full justice to the significance of this component. It appears that the unique bond our participants have formed is more than merely an attitude or a disposition – it constitutes a deeper, more intimate and chronically accessible connection that has a more direct impact on one's ongoing behaviour. One might posit that this motivational construct's effectiveness has, in some sense, been expanded past ordinary boundaries by the affective component of our participants' experiences. In other words, the learners' L2 motivation intertwines with their positive emotional experiences, forming a unique bond and energising their relationship with the L2. Once the bond has been formed, the L2 becomes attached to one's overall identity, which is an issue that we will return to in Chapter 12.

The examples reported in this chapter demonstrate that there are several different channels that can lead to forming a unique bond with the L2, and participants could also find themselves travelling along more than one channel. For example, while Livia's initial motives for learning L2 English may have been pragmatic ones, she soon developed a relationship with English language music and special attention to the sounds of her L2 (as we will see in Chapter 7), and later through community contact after she moved to the UK. Although for certain participants such as Colin, the role of visits to L2 communities (e.g. through travelling or study abroad) was paramount, so was becoming aware of various cultural and pragmatic aspects associated with the L2. None of the above factors, whether they involve community contact or cultural products, guarantees bonding by themselves, but they do create opportunities for forming an intimate personal relationship that can lead to, at some point, something 'clicking' for the learner.

Offering such opportunities has traditionally been well covered in the motivational strategies literature (see e.g. Dörnyei, 2001; Lamb, 2019), except for one notable aspect: the development of a special liking for certain linguistic properties of the L2. In particular, we were surprised to hear about the strength of the connections that participants recalled having with specific aspects of their chosen languages. While it is largely agreed that the development of metalinguistic awareness is vital for language learning and literacy development (see e.g. Roehr-Brackin, 2018), very little attention has been paid to its potentially motivating side effects. This is in contrast to our participants' accounts, which suggest that it is, in fact, possible to find personally meaningful and pleasing aspects of a language code. We suspect that for 'ordinary' – and especially monolingual – L2 learners, discovering this affective dimension of metalinguistic awareness is likely to be something that needs explicit encouragement and facilitation. Uwe's explanation of how he is trying to master Hungarian – the language of the country he currently lives and works in – is enlightening in this respect. He initially felt that Hungarian 'wasn't a pleasing language to my ears', which constituted a kind of 'barrier' to learning it for several years. However, he noticed over time some of Hungarian's similarities to his L1 German, and this became his 'ticket into the whole thing', that is, into his slowly 'developing a relationship with Hungarian'. As a result, he says he is 'now beginning to see the beauty of it' and, accordingly, he offers the following general advice:

> Observe and notice if something's beautiful in the language that attracts you; follow the light, and just be drawn in, and it'll work out by itself. If you pay attention, you will know where to go and where not to go.

Uwe concludes that his learning journey with Hungarian involves more conscious experimentation than the process he followed with his native-like English, but that this intentional engagement to build bridges with the language is 'slowly working out. And I'm not rushed.... We'll get there like a long-term relationship'.

6 Cognition and Other Facilitative Learner Characteristics

Chapter 2 surveyed a number of different learner characteristics that can underpin one's aspiration for excellence in language learning, and given that our participants have proven to represent such excellence, it should not come as a surprise that we find in our data set examples of virtually all the features mentioned there. In mapping these learner characteristics, this chapter adopts an established structure, dividing them into cognitive, motivational and personality factors. However, the familiarity will largely end there, because our emphasis will be on describing variables that have not been in the spotlight of second language acquisition (SLA) research in the past but that have emerged in the present study as potent contributors to second language (L2) learning success. While these learner characteristics offer intriguing additions to our understanding of individual difference variables, we can state as a preliminary that we have not found any 'magic keys' to achieving excellence in language learning, in the sense that no facilitative factors, not even the most potent ones, have been shared by everyone in our cohort. In fact, as we will see below, even in areas that one would usually regard as basic conditions for L2 learning success – language aptitude, for example – certain participants displayed only average quality, if that. This confirms a point made in the previous chapters, namely that it is the *optimal combination* of individual difference variables and other factors that have helped our participants to qualify for the language learning elite of nativelike L2 speakers.

6.1 Cognitive Endowment: Language Aptitude and Other Learning-Specific Factors

We started our investigation with the expectation that all of our participants would display a high degree of *language aptitude* – after all, how could someone perform exceptionally well in any domain without having an exceptional ability level? Things, however, proved to be somewhat more complicated because – as was pointed out in Chapter 1 – language aptitude is not a unitary factor, and while all of our participants possessed a high level of *some* aspects of this composite cognitive construct, their above-average quality did not always transfer to other components. Furthermore, while language aptitude is defined in the literature as language independent (i.e. it is expected to affect every L2 that a learner studies equally), the picture our participants painted did not fully support this position. Finally, we also came across certain cognitive factors with a strong impact on participants' learning progress that did not comfortably fit into the traditional construct of language aptitude. In sum, our study of the cognitive foundation of L2 learning success turned out to be a journey offering a series of new discoveries and surprises. Let us start our exploration with the most general aspect of this domain: language aptitude.

6.1.1 Language aptitude

Language aptitude is not unlike intelligence in that (a) everyone believes that it exists, (b) it can be measured fairly accurately and yet (c) nobody quite knows what an aptitude score really represents (for the 'mystery' of the IQ score, see Dörnyei, 2009b). There is no doubt that aptitude matters, because language aptitude test scores have produced consistent positive correlations with learning performance over the past five decades, but there is no consensus in the literature on how to break down this composite score into subcomponents, with several divisions proposed over the past decades (for reviews, see Li & Zhao, 2021; Wen *et al.*, 2017). Although we did not explicitly test our participants in this area, our data set indicates a high overall aptitude characterising them, manifested through frequent references in the participants' interviews to their relative ease when learning languages. Hanna, for example, explains: 'I do think that some people are just naturally more wired to learn languages. We know that some people find language learning easier, and I've always been like that... I've always been like, "Okay, I'm good at this"'. Judith's case corroborates this general impression, particularly because she was not always good at other subjects: 'There were other subjects I didn't get top marks in, so I assumed I was just good at languages. And I found them fairly easy'.

One source of L2 learning ease in our investigation has been a good *language memory*, which is in line with findings about gifted learners in general (Biedroń & Pawlak, 2016). Ira for example states: 'Somehow I just seemed to have a knack for it. I think one of the main things is that I am just good at learning things by heart, and that kind of worked with the way our English was taught'. Lesley concurs, 'I am fortunate enough to pick up most things quickly and have a good memory'. In a similar vein, Sara concluded that her L2 'was always something that came naturally', and Theresa elaborates on this as follows:

It's just natural, I think. I don't see learning a language as something I have to do.... And maybe I'm gifted that way, that I'm just able to absorb it and bumble along in my life. I never felt as though it was a chore or a duty... I just think it's fun.

Sara adds an important point to this commonly held view, namely that the ease of L2 learning is also manifested in difficulties not causing major setbacks:

And then if there were problems that I stumbled upon in English, it didn't take all the motivation out of me. For somebody who's struggling with English, every little thing can just take the motivation out of them, but I was like, 'Okay, this is just like a minor thing, a minor setback'.

Surprisingly, however, in contrast to such positive appraisals we also find dissenting accounts in our data set, as certain participants did, in fact, experience cognitive difficulties with language learning. Uwe, for example, 'got bogged down on the grammar early on' in his French studies. Carl appears to be in a similar situation: 'I'm currently learning German as well, which I'm not really fluent in. It's a difficult language'. Moreover, at the time of being interviewed by us, William, who had picked up English effortlessly, said that he was seriously thinking of dropping French as a school subject, 'because it's very hard. Of all the courses I'm taking, I think it's the hardest'. To cite one more example, Kerry drew up a direct contrast between learning two different languages:

When I was in Japan, I remember kind of going, 'This language is driving me crazy!' I remember my brain just going 'ugh ugh ugh ugh, this is so hard!'... Italian never felt that way. I never felt that anything [with Italian] was really difficult.

While other factors such as first language (L1)–L2 linguistic distance may have influenced the above learners' performance, particularly salient were accounts in which learners' average – or sometimes even below average! – cognitive functioning initially concerned the very signature language in which they later became nativelike. For example, Denny remembers that when she started to learn her now-nativelike German, 'there was always a struggle. The grammar was difficult. No question about it'. Heidrun also recalls memories of her early English studies that will resonate with many ordinary language learners: 'I wasn't very good at all... I could say a few things, but it was very bad'. Similarly, Livia describes her initial English proficiency – which she then perfected to a nativelike level – as merely 'average', and Rianne goes one step further when she admits that 'I never had a really big affinity with German in high school; actually it was one of my worst grades because I really didn't like it'. Yet, something along these individuals' learning trajectories shifted and jump-started their cognitive functioning to allow them to reach the ultimate mastery they later attained.

The most puzzling example in this respect has been offered by Kristopher, whose memory for Chinese characters – as discussed earlier – was impeccable: 'When I read new Chinese characters, I don't forget them. It's wonderful. It's strange, but I don't forget them'. However, he also states:

> My memory is awful for everything except language. With words, I can remember words; I can remember languages. But that's about it. It's actually a big struggle for me... I have to take a lot of notes, otherwise, I just can't remember anything. For daily life, I have to write everything down otherwise it's gone.... You see, I'm very slow with most things other than language.

Kristopher's case might be regarded as especially exceptional, and one can argue that his memory problems concern only non-linguistic matters. However, we should remember that his first experience with language learning – studying French in primary school – was so 'awful' that it 'really put [him] off of language learning', and as he recalls, he had 'no idea' that he could learn languages. As such, it is frankly astounding that this same person then succeeded in learning both nativelike Mandarin and Japanese!

These unexpected accounts have some important theoretical implications. They suggest that even when a learner possesses highly effective cognitive faculties – which are evidenced by their exceptional L2 ultimate attainment – these faculties need to be primed by other factors in order for them to deliver outstanding performance. In the absence of such priming, even the outstanding learners of our study operated at a rather average level. Even a seemingly straightforward area of language aptitude such as language memory – straightforward in the sense that one would expect it either to be there or not – appears to fluctuate in an individual depending on the phase of learning and the specific language one studies. We will return to this phenomenon in Section 6.4.

In sum, with regard to language aptitude our data set offers a mixed picture. On the one hand, there were participants who had the subjective impression that they had a definite general 'flair' for language learning. On the other hand, certain accounts question the general predictive power and context independence of the language aptitude construct (at least beyond a certain proficiency level), and it remains puzzling as to why learners who master one language at a nativelike level might struggle with other languages.

6.1.2 Other cognitive factors

As we analysed the interviews, we noticed that certain participants also underlined the facilitative role of certain cognitive factors that have not been documented in established surveys of L2 individual differences. Let us illustrate this with Joy's case.

JOY: THE IMPORTANCE OF MIMICRY, MUSICALITY AND SELF-MONITORING

As the daughter of two missionaries, Canadian Joy found herself living in Brazil at the age of nine, and she soon mastered Portuguese at a nativelike level. Although this early language acquisition did not qualify for our analysis and our focus has been on her mastering nativelike Icelandic in her twenties, it is obvious that some of Joy's cognitive features played a decisive role in both learning processes. To start with, in her recollections Joy emphasises her *mimicry ability* as having had a substantial impact on her learning:

> I think I've always tried to mimic pronunciation. Where did all of this start? It goes back to my earliest memories. I remember, as a little girl – I couldn't have been more than five or six years old – I was sitting in a church service, and there was somebody from another country and for whatever reason, they were teaching the congregation to say something [in their language], some simple phrase. And I remember trying very hard to say it exactly like they said it. I wanted to do it perfectly, just because I wanted to see if I could fool people into thinking that was *my* language. There was just some innate desire to be perfect. I was just a little girl, but it was this thrill of being able to speak and sound like a person from another country....
>
> When in Brazil, my sister and I occasionally sang songs in Portuguese, mimicking my parents' less-than-perfect accent, frequently resulting in convulsions of laughter on the part of all, sometimes even to the point of tears running down our faces, including the faces of those being imitated!...
>
> In Iceland, I did try to mimic Icelanders; I did try to sound like them.... I wouldn't just listen to individual pronunciation, but I would try to imitate it. I loved to listen to the reporters on the news, the radio or TV. I loved the way they sounded, and so I'd try and mimic that.

Significantly, Joy relates her mimicry practice to her *musicality*, which she associates with social interaction and the aesthetics of communication:

> For me, in a way, [mimicry] was like playing music by ear, not just by note. As a child, not only did I grow up participating enthusiastically in congregational singing, but from an early age, we would also sing as a family. In Iceland, singing was similarly a regular part of my church involvement as well as most gatherings with my husband's

extended family (a practice common in Iceland). For me, music has never been first and foremost about entertainment or performance, but rather about belonging and participation. It represents a shared form of enjoyment and interaction.... Apart from the social meaning, music has also been important to me for what the composition or text communicates, and linked to that is acoustic beauty, not least harmonies and rhythms.... In my case, at least some of the connection between musicality and language learning goes beyond just 'having an ear' for music, and has to do with all of the positive associations (e.g. social, spiritual, aesthetic) that are also, for me, part of learning another language.

Finally, Joy mentions another important learner characteristic, which she actually describes as her greatest L2 learning asset: her *self-monitoring capacity*, coupled with a desire for perfection. She recalls that she always wanted to avoid looking like 'a bumbling foreigner': '[In Iceland] there were plenty of examples of people around me who had fossilised. But that was never an option for me. I didn't want that for myself'. So, she concludes, 'I do monitor; I want to get it right. Often it's almost like I'm playing a game with myself, well expressed by the saying I saw on a poster years ago: "Find your limits. Exceed. Repeat"'.

The three learner characteristics Joy highlighted – mimicry ability, musicality and a self-monitoring disposition – are noteworthy for two reasons. First, they are not usually regarded as part of the traditional set-up of individual L2 learner differences (e.g. Dörnyei & Ryan, 2015; Pawlak, 2012; Williams *et al.*, 2015), and yet in her case, they proved to be vital for achieving excellence. In fact, without considering their role we would find ourselves hard-pressed to fully decode Joy's wonderful L2 learning journey. Second, Joy was not the only one in our sample who found that these three concepts played a significant role in their learning experience, and we explore the idiosyncrasies of how these concepts could play out below.

6.1.2.1 Mimicry ability

Participants such as Joy, Ira, Colin, Denny and Livia reported having a special knack for imitating people and 'doing loads of different accents' (Ira). They take pleasure in exploring accents and emulating them, thereby producing different voices. This was evident in Joy's account above (as she remembers mimicking her parents' not-so-great Portuguese pronunciation), and Zoltán believes that his wife, Sarah, can speak better

Hungarian-accented English (for fun) than he does. English Colin also connects his ability to mimic with his flair for comedy:

> When I was young, I'd always mimicked adults and uncles and aunts and done accents. I loved putting on Irish accents and Welsh accents – I've always been able to do that and always liked that. And of course, part of it is that I like comedy enormously. I've always loved comedy, and making the kids laugh at school has been incredibly important. And a lot of the time I would make them laugh by using a different accent.

Denny has been particularly expressive about her mimicry skills:

> There's something really magical and something really empowering about hearing something and then trying to imitate it, trying to reproduce it. Imitating sounds has always been something that I've really enjoyed and something that I was probably best at. Being able to imitate sounds fairly convincingly is, ultimately, what draws me to a language.... I think that this fascination with sound and imitation is a big part of me being sometimes mistaken for a native speaker in English and in German.

Such imitation can also happen on an unconscious level and is not restricted to L2s. Livia, for example, finds this happening in both her L1 and L2:

> There have always been things that point towards me having a natural tendency to parrot sounds that I hear. I change my accent a lot, and I don't realise it at the time. I tend to slide into other people's accent.

Likewise, Amelia reports that 'I do pick up accents in [my L1] English very easily as well... There's a thing when you're talking to someone, you start to mirror their accent – it's a way of building empathy'. This unconscious imitation also occurred throughout the duration of Carl's interview: Katarina noticed that he often switched his usual aspirated British *t*'s to her more American *t*'s, and after a while he even became conscious enough of it to mention it explicitly. In Chapter 1, this phenomenon was discussed under the label of *phonetic convergence*, and Rianne describes the phenomenon very well:

> What I do notice is that depending on the person I'm speaking to, if I'm speaking to some UK natives, I have a tendency at the end of the conversation to have taken over a bit their way of English, like more British sayings or slightly with the accent, whereas when I hear myself talking to Americans, I notice at the end of the conversation that I kind of adjust to that kind of way of speaking English.

Participants' accounts of speech convergence also went beyond imitating solely pronunciation; for example, Rianne adds that in her L1 'depending on which side of the family I spoke to, I kind of started to take over their way of saying things', and similarly, Theresa recounted that often when speaking with friends, 'I would start mimicking the language, the vocabulary that they use, or the phrases they use'.

Let us conclude this section with Peng's account, as he can distinctly recall the origins of his awareness of dialects and his mimicry skills. Moving across China as a child, he grew up speaking standard Mandarin at home, but he realised that there was a 'very strong dialect' locally. This contributed to an early awareness of pronunciation and its social benefits: 'I was fully aware of circumstances or contexts where I had to speak with a little bit of an accented Mandarin – whenever that was going to work in my favour or to my advantage, I was going to use that'. As a result, Peng became able to 'impersonate' the local dialect 'just enough for me to blend in with my community'. Interestingly, he attributes his early attention to and success with pronunciation to his mother being a music teacher and his childhood vocal training and singing practice. Musicality and singing also intertwined in Joy's earlier account, so let us take a closer look at this intriguing association.

6.1.2.2 Musicality

We saw in Chapter 1 that various aspects of musical ability have been repeatedly associated with L2 learning success over the past decades, without however establishing a conclusive link. Musicality has also emerged in our data set in multiple ways. To start with, it was striking to see in Chapter 5 that for certain participants the strong bond with their L2 was rooted in the perceived musicality, melodic qualities and aesthetic beauty of the target language. They perceived an aspect of the L2 that for most language learners remains hidden; Peng for example states, 'The English language is just so musical. And it's a beautiful language when you read poems out loud. So it enriched my aesthetics, and has given me a lot of pleasurable experiences'. Such a sensitivity could be coupled with at least some form of musical training in our sample, and at the time of being interviewed, participants such as Colin, Sarah and Joy were also active members of non-professional orchestras and/or choirs. They would all agree with Kristopher's conclusion: 'I love music with my heart. And I've always thought that my music, my love of music, is somehow related to my love of language and pronunciation. It must be'.

In her earlier account, Joy emphasised the significance of singing in her L2 development, and others had similar experiences. Ira, for example, recounts: 'I do love to sing, which is a big part of my exposure because I started singing English songs before I spoke English. So I'd kind of just imitate the sounds a little bit'. Marjan also recalls hearing English on the radio in the Netherlands and singing along. Denny explains that although she 'never really got on well with the actual process of developing a classical music education, it was all about listening to music and trying to imitate or trying to reproduce it'. Uwe recounts learning to sing and play guitar, and replicating songs he heard on the radio, as a 'very important' and 'parallel process' to his formal L2 English education. Kristopher explicitly states that his Japanese learning involved 'a lot of singing. I love singing and there was a lot of singing there. Old folk music; we sang together a lot. And that helped me learn'. Colin both sings in a choir and conducts one, and Sarah similarly is the chair of the choir she sings in. Last but not least, among her many other professions, Heidrun is a music teacher.

However, before we jump to the tempting conclusion that musical abilities are the key to L2 learning excellence, we ought to note that four of our participants have had absolutely no musical training or experience whatsoever, and three others were distinctly *bad* at singing: both Amelia and Judith were told when they were young, 'Don't sing, just mime', because they were so unmusical. As Amelia puts it, 'My singing is truly awful. And I haven't got a musical bone in my body', and when Thamarasie started singing classes at the age of seven, her teacher 'listened to me and put me out of the class saying, "If you sing, everybody else will go wrong". And for seven years, I was not allowed into the singing class'.

6.1.2.3 Self-monitoring with a view to perfection

Although mimicry and musicality were both vital to her experience, Joy characterised her self-monitoring practice as her 'greatest L2-learning asset', as it helped her to process and improve her L2 production. Peng also states that he tends to listen to a 'mental recording' of himself to reflect on it: 'As soon as I finish a conversation with someone, both in English or in Chinese, a lot of the clips will flash back to me, and then I'll think, "Oh, I made that mistake. Oh, my God, that's so embarrassing"'. Focusing on accuracy in self-monitoring appears to be another feature of certain participants, even though in language teaching circles the communicative approach prefers to highlight the significance of fluency even if it comes with mistakes. Timur has been well aware of this contradiction:

> When I used to work as a teacher, I would always tell my students, 'You have to be a child again. You have to forget all of this embarrassment. You make mistakes and you say something you didn't mean, and you have to just let it go'. But you know, I am just being basically contradictory to myself, because that's my biggest problem: I don't *want* to make those mistakes. I don't *want* to be a child again.

In a similar vein, Theresa compares herself to her brother:

> He embraces any language. In any country that he goes to, he tries to speak the language, and he honestly does *not* care whether he makes a fool of himself and just says something that is completely wrong. He does not care! Whereas I'm the one who, unless I know it's right, I'm not going to say it.

Likewise, Lesley was possessed by the determination to not make mistakes, in part because she was afraid she would lose her job, but also because of her 'perfectionist' personality. When others corrected her, she saw it as a learning experience and determined not to make the same mistake twice. The desire to be correct was strong, and it took her about four to five years to feel 'comfortable' in German. As she recalls,

> I'm very ambitious. It was a challenge, and that was the goal: 'I want to speak this language *properly*'. And I didn't give up, and I kept working on it; I was constantly learning. To this day, if I can't remember how to say something or a grammar rule, then I always look it up. Maybe I'm just a perfectionist.

Colin, too, has been critical of his proficiency level throughout his journey, admitting that 'all the time you're aware of what you don't know'. In Section 6.4, we see that such a desire to be perfect can become a double-edged sword, as it can actually hinder L2 development, but participants such as those above simply would not compromise: they wanted to make sure that they got things right.

In contrast to the perfectionist approach, other participants in our sample believed in exactly the opposite strategy; for example, Rianne explained that a 'key learning strategy is to just start speaking, regardless of if you don't know anything at all. Just start speaking, and if you don't know a word, then just describe it in the simplest words you *do* know'. Lisa agreed:

> I also think what makes me successful is that I'm not afraid to just talk. I don't have a problem with just starting to talk. And I think that often, people I know who take a long time with language, they're not starting to talk. They won't start until they're perfect. In my experience, that is not how you start to learn a language. You have to just get in there. If it's wrong, it doesn't matter.

However, it is noteworthy that after Lisa said, 'If it's wrong, it doesn't matter', she added, 'I mean, obviously, now I'm at work, and if it is wrong, it *does* matter'. In the process of reaching her nativelike level of L2 proficiency, therefore, she still needed to start paying firm attention to accuracy at some point. Returning to our first example with Peng's self-monitoring, despite his statement above, Peng describes himself as a communicative and spontaneous rather than careful speaker:

> I have two modes of speaking English going on at the same time, but they're different. I think my strategy is, when I speak, I'll only use the former mode, which is to speak whatever I want. But then normally, I'll listen to my [mental] recording, or try to reflect…. So I was able to keep note of it, and then try to avoid that in the future. But I think I'm more of the first type of speaker. I like to speak whatever I want.

We should note that Joy, too, finds that she sometimes needs to take a step back from perfectionism: 'I see my self-monitoring capacity as a two-edged sword…. particularly given the possibility of it leading to a debilitating focus on potential or actual failure'. She recalls remedying this by being 'intentional about monitoring [her] self-monitoring', 'reframing' her experience in a more positive light, which helps her to 're-route' her focus back to her original instance of 'Find your limits. Exceed. Repeat'. In the end, each participant found their own unique balance of communication and perfectionism, but it is safe to say that accuracy and self-monitoring played a significant role even in the most communicative of participants.

6.2 Personality Factors

We saw in Chapter 1 that the scarce research on personality factors in gifted learners uncovered only one consistent personality dimension associated with L2 learning success: openness to experience, referring to a novelty-seeking, curious, flexible and artistic character strand. Amelia's self-reflection illustrates some aspects of this personality trait really well:

> I was 13 years old when I first went to France on my own. I had no fear about flying on my own, travelling on my own. I've always been not short on the confidence front, trying new things out… 'Oh I've not done that before, I'll give it a go!' So, I certainly had an openness and a confidence and a curiosity.

Musicality (as discussed above) may also relate to the artistic-creative aspect of this trait, and so is what we refer to as a *cosmopolitan orientation*, a salient personality feature that characterised many of our participants. We start the personality section of our discussion with this intriguing international disposition before addressing another important thread in our data set, the complicated question of introversion versus extroversion.

6.2.1 Cosmopolitan orientation and an interest in foreign languages

Many of our participants talked about a strong interest in everything foreign – languages, people, cultures, etc. – that they experienced from an early age onwards. As discussed in Chapter 4, sometimes this interest is instilled in learners by their family and early influences; other times, as we will see, the source is less obvious. When Samuli was asked when his international interest started, he answered, 'I don't know... I've always had it; I mean, as far as I can tell, I was kind of born with this – it's always been there for me'. In certain cases, this interest took the shape of an almost inexplicable travel bug, or wanderlust that might shift towards escapism. Amelia expresses the link between L2 learning and her cosmopolitan interest very clearly: 'I think going abroad because I wanted to improve my languages was primarily an excuse; really, I just wanted to travel and have experiences and independence and do new stuff and do unusual things'. In all cases, whether this orientation derived from early international exposure, family influence or through spontaneous generation, our participants found this personality trait an important factor that fed their motivation to learn the language in which they later became nativelike.

Similar to our observation of a cosmopolitan orientation is the notion of an *international posture*, which was first proposed by Yashima (2002) to describe the more general, global sense of integrativeness she observed in Japanese learners' motivation to learn English. Although debate remains regarding the exact definition and components of an international posture, the variable has since been adopted primarily to describe this aspect of English language learning motivation (for a recent review, see Botes *et al.*, 2020). What is surprising in our data, then, is that the cosmopolitan trait appeared strongest and most motivating in our anglophone learners – learners studying languages *other* than English (LOTEs). Although there has been some recent research into international postures in LOTE learners (e.g. Amorati, 2020), this area of interest remains a blind spot regarding the trait's general stability, its manifestation depending on the L2 studied and also its relation to personality traits such as openness to experience (which as discussed in Chapter 1, has been linked to gifted language learning). Overall, while similar, the cosmopolitan orientation we encountered in our learners appeared to be stronger and more energising than the more general 'global attitude' that an international posture usually involves. To demonstrate, we will close this discussion with Sarah's account, which conveys the full power of her longing to go abroad, ultimately leading her to L2 Hungarian nativelikeness.

SARAH: YEARNING TO BECOME INTERNATIONAL

Sarah comes from a 'very British' background in the sense that nobody in her family spoke any foreign languages well and her childhood holidays were always spent in the UK, never abroad. Despite this, Sarah knew by her early teens that she wanted an 'international life'. To describe this feeling of longing to travel and live abroad, Sarah uses the German word *Sehnsucht*, which expresses an intense yearning, in this case for something she had not yet experienced:

> I knew all along when I was a teenager that I was different. I didn't want to stay in the UK when I left education. People say that school days are the best days of your life, but even at the time, I thought, 'No way! I know these are not the best days of my life. I'm going to be living and working abroad, and life is going to be much better than it is now'. I didn't know where, but I knew I wasn't going to stay in the UK. And I felt it all the way through university even though I still didn't know where I was going.

Sarah's earliest realisation of this *Sehnsucht* for an international life was when she was around age seven or eight, watching an advert on her great aunt and uncle's TV in Sheffield. They had a large colour TV (unusual in the early 1970s), and she remembers vividly the effect the scenes and music had on her:

> I saw an advert on TV — I think it may have been for a car but that wasn't the important thing. This car was driving up a hillside around hairpin bends on maybe the Amalfi coast in Italy. The background music was from *The Godfather*, the Sicilian theme, played by a full orchestra with all the 'hearts and strings'… this car then went up a dusty road and arrived at like a farmhouse, and it was sunny and had olive trees and grapevines. And then they showed a wine cellar with a shaft of dusty sunlight, music playing, and I just had this real longing to be there. I remember thinking, 'I really want to travel. I want to go and see those kinds of places'.

Another memory from around the same time concerned foreign languages more specifically. This time, Sarah was at home with her parents watching a TV programme that featured an interview with singer Petula Clark:

> Petula Clark was interviewed on one of the news programmes. She had just married a French guy, and the interviewer said a few words

to her in French (probably very basic things). But it was when she answered in French that I got that feeling again! The Sehnsucht – I just felt this real longing to be able to speak a foreign language like she did.

Sarah has not yet been to the Amalfi coast (although she has been to other places in Italy), but she did go on to study modern languages (German and French) at university. In her final year, she met Zoltán and went to live with him in Budapest after graduating. She subsequently spent nearly 10 years living and working in Hungary (and learning to speak nativelike Hungarian) before returning to England with her young family in the late 1990s.

6.2.2 Introversion, extroversion and a 'theatrical streak'

As discussed briefly in Chapter 1, although many exceptional L2 learners have been found 'socially outgoing', the personality trait of extraversion has not emerged as a defining feature of gifted learners (Biedroń, 2011b; Hu & Reiterer, 2009). Our data is consistent with this seemingly contradictory situation. On the one hand, there is no doubt that in order to become a fluent communicator one needs to practice the various communication skills, and this requires some form of social engagement with speakers of the L2. This would suggest that extroverts – that is, people who relish social interaction – might have an advantage, and indeed, we do have participants in our sample who may be characterised as highly outgoing types. A case in point is Lou, an activist who does stand-up comedy and whose favourite times in English class were when they had to do an oral presentation: 'I was able to talk about myself in front of the class in another language and show off. I liked that. I guess that helped'. Similarly, Kerry describes herself as a chronic joker and admits to having 'a bit of a theatrical streak'; Heidrun confesses sometimes being 'a bit over-the-top enthusiastic' and Ranko states: 'If I want to ask something, straight away I'm going for it. So I'm not shy'. Amelia explains that such proactiveness does not necessarily mean, however, that one needs to be a true extrovert:

> It's about having the courage to go out there. It's not about being by nature extroverted, but knowing that that's a good thing to do, so doing it anyway. Because language is something that has to be used, and you have to be engaged with it. And maybe that is why it's a lot to do with having the courage to get it wrong. When you're learning a language, I

think you've got to be able to cope with mistakes, have the courage to put yourself out there, and be willing to be judged, because you are judged on your speech all the time.

It appears from our interviews that the secret instead lies in our learners' ability to overcome any natural shyness or introverted tendencies for the sake of the benefits of L2 practice; as Sarah put it, 'you have to be more thick-skinned, I think, if you want to become [proficient]'. Other learners were also witness to this principle; for example, Timur described how he went up to strangers in the street if he heard them speaking English: 'I'm a bit shy naturally, and I would never start a conversation with a stranger, you know? But back then, I was like, "I want to practice English, I don't care"'. Likewise, Ira says,

> I'm quite a shy person naturally. So I kind of have to force myself to go out of my way to talk to people sometimes. It would be easier not to, I suppose. But then you do get that satisfaction of like, 'Oh, I've pushed myself to do this, and it's actually been really good'.

In addition to overcoming inhibitions, certain participants developed specific compensatory strategies. Sarah for example explains:

> I'm a massive introvert and I'm quite shy, socially. So I wasn't one of those people that 'went out there and looked for opportunities to communicate!'... One thing that actually helps is having conversations with myself. I find that really helped with my fluency, rehearsing it, sometimes in front of the mirror. I realise I also do that in English... That can actually work well for us shy people who aren't naturally that good at going out there and finding random native speakers to have conversations with.

Amelia and Sara (and even extroverted Lou!) also recall using the same strategy. Others instead have relied on spending extensive periods simply observing people. Joy, for example, recounts that 'it's the shyness that enabled me to listen... I'm happy in the back of a room, just listening and observing... being shy and being quiet gives you an opportunity to observe how people communicate. And that has served me well'. Kristopher also used silent observation to good effect in both his Mandarin and Japanese studies. After he met a Chinese couple in Canada, he bluntly asked them if he could visit them:

> They said, 'Well, why not?' That's how it started, and then I went to their house. I did not understand anything, but I just sat with them in the living room, and I just listened. I went there every day after school, I just listened and listened and then somehow got to pick it up.

In Japan, he pursued the same strategy:

> Then I did my regular method: I found a nice *izakaya* [traditional pub] and I went there basically every night… and I sat there just as an excuse to listen. And I just listened every night. Listen, listen, listen, to how they talk. Then I started to talk, pick it up.

Thus, while extroversion itself was not a recurring personality trait in our gifted learners, social interaction remained an important part of their learning, and they developed a wide variety of strategies to help them overcome the potential disadvantages one might associate with introversion and shyness.

6.3 Motivational Factors

Earlier, we heard from Rianne that during her secondary school studies she received one of her worst grades in German 'because I really didn't like it'. Later, however, when her negative disposition was replaced by a positive one, the same Rianne excelled in the same language to a degree that is unreachable for most ordinary L2 learners. We must realise that the only difference between the two extremes concerned a single notion: *motivation*. Of course, when we say 'single' notion, we do not mean a unitary concept, because language learning motivation is a multifaceted construct (see e.g. Dörnyei & Ushioda, 2021), which means in practical terms that there are many diverse motives that can energise – or thwart – someone's learning process.

Some powerful motives were already discussed in Chapter 5, because *forming a unique bond with the L2* – which includes an attraction towards the language, its culture and its speakers as well as the pragmatic benefits of L2 proficiency – constitutes a potent source of learning energy. Earlier in this chapter, we also described our participants' *cosmopolitan orientation*, which again serves as effective fuel for action. In this section, we highlight three further motives that emerged in our data as substantial stimulants for L2 learning effort: the *desire to integrate*, *success which breeds further success* and *directed motivational currents*.

6.3.1 Desire to integrate

Participants could also be motivated to achieve excellence in their L2 development by the desire to be able to blend in or integrate into a particular L2-speaking community. As Lesley put it, such integration means that 'well, you don't stand out from the crowd anymore'. Ranko, an asylum-seeker in the UK, saw his future life goals and his professional dreams as dependent on his ability to integrate in the country, which he in turn linked to his English proficiency level. In a similar vein, Shinhye also saw nativelikeness as something necessary for her future success in American employment. The desire to integrate is an obvious (and well-known) motivational precursor (see e.g. Al-Hoorie & MacIntyre, 2020; Muir, 2021), but let us consider here three aspects of integration that deviate somehow from the standard meaning and implications of the notion:

- *Integration to avoid profiling.* Canadian Kerry recalls much of her Italian learning being motivated by the fact that 'I really did not want to be seen as the "ugly American", the stereotype of the demanding, loud-voiced foreigner who assumes everyone else speaks English and responds to incomprehension by speaking more loudly'. In a more appalling example of profiling, Theresa recounts that as a young German settling in the UK, she and many of her German friends were the victims of 'some really bad stereotyping'. This led her to 'try and disguise who you are. Initially quite intentionally, because I've had everything from "Heil Hitler" to "Eva Braun"'. Timur also reports that his learning efforts involved stepping away from sounding Russian and towards becoming unmarked: 'I just didn't want to sound Russian because we all know these movies where you have Russians and they speak English with a terrible Russian accent and everything. Well, I just didn't want to have that'.
- *Integration to overcome boundaries.* In a more positive light, Heidrun was enamoured with British society and wanted to achieve the total freedom to mix with every aspect of the sociocultural fabric of British life on her visits. Her dream had always been to be able to go to England and 'not to have any problems and no boundaries in who I talk to and what I can say, and also have the confidence... I think I've achieved that to a certain degree'. Similarly, 'no boundaries' was also the phrase Capucine used in reference to her nativelike English.
- *Integration to avoid standing out.* Finally, for Sara blending in was linked to a deeper psychological disposition:

> I like to say that my goal in life is to be average and to blend in. So, by imitating I become 'okay I'm more like them, I'm blending in, and I'm not standing out...'. And I have wondered if that may also have had an effect on the way I speak English.

Similarly, returning to Lesley's account:

> I was so determined to learn the language properly, so that I could just fit in! Because if you've got an accent and struggle to speak or express yourself properly, you stand out, and I didn't really want to stand out'.

Integrative motives are a well-established concept in L2 learning motivation theory (Gardner, 2019), but are usually associated with a positive, promotion focus (i.e. simply liking a culture and wanting to learn more about it) (see e.g. Papi *et al.*, 2019). The three types of integration explored here offer a surprisingly negative twist on the traditional construct, with participants alluding to prejudice, 'boundaries' and 'standing out'; we will return to this theme in Chapter 9.

6.3.2 Success breeds success

Certain participants found language learning at school relatively easy (as discussed above), and they typically experienced initial success in their L2 studies, which in turn generated further motivation. As Lou explains, 'When you know you're good at something and you can easily show off, that really motivates you… that would be my identity at the time'. Lou's sister, Capucine had a similar experience:

> I was actually going through a bit of a rough time, like I was a little bit bullied, but people had respect for me when I spoke English, because I was good at it. In a weird way, English became a sort of a shelter, a safe space in school, where if I had a presentation, people would praise me, and they would be really positive about me. That really sort of forged a deep interest for the language.

Interestingly, even Sara, whose psychological inclination has been to blend in as much as she can (discussed above), considered standing out in terms of her L2 proficiency to be a positive feature: 'Having a native-like proficiency was something special that made me stand out a little bit from others. I think we all sometimes like to know that there's something that we can do really well'. She then reiterated, 'That was one thing that made me like, stand apart'.

Experiencing success, especially early on in the learning journey, can provide learners with a self-fulfilling prophecy of positivity: they think they are good at language learning, and so they are – learners' sense of self-efficacy is a well-known construct in L2 motivation (for reviews, see Ahn & Bong, 2019; Schunk & DiBenedetto, 2015). This was particularly salient in Marjan's case: 'People around me were complimentary about my English all the time… so my confidence just grew, I think, because of all of that feedback. I took on more things, I just pushed myself therefore to do more'. Our learners also experienced a sense of success as a result of social comparison, and Lou underlined this aspect in a marked way: 'When you're already good at something, you want to keep being the best'. An even more pronounced example of this competitive motive came from William, who admitted that 'my goals have usually been just to be like, better than everyone else'. While competitiveness as a personality trait and competition within the learning environment have both been largely overlooked in the recent language learning motivation literature, studies show that competition can lead to higher creativity and classroom performance (Baumann & Harvey, 2021; Eisenberg & Thompson, 2011).

Finally, while success can undoubtedly breed further success, there are two sides to every coin, and to illustrate this let us conclude this section with a contradictory point made by Carl:

> Sometimes, especially if the language is easy for you, as it was for me, it is very hard to find motivation. Like when I went through primary school I didn't really focus on the classes, which kind of ruined the foundation of grammar for me. But I was able to pick it up later... being able to speak the language makes it very discouraging to learn [in class] even more.

6.3.3 Directed motivational currents

Directed motivational currents – or DMCs, as they are usually referred to in the literature (see Dörnyei *et al.*, 2016; Muir, 2020) – are powerful surges triggered by a specific event that motivate individuals to achieve a salient goal/vision, and they can drive the person caught up in them towards a well-defined goal in a highly effective and sometimes unstoppable way. We find instances of DMCs in our data set concerning important goals externally set for certain participants; for example, soon after starting a PhD programme in Austria and mastering nativelike English, Dutch Rianne was informed by her supervisor that she would be expected to teach in German the following year. From that moment, she knew she had one year to get up to speed, and she threw herself into it: 'It was kind of out of the question for me that this language would be the reason that I would not be able to continue to make progress'. So, she rose to the challenge and began taking language classes while also shifting all of her extracurricular activities (e.g. reading and watching TV) to German. Rianne's story is reminiscent of Lisa's account in Germany after she found a job and was given six months to improve her technical German. As she recalls:

> That was a motivating factor for me, because I really had to be able to function better. So that was half a year of doing a lot of language work.... In that period, we'd switched over to just speaking German at home [with my German husband]. Only watching German telly, only reading German magazines. At work, I was reading a lot of reports in German, which I had never done before. All of this really to start getting up and running properly in German, giving myself half a year to get up to speed.

One of the main types of triggers for a DMC is a negative experience, which can initiate a strong sense of psychological reactance, defiance or determination never to let the same thing happen again. Lesley's story is a perfect illustration of this 'I'll show you...' kind of surge:

LESLEY: 'THIS IS *NEVER* GOING TO HAPPEN TO ME AGAIN!'

After graduating from university in Scotland, Lesley moved to Germany as an au pair, and although she took some German classes, her German did not improve as much as she hoped because she was hired to speak English with her host family. After a year, she decided to move to a bigger city and, with her still quite rudimentary German, found work at a restaurant. Her desire to master German completely, however, was sparked by a particularly negative encounter with a pair of rude customers:

> One of the women said something, which I didn't understand, so I asked her to repeat it... and although I didn't understand exactly what she said, I knew that it was very rude and condescending. Her body language and the way her friend reacted made it clear... And I think that was a turning point for me. I just thought, 'Okay, so I'm going to have to buck up my ideas and learn more German – this is *never* going to happen to me again!'... [They] did me a favour, because after that I said, 'Right. That's it, you're going to learn German properly!'

She did indeed do so. In the evenings after work, she made a conscious effort to watch more television and read the newspapers. The internet did not yet exist, but she tried to immerse herself in German media and life. She watched a lot of films, and specifically documentaries as well, which she recalls diversified her vocabulary. It was also around this time that she moved in with a German partner, who in turn did not want to speak English with her, leaving their relationship and daily interactions primarily to German. As she improved, she began working in the office side of the restaurant, and soon after transferred to work at an office job – entirely in German.

Ultimately, while DMCs did not appear to be a common experience across all of our participants, the learners who did experience a DMC did so at the tail end of their learning trajectory to nativelikeness; perhaps then DMCs were the final surge that was needed to push themselves over the edge to nativelike mastery.

6.4 Discussion and Some Lessons to Draw

Compiling the material for this chapter was a stimulating exercise because it offered an overview of L2 learner characteristics with a difference: while much of what our participants reported aligned relatively smoothly with established theories of individual differences in language learning (e.g. Dörnyei & Ryan, 2015), a number of unexpected priorities emerged from our findings and a few surprises too.

The main lesson about our participants' *cognitive endowment* was that simply stating that these learners had a high degree of language aptitude does not offer a sufficiently accurate characterisation of their actual learning capabilities. Cognition is typically discussed in the SLA literature separately from other factors, implying – even if it is not stated explicitly – that the various cognitive variables are fairly static and situation independent. Although there has been some recent discussion about the trainability of aptitude (see e.g. Sáfár & Kormos, 2008; Singleton, 2017), the general assumption has been – to put it broadly – that someone is either good at learning languages or not. As Hyltenstam (2021: 58) summarises, 'A fundamental assumption is that language learning aptitude is an innate, relatively fixed talent for language learning'. In contrast, our data set produced a more complex picture. To be sure, our learners appeared to display good cognitive capabilities on balance, but for certain learners these capabilities only materialised once the particular individual became fully engaged with the learning of a specific L2. How can this be? How could an individual display average learning skills before something 'unleashed' their full learning potential and propelled them towards achieving nativelike L2 competence? A similar puzzle appears in a different form with participants who proved to be outstanding while learning one specific L2 but were not particularly successful – and even struggled – with another language.

The most tempting solution to this dilemma is that learners' cognition needed to be primed or activated by sufficient *motivation*. However, it is unclear what the specific mechanisms involved in augmenting one's cognitive abilities are, and in any case, the picture is bound to be more complex given that motivation itself is a multifaceted construct. Nonetheless, this draws attention to a broader underlying dilemma in psychology, namely to the insufficient understanding of motivation–cognition interactions: in the Introduction to a pioneering volume on the subject, *Motivation and Cognitive Control*, Braver (2016: 15) for example laments that the scientific literature in this area 'is still relatively young and not fully mature'. What evidence we do have suggests that motivation can indeed affect cognitive processing and control (for reviews, see Braver *et al.*, 2014; Ferdinand & Czernochowski, 2018; Hughes & Zaki, 2015), and there is even evidence that sufficient motivation is capable of overpowering certain cognitive age effects (Yee *et al.*, 2019). Nonetheless, most studies thus far on this topic report on short-term motivation and real-time performance, usually through the use of a participant reward system (e.g. Hall-McMaster *et al.*, 2019), and there remains little known about how the motivation–cognition relationship plays out in the long term. Future research is likely to shed more light on how motivational signals influence the selection, activation, intensity level and duration of cognitive processes, and our interviews provide evidence of the reality of these phenomena (for more discussion, see Dörnyei, 2020: 51–52).

Returning to our data analysis, we had the growing impression that success for each of our participants depended on the optimal *combination* of a number of cognitive, motivational, personality and contextual factors, which together formed a 'dynamic facilitative ensemble'. The best way to characterise this is comparing the process to an upward spiral: when the various circumstances aligned with each other favourably, the learner embarked on an increasingly profitable L2 learning journey where success bred more success and where the psychological and pragmatic benefits became increasingly palpable. Such momentum is, in fact, a key component of long-term motivation (for recent overviews, see Dörnyei, 2020; Dörnyei & Henry, in press), and so let us now briefly survey the specific cognitive and motivational components contributing to such L2 learning momentum.

6.4.1 Specific cognitive factors

In terms of cognitive factors, a relatively under-researched capacity, *mimicry ability*, emerged as an unexpected key element, with many participants displaying it in both their L1 and L2 use. This was related to a theatrical streak in some of them, but even learners who were shy by nature found the reserve to step out and engage proactively with the L2 learning process, trying to absorb and imitate the input. The role of conscious imitation in language learning is a familiar one, in particular with regard to the sociocultural theory of language acquisition (see e.g. Lantolf, 2006). As Lantolf (2012: 59) explains, learners use imitation to 'build up repertoires of resources for future performances', but specifies that these repertoires are not often 'precise replicas' of their original input. Imitation in both the first and second language acquisition literature is thus largely considered to be a process of slowly building up linguistic structures gained from input and creatively reproducing them. Yet, alongside this there also appears to be an underlying ability regarding the phonetic component of imitation, which we refer to here as mimicry ability (see e.g. Hinton, 2013; Reiterer *et al.*, 2013).

The phonetic side of speech imitation ability was, in fact, one of the measures used by Lewandowski and Jilka (2019) to test language talent in their investigation into speech convergence, and they found that phonetically gifted individuals tended to phonetically converge extensively more than their non-gifted counterparts. This suggests that learners' speech can benefit from a mimicry ability both on a conscious and unconscious level and indeed, Moyer's (2021: 51) recent overview offers a similar conclusion: 'Perhaps mimicry ability is a special kind of aptitude, indicative of either exceptional tonal and suprasegmental perception and/or bilateral language processing'. Our learners' accounts corroborate such an emphasis, and they also suggest that speech accommodation may be linked with gifted learners even beyond pronunciation mimicry, which is consistent with the effectiveness of an innovative learning method called 'shadowing' (e.g. Hamada, 2019; Kadota, 2019).

Mimicry ability was also linked to *musicality*, which makes sense in light of the review of the relevant literature in Chapter 1, and our participants' considerable involvement in music in one way or another was unmistakable. The difficulty of directly associating musical ability with specific SLA processes, however, is that the former is itself difficult to define. A variety of concepts have emerged related to music skills: musical aptitude, musical intelligence, musical giftedness and musicality, to name a few, and all of these can consist of a range of innate and/or trainable factors depending on the concept and the scholar using them. Musicality specifically is, as Nardo and Reiterer (2009: 245) summarise, 'a multi-faceted and fuzzy concept conveying the meaning of a collection of musical abilities which rely on both innate predispositions and experience'. In other words, the musicality we intend here is musical ability as a 'complex skill stemming from the interaction between innate and acquired factors' (Nardo & Reiterer, 2009). Musicality is therefore an umbrella construct similar to language aptitude in that it is a constellation of individual characteristics and trained skills. This complexity makes it a challenging task to find the right interface with the equally complex domain of L2 skills, and it remains to be seen whether the relationship between musicality and exceptional language learning we have seen here stems from learners' innate abilities or their musical experiences or a combination thereof. Nonetheless, musicality and indeed the use of music in language learning appear to have further potential as a future research topic for both the exceptional and the ordinary language learner (see also Fonseca-Mora & Machancoses, 2016).

A final cognitive component, a *self-monitoring disposition with a view to perfection*, evoked some inconsistent accounts, which is, in fact, in line with relevant findings in the scholarly literature. In his classic work, Krashen (1978) distinguished between two types of L2 speakers, *monitor underusers* and *monitor overusers*: speakers in the former group were found to speak fast, did not worry about making mistakes and did not repair their utterances frequently. Monitor overusers, on the other hand, tended to speak more slowly and precisely, and seemed to be disturbed by mistakes (for a review, see Kormos [1999], who argues that learners have a steady disposition concerning the allocation of attention to monitoring, which suggests that there might be an individual trait responsible for this). Self-monitoring therefore can be seen as a double-edged sword in exceptional language learning in the sense that it promotes nativelike accuracy but hinders nativelike fluency. It appears, therefore, that a special talent of our learners has been their ability to find a way of sustaining each function without one coming at the expense of the other.

Interestingly – and to bring us full circle – some evidence suggests that individuals who tend to self-monitor more also tend to unconsciously mimic their interlocutors more than their peers (Cheng & Chartrand, 2003), although further investigation is necessary regarding what this means for both gifted and ordinary language learners on a broader scale. Such an investigation, however, is also warranted by Moyer's (2021: 48) conclusion that 'nearly everyone [gifted language learners investigated in the literature] cites a propensity to self-monitor and attend to difficult features (phonological for the most part). Nearly all enjoy imitation as a learning strategy'.

6.4.2 Specific motivational factors

Specific *motivational factors* have been discussed in Chapters 4 and 5 as well as in this chapter, and the range of motives documented in our investigation reflects the wide variety of motivational components discussed in the literature (see e.g. Dörnyei, 2020; Dörnyei & Ushioda, 2021):

- family support
- L2 resource access
- social expectations
- rewarding contact with the L2 community
- attraction towards the L2 culture and cultural products
- pragmatic benefits of L2 proficiency
- attraction towards specific aspects of the L2
- an international posture
- the desire to integrate
- experiencing success

This list raises one big question in particular: do any of these factors stand out in terms of their significance for achieving exceptionality in L2 learning?

In short, in a qualitative study such as ours, the sample is by definition non-representative. This means that in a strict sense, it does not make any summative difference if a motive has been mentioned once, twice or thirty times. Therefore, there is no principled way for us to assign special significance to any of these factors, given that each has played a decisive role in at least one participant's learning history. Moreover, we have also seen that what really matters in this respect is not the individual factors themselves but rather their cooperative interaction with other variables, thereby forming optimal combinations. Having said that, qualitative research also recognises the importance of the researchers' subjective experience and assessment, and during the analysis of the interviews we did develop a sense of two higher-order motivational themes emerging in our sample:

- The first theme concerns the *creation of an intimate bond with the L2 and what it represents to the learner*. We have found that one of the most distinct features of our participants was that they had developed a special, personal relationship with the L2 and with some of its manifold aspects (e.g. aesthetic quality, non-gendered nature, cultural applications as well as the appeal of the land and the community where the L2 is spoken). Our interviewees considered the L2 not so much a subject to master but as a holistic enrichment of their lives and very identities. We will return to this broad issue in the final chapter of this volume (Chapter 12).

- The second higher-order motivational theme emerging from our interviews concerns the *desire to become an unmarked member of the L2 speech community*. Almost all of our interviewees expressed a desire at some point in their learning journey to become an unmarked L2 speaker, and even those who did not still acknowledged the benefits of having found themselves at the far end of this goalpost. We saw in Chapter 2 that the specific benefits of becoming linguistically unmarked can have a wide range, from overcoming more problematic aspects such as work requirements and linguistic discrimination to the more positive ones such as facilitating a personal sense of belonging, and in the most general sense it referred to a sense of freedom without any constraints.

6.4.3 In summary

The main lesson we can draw from this chapter is that although there is a range of potentially facilitative learner characteristics that can serve as a springboard into a positive spiral of L2 learning progress, none of them proved to be indispensable for reaching excellence – for each positive attribute identified in our investigation there were at least one or two participants who did not share it or who even displayed the opposite. While we cannot definitively say that all of our participants were not, in fact, born 'naturally gifted linguists', our findings suggest they may not have been, and also that, as Mercer (2012: 27) puts it: 'The factors contributing towards an individual's continually emergent abilities as a language learner are potentially complex, manifold, and intimately interconnected with the person's environment'. This is good news for the ordinary learner; while an exceptionally high cognitive endowment or specific personality factors might certainly help in advanced language learning, no factor appears to be indispensable, and in fact learners' affective and motivational relationships with their languages appeared to have a much stronger link to their success. Thus, the only magic key we can offer to open the gates of successful language learning is that one needs to relate the L2 to some aspect of one's core personality. If such a link is successfully formed, as it has been in each and every one of our learners, it can be nurtured into a mature, lifelong relationship, not unlike a great fire can be kindled from even the smallest of sparks.

7 Attention to Pronunciation

Why does a relatively narrow topic such as 'attention to pronunciation' merit its own chapter (even if a relatively short one), when other critical factors like language aptitude had to share a chapter with other subjects? Admittedly, our initial plans did not include giving that much attention to the matter of pronunciation, but during the interviews and data analysis we came across quotation after quotation such as the following:

> That's basically all I care about: pronunciation. That's all I focus on. That, to me, has always been the most important thing when I learn a language. And then beyond that, it just comes. When I started learning Mandarin, I was obsessed with tones, and I wanted to get each tone exactly right every time. And I did. And after that, everything is very easy. Once you've got the pronunciation, I find everything is just effortless. (Kristopher)

> I do think that a lot of passing for a native in all kinds of languages involves, first of all, speaking in an idiomatic way. And second of all, getting the pronunciation roughly correct. And then they won't notice any grammatical mistakes you might be making. (Judith)

> I suppose my most reliable friend has probably been sound and pronunciation. It's my one because it's where the satisfaction comes from. (Livia)

> For me what was important was the accent…. That was somehow super important to me. So I did lots of training, trying for all the sounds and everything. (Timur)

> I used to think accents really mattered. So I used to try and work on my accent a lot. And yeah, practice my accent, I guess, like speak to myself in my room to practice. (Capucine)

> One thing that I've concentrated a lot on in all the languages that I have been learning is the correct pronunciation. That's the only thing I've actually actively concentrated on and tried to perfect from the beginning. (Samuli)

[Nativelikeness has] kind of worked as a symbol for me, that achieving an accent means achieving the language. (Carl)

The consistency of such statements and the amount of time our interviewees devoted to talking about accent-related issues made us elevate the matter of pronunciation to a place of greater significance than we had originally expected. This increased attention is also warranted by the fact that in many language teaching situations – including ones we ourselves have experienced both as learners and teachers – pronunciation tends to be treated as a rather secondary issue if that: it is rarely addressed, taught or tested explicitly (see e.g. Foote *et al.*, 2016). This is in stark contrast to the message communicated by our participants, which makes us wonder whether this established practice is partly responsible for there not existing more second language (L2) learners with outstanding – or even nativelike – L2 proficiency. Therefore, let us take a closer look at this question and examine what lessons our investigation might offer in this respect.

7.1 Triggers of Attention to Pronunciation

It was striking to see the special attention our participants paid to pronunciation. While, as we saw in Chapter 2, pronunciation is indeed one of the keys to nativelike L2 mastery, it is certainly not the only one. So where did this emphasis originate in our learners? Our interviews showed that the sources could be quite varied and overlapping.

7.1.1 First language experience

A recurring source of the allocated attention to pronunciation concerned the participants' first language (L1) rather than their L2 use in the sense that it could be L1-related events that highlighted for them the significance of variation in accents in general. For example, Sarah moved from the south of England to the Midlands at the age of 10, and she soon realised that unless she changed her 'posh' southern accent to the local one, she would not be accepted by her new peers. This heightened her awareness of accents, and her experience was not unlike that of Lesley, who was aware quite early on that with non-Scottish people she should use a less thick accent of her Scottish dialect than she did with her family. In a similar vein, from an early age, Peng also became aware of the benefits of different dialects and accents in varying contexts due to his family's transfer across China, as we will see in his story below. Thus, from these and comparable cases, we observed learners developing metalinguistic awareness about the communicative importance of pronunciation long before ever encountering the L2.

7.1.2 Family emphasis

Similarly, and often overlapping with L1 experiences, some participants attributed their early attention on pronunciation to their family's influence. In addition to her experience with Scottish English, Lesley also describes her parents' influence on her attention to pronunciation: when she was growing up, her parents 'always made sure that we spoke properly and pronounced the words properly... it was very important. My mum and dad aren't snobs, not at all, but they wanted us to speak properly'. Colin's parents took a similar approach: 'Where I came from... [had] an accent where you dropped your *t*'s a lot... my parents didn't want us to speak like that. They were very poor, but they had a kind of middle-class way of speaking clearly'. While the previous two examples involved participants' L1s, participants were also influenced by family members' opinions on L2 pronunciation. In William's case, it was his brother who first drew his attention to pronunciation issues in the L2: 'My brother said that it was wrong to say [the number three as] "tree" and it was better to say "three", and he was my brother, so I obviously thought it was right to do that'. Kerry's grandmother similarly had strong opinions on the L2 French pronunciation taught in Canadian schools, calling it 'debased'. Thus, it appears that family members can have a strong influence on learners' focus and attention in both the L1 and the L2, in this case on pronunciation in particular.

7.1.3 Music and radio

In Chapter 6, we explored the idea of musicality facilitating language learning and nativelike L2 mastery. It turns out that musical interest also acted as certain participants' entry into the world of pronunciation attention. For example, Livia relates her awareness of accents to her passion for music: 'I used to obsessively, like *obsessively*, listen to music. And I think that plays a major function in terms of understanding where an accent falls in a word or a sentence'. As an Italian youth, she used to help her friends to write songs in English by adjusting their lyrics so that they were singable. She considers this 'the key thing, to associate words to certain patterns, and music has helped hugely... I think that was the starting point'. Uwe was also keen on English songs and their lyrics, and his love for the radio also led him to 'another really important discovery, a very East German one' when he came across the radio station of the British Forces Broadcasting Service: 'I noticed that these guys were all speaking a very different English. So it wasn't the Queen's speech; it was Irish, Northern, Scouse, anything'. As he recalls, 'That's when a sort of a "mongrel" version started happening in my head, of things that my brain acoustically liked and stored'.

7.1.4 A 'good ear' and noticing capacity

As we saw in Chapter 6, participants benefited from at least some degree of high language learning aptitude. We also found that this ability could manifest in a 'good ear' and noticing capacity. For example,

Kerry describes her learning approach as 'the soaking up way', involving 'being very open, being very curious and paying close attention. I think I was naturally somebody who would notice it, and I would ask about things that I had noticed'. Marjan also recounts that she was 'quite proud of the ability to develop my language... I wanted to be good at it, so I would check that it was how you pronounce it and how you would say it'. Peng adds that being an English tutor developed in him a noticing capacity of other people's mistakes, and as such he would try to avoid making the same mistakes he heard. A special and highly potent version of a focus on pronunciation based on other people's mistakes has been some of our participants' desire to avoid the stereotypical heavy L2 accent used by their fellow nationals: Kerry for example thought, 'That's got to go. I *cannot* sound like that' upon hearing some fellow North Americans speaking Italian, and Timur was equally keen: 'we all know these movies where you have Russians and they speak English with a terrible accent and everything. Well, I just didn't want to have that'.

7.1.5 Pronunciation in the curriculum

From a practical perspective, it is reassuring to learn that according to our participants, schools can also make a big difference in enhancing one's focus on pronunciation. Although they are in the minority, some L2 teachers and courses do emphasise the way the L2 is articulated and pronounced, and this can have a lasting impact on learners. Denny, for example, recalls being corrected on her pronunciation of German and slowly beginning to develop an ear for the unfamiliar sounds of the language: 'There were particular phonemes that I thought I could pronounce well, but actually I couldn't... looking back now, I can see how your ability to hear those sounds kind of develops over time'. Timur recounts that:

> every time I wanted to say something with a *t*, like, 'top' or 'tea', it just sounded wrong. And it just felt like, 'I don't know what to do!' But once you get the sort of new set of tools like I did in my linguistics classes, it's like, 'Oh, I know what's wrong with my *t*'s now! They're unaspirated, so I just need to aspirate them'.

Interestingly, in some teaching environments the curricular emphasis on pronunciation was caused by having to differentiate between a British and an American English accent. In Ira's class in the Netherlands, for example, students were given the choice to speak with an 'American' or a 'London' accent, and for presentations they would be asked to identify their peers' accents and were given teacher feedback. Consequently, Ira placed a high value on accent, as she valued her grades. Finally, in some cases negative criticism by the L2 teacher made a big difference in the long run; Shinhye, for example, recounts a highly unpleasant episode that changed her attitude towards accents:

> I had a very unpleasant memory about pronunciation in my first year in college. When I presented something in class, the professor told me, 'You speak English with a Kyungsang dialect'. That was the first time someone told me that my pronunciation was not good. I felt ashamed... because of that, I became more conscious of pronunciation.

While Shinhye's was a decidedly negative encounter, classroom experiences like hers (as well as our other participants' more positive equivalents) can instil in language learners an attention to pronunciation that follows them through their learning trajectories.

7.1.6 Awareness of the social benefits of good pronunciation

Perhaps one of the most pronounced sources of pronunciation attention in our interviews was that, in many contexts and cultures, a special dividend is attached to good L2 pronunciation. For example, Shinhye explains that 'Korean people give more credit, or give more praise, when they hear good pronunciation: "Wow! Yeah, your English is very good"'. Interestingly, she adds that 'it's not related to grammar or writing or any other skills. It's a direct reaction to pronunciation, and I've seen it a lot. So because of that I paid more attention to the pronunciation'. A closely related issue to this social recognition of good pronunciation is the fact that L2 speakers are often judged more positively if their pronunciation matches specific native speaker norms, regardless of what their L2 proficiency truly merits. This, in turn, can offer certain concrete benefits, such as being hired for a job. Sarah, for example, explains:

> A lot of people listen to the pronunciation in their judgment.... They kind of think that somebody's nativelike [in English] if they sound like a British or American person when they speak, even if their vocabulary is skin deep.

As she recalls about her learning Hungarian, 'I was probably only intermediate level, but I sounded like a Hungarian by that stage, and even if people didn't mistake me for a native speaker, they thought my competence was much higher than it was'.

Amelia summarises the underlying issue clearly: 'One of the defining things is pronunciation, because that's the thing that hides other sins. If you sound authentic, even if you're making mistakes, people don't hear it. They just hear the authenticity of the accent, the pronunciation'. This is corroborated by Judith who, when asked whether good pronunciation was something that was important to her, said: 'Yes, because I quickly realised that if I was being taken for a Norwegian, it was because I had good pronunciation'. William aptly adds that if one has a good accent 'then other people view you as if you know what you're talking about'. Thus, participants' attention to pronunciation often stemmed from their knowledge of the social benefits associated with good pronunciation.

While we have explored six specific and distinct triggers above, the learning experience (and indeed life in general) is often more complex than the seemingly linear relationships presented here. As is evident from our discussion thus far, participants could also experience multiple triggers that worked together to reinforce the importance that the individual placed on pronunciation. To sum up this section of our discussion, we will end with Peng's story, which illustrates well how these triggers can intertwine to culminate in nativelike pronunciation:

PENG: CREDIT WHERE CREDIT IS DUE

From a young age, Peng had a particular awareness and talent for pronunciation, which he attributes to three main factors: his early musical training, his experiences moving provinces as a young boy in China and his awareness of pronunciation's social benefits.

Peng's mother, a music teacher, trained him from a young age in singing, and Peng subsequently sang in a chorus from the age of eight throughout his school years. Looking back, he finds this early music experience gave him 'the ability to make sense of those subtle nuances and pronunciation or tonal differences in languages'.

Parallel to this experience, Peng and his family moved provinces several times due to his father's job. Even as a young boy, one of the first things he noticed was the difference in dialect and pronunciation, and he reflects that 'local kids had access to more cultural resources or social resources' than he did because of his linguistic and cultural differences. This early experience instilled in him an attention to pronunciation differences in his L1, which he was eventually able to take advantage of: 'I was fully aware of circumstances or contexts where I had to speak with a little bit of an accented Mandarin – whenever that was going to work in my favour or to my advantage, I was going to use that'.

Thus, when it came to learning L2 English, Peng was already on track to having good pronunciation. What gave him the final push was the affirmative feedback he received for his budding pronunciation talent. Although pronunciation was not explicitly taught in his English curriculum, as he explains:

> You talk to people and then they appreciate your good pronunciation – they tend to give you more credit for that. And then later on, you just

feel, 'I should work on it, because I get more positive feedback', and then you just spend more time on it. It's like a positive feedback loop.

This positive feedback on his pronunciation followed him past the classroom to his later job hunt, making him realise that good pronunciation also offers tangible benefits:

> I sort of discovered that myself, that with good pronunciation you can easily find a good job. And during the interview process when I graduated, as I interviewed with different companies, I got that feedback as well. Because pronunciation is the easiest thing you could tell from a possible candidate.

Ultimately, while Peng's nativelike mastery was the result of a combination of his attention to a variety of other factors as well as pronunciation, pronunciation holds a special status for him as something that 'opens up more possibilities'.

7.2 Developing a Nativelike Accent

Some of our participants managed to pick up nativelike pronunciation without putting in much conscious effort, although such a statement does not fully reflect the actual situation, because such implicit learning requires receiving a lot of authentic input that can only be ensured through determination. For example, working as an au pair in Norway, Judith had relatively little to do during the day, and she used this time to listen to the radio:

> I was at home, doing nothing except a little bit of light housework. So – and this was a long time ago – there was the radio, and I just turned the radio on all day long. I'm convinced I learned an awful lot just from listening to the radio... the pronunciation and how I speak Norwegian in a natural way, I'm pretty sure it came from listening to the radio throughout the whole of that year.

However, for other participants, acquiring a nativelike accent in the L2 required putting in more conscious effort and practice than merely listening to the radio or, in Kristopher's case, listening to native speakers of the L2 in their homes or at the local pub. Samuli, for example, explains:

> I tried my best to pronounce the words the way the pronunciation was described. Because I've seen many people who pronounce words more

based on how they would pronounce them in the languages they already know, instead of concentrating more on the correct way to pronounce the words in the target language.... One thing that I've concentrated a lot on in all the languages that I have been learning is the correct pronunciation. That's the only thing I've actually actively concentrated on and tried to perfect from the beginning.

Our interviews suggest that two strategies stood out in particular in terms of how our participants developed their nativelike accent: applying *conscious mimicry* and imitating specific *role models*.

7.2.1 Conscious mimicry

We saw in Chapter 6 that the ability to mimic accents was an innate characteristic of certain participants, who exercised mimicry both unconsciously and consciously. Our current focus is on the latter process, when imitation of the sounds and intonation of the L2 was practiced intentionally and with a view to improve. Colin's fascinating account of trying to imitate birds while on holiday shows how deeply such an exercise was ingrained in his nature:

> I remember being in the Amazon and hearing birds. And I would try to imitate the birds, the sound with a kind of different whistle effect. And it was incredible, because sometimes there are certain sounds which are very hard to imitate. But other ones I was able to get exactly the pitch. And I think sometimes if I hear something right, I would pitch that out of the blue, exactly the right note. And I think that's got to do with the fact that you can hear a German say a word and you can recreate that word, exactly as he said it.

This mimicry skill may have helped Colin to achieve the remarkable feat of learning both German and French at a nativelike level and maintaining this competence for decades while living and working in the UK. Other participants also report various forms of mimicry practice:

- 'If I'm talking to someone in English, I usually go for their accent. Unless it's really local and strong, and there's no way I can embrace the accent, I usually imitate what I hear'. (Capucine)
- 'I quite like trying to imitate local dialects. I really find that very interesting. And actually, sometimes I do it without realising and it gets pointed out to me'. (Denny)
- 'I trained with mimicry – I stumbled into it: I found this little DVD kind of program, where you could superimpose your voice or record your voice over somebody else's, and you could see their lips

moving, and you could hear your voice over the other person's...'. (Timur)
- 'I've always tried to mimic pronunciation.... In Brazil and in Iceland, I did try to mimic; I wouldn't just listen to individual pronunciation, but I would listen and try to imitate'. (Joy)
- 'And then I started to talk with the same accent [Connecticut English] as this girl because we were friends. I don't know if I'm that good at mimicking, but that was my goal at least'. (William)
- 'I copied the people I wanted to sound like. You know, so I thought, "I wanted to sound like her", so I copied them'. (Heidrun)

Ultimately, while various (sometimes immutable) factors may determine whether a language learner mimics unconsciously, conscious mimicry is an accessible learning strategy that our participants utilised. Indeed, similar strategies for teaching pronunciation have been proposed, such as 'interactive alignment' (Trofimovich, 2016), but there remains a plethora of research potential in this area of pronunciation instruction.

7.2.2 Role models

The last two excerpts by William and Heidrun draw attention to the fact that an important aspect of mimicry is *who* someone tries to imitate, which brings up the issue of *role models*. In their large-scale international survey of L2 role models, Muir *et al.* (2019) found that one of the four main dimensions of learners' role models was based on accent and L2 variety. Indeed, certain participants in our project based their pronunciation on such role models, though exactly who these role models were turned out to be slightly more complex. For example, Denny's account in this respect is similar to Heidrun's in the sense that she follows an aggregate role model made up of several speakers: 'I think I probably have more of a composite image in my head of people that I've come across whose pronunciation I really liked – I think that there's maybe a composite role model there in terms of sound'. Denny's concept of a composite phonetic role model is echoed by Livia:

> There are patterns I've picked up, and I feel like I carry like a tiny fragment of a lot of people I met at pivotal points in my life... but I can't pinpoint a single person; it's more like in different contexts, and looking at somebody and being like, 'That person is comfortable', and figuring out how. It's happened over time, though, with lots of different people.

Ranko instead selected a specific group of speakers to imitate:

> The best English I have ever heard was my [community organisation] friends'. They talk to me in a different way from what I have learned

before, they speak using a high quality of English words and level. On the street, in reality, they don't speak like that.... I'm trying to use my skills to speak English at as high a level as I can.

Others, too, have more specific linguistic role models. The people Heidrun wanted to sound like were the comedy troupe Monty Python, and she and her friends could repeat their sketches verbatim. For Joy, the obvious choice was her husband ('I was aiming to sound like my husband') and for Kristin and young Shinhye it was their English teachers, although Kristin adds, 'Maybe I got a bit from YouTube. I remember watching a lot of Zoella, like Zoe Sugg... So I think I tried to like channel my inner Zoe when I spoke'. Regardless of who they modelled their pronunciation on, whether it was every person they encountered, a composite group of people or a specific individual, mimicry played an important role in acquiring nativelike pronunciation for these learners.

7.3 The Flip Side of Good Pronunciation

One would assume that in language learning circles the more authentic one's pronunciation, the better. While in many learning contexts this is indeed the case, there are a surprising number of exceptions. Let us consider Capucine's account as an illustration.

CAPUCINE: THE 'WEIRD RELATIONSHIP WITH ACCENTS IN FRANCE'

When Capucine was in secondary education, accent was incredibly important to her:

> So back when I was growing up at school and so on, a peak language speaker would be someone with a great accent. Obviously, when I say a great accent, I mean either BBC or an American accent...

As a result, she 'used to try and work on my accent a lot'. She explains, however, that there is a paradox in French society, whereby an authentic accent is highly valued, but at the same time an L1 French speaker with a good accent may also be considered pretentious or too much of a try-hard. She recalls that, in general, good English pronunciation was highly appreciated among French teenagers: 'If you have an English accent and you can speak English properly, you go from being a 5 to a 10 in girls' views, most of the time. It was really praised'. However, she admits that this was not representative of the typical experience, because 'there's a really weird relationship with accents in France: if you're French, and you try really hard to get a good accent, people will most likely think that you're being arrogant, that you're trying to show off'.

This would result in earnest students being 'teased or mocked' in class. Luckily for Capucine, her class in high school was different largely due to the influence of a particularly observant teacher:

I had a really good teacher in high school, who immediately said, 'If I hear anyone, if I see anyone, if I suspect anyone of making fun of someone's accent, you're out. I don't want to see you in my classroom…'. That's so good because it helps both the people with a strong French accent that feel insecure about their accent, and the people that are actually enjoying English, trying to embrace an accent. It protects them both, in a way. So that was definitely the best.

Capucine's sibling Lou confirms the existence of such a flip side of good pronunciation: 'I used to be called a super snob. Because in France, when you have an English accent, like a proper one, you look like a super snob. So, it made me shy to speak English in France'. Such an ambiguous attitude to a nativelike English accent is not restricted to France alone. Ira has experienced the same phenomenon in the Netherlands:

When I was speaking to my classmates, I would speak in the more Dutch accent that I have…. It's just when you constantly hear people commenting on other people's accents and saying, 'Oh, they're so pretentious for doing that. Why do they do that?' You kind of get a bit like, 'Oh, I probably shouldn't do that'.

Kristin, in turn, explains that sounding nativelike in her English class in Norway was 'a bit awkward', and trying to use a non-Norwegian accent made you 'sound stupid'. Shinhye explains that among her fellow Korean international students in the United States, using an authentic English accent suggests that 'you try to be different'. She continues:

And that is something that made them feel a little uncomfortable: 'You're a Korean, so act like a Korean. And don't act like you are in the native speakers' group, because you're not. Don't act like you don't belong to the Korean international student group'.

Such accounts confirm the fact that good pronunciation is much more than accurate L2 use only, because pronunciation touches upon deeper layers of meaning both in the speaker and the listener. As an extreme, in some learning contexts it may even be seen as a betrayal of one's national or community identity, and this can solicit both implicit and explicit disapproval.

Luckily, at least in the institutional context, as we saw with Capucine's teacher, there are ways to mitigate such negativity around accents, both for learners who struggle with pronunciation as well as for learners who excel.

7.4 Discussion and Some Lessons to Draw

In the theoretical overview in Chapter 1, we saw that pronunciation is a core area of linguistic self-representation in one's L1 and L2, and it is therefore closely associated with – if not a reflection of – aspects of one's identity; as Guiora (1972: 144) famously put it, pronunciation 'is the key to the extent to which the individual is psychologically capable of stepping into a new system of communication'. The discussion in this chapter has been consistent with such a view; our participants assigned much more importance to the matter of pronunciation than to many better-known topics in second language acquisition (SLA). Indeed, certain participants considered it to be one of their key concerns in L2 learning, and learners like Shinhye, Peng and William articulated the view that 'pronunciation hides many sins'. They mean this in the sense that if one sounds more like a native speaker, their interlocutors will treat them as more competent, often beyond their real proficiency level – not only will they likely overlook any linguistic mistakes, but, as William noticed, they will also take the content of what is said in good pronunciation more seriously.

Our participants' perceptions of positive attitudes towards speakers with more nativelike pronunciation are backed up by the literature. Derwing and Munro (2009) distinguish between three different evaluations of L2 phonetic performance: accentedness, comprehensibility and intelligibility. Accentedness is a (relatively objective) evaluation of how speech patterns actually differ from local varieties. Comprehensibility, on the other hand, regards the listener's evaluation of how easy it is to understand the speaker, and intelligibility involves the degree of the listener's actual comprehension of the speaker. It turns out that these three dimensions diverge in important ways. For example, in Hendriks *et al.*'s (2021) study on students' evaluations of differently accented lecturers, they found that non-native speaker students evaluated slightly accented and native speaker lecturers more positively than their heavily accented counterparts in English – despite all three kinds of lecturers being equally intelligible. In addition, studies have shown that educational attention to L2 prosody tends to account for the greatest amount of variance in both comprehensibility and intelligibility for L1 listeners (Kang *et al.*, 2010; Leather, 1999). On the other hand, L2 listeners' evaluations of comprehensibility and intelligibility tend to be affected more by bottom-up factors in pronunciation such as segmental and nuclear stress errors (Field, 2003; Wilson, 2003). Taken together, these studies suggest that an increased focus on pronunciation is vital in L2 education, and furthermore that attention to both segmental and suprasegmental pronunciation is important for robust pronunciation development (see also Lee *et al.*, 2015; Pennington & Rogerson-Revell, 2019). While listener attitudes to L2 speech are, of course, moderated by a variety of background factors (see e.g. Nagle *et al.*, 2021; Saito *et al.*, 2019; Winke *et al.*, 2013), the effects of pronunciation on attitudinal evaluations can have long-lasting impacts, particularly in the workplace but also in everyday life (Lippi-Green, 2012).

The fact that an authentic accent is extrapolated to areas that extend beyond linguistic form was also highlighted by reports in our data set that in some contexts a nativelike L2 speaker can be seen as pretentious, arrogant or even a traitor to their culture. As a consequence, in order to avoid any form of peer pressure, learners might deliberately choose to increase the foreign sound of their pronunciation. On the converse side, the study by Hendriks *et al.* (2021) also found that Dutch students (compared to their international or English native speaker counterparts) were the harshest on moderately Dutch-accented lecturers, suggesting that interlocutors are more critical with accented speakers who share the same L1. Both instances of peer pressure follow Capucine's observation about students being bullied in the classroom for being on either end of the spectrum of pronunciation talent – a double standard in which L2 speakers can be neither too good nor too bad at L2 pronunciation.

Two obvious lessons for everyday learners emerge from the participants' accounts in this respect. First, Capucine's example shows that any negative peer evaluation of an authentic accent *can* be stopped by decisive *teacher intervention* right from the beginning, thereby creating positive group norms that favour constructive performance in this area. This requires, among other things, an open discussion of the matter and bringing the majority of the students to a consensus (see Dörnyei & Muir, 2019). Gluszek and Dovidio (2010) also make the point that this kind of intervention can also work both ways as it did in Capucine's classroom, by de-stigmatising non-native accents and creating a more constructive classroom environment on the whole.

The second lesson concerns the widespread observation that L2 instruction too often pays too little attention to improving learners' pronunciation (see e.g. Trofimovich *et al.*, 2016). There are several reasons for this, but this is in stark contrast with the message consistently communicated by our participants, namely that in order to modify your accent, conscious attention needs to be paid to this matter. While becoming specifically nativelike may not be every ordinary learner's linguistic goal, the importance of pronunciation in everyday life suggests that some learners may desire the skill set to be able to play an agentic role in their pronunciation, yet the topic is often an overlooked facet of language teaching. In fact, Szyszka (2011) found that learners with positive perceptions of their pronunciation competencies were also less likely to experience high levels of foreign language anxiety, further suggesting that an increased attention to pronunciation instruction could benefit learners' L2 development and their well-being (see also Baran-Łucarz, 2014; Szyszka, 2017).

Fortunately, interest has been slowly rebuilding in the area of pronunciation instruction over the last few decades (see e.g. Pennington, 2021), and our participants' accounts suggest at least two additional potentially effective routes into pronunciation instruction: conscious mimicry and role modelling. A further avenue presented by our data, as in Timur's case, is intensive L2 perception and production training, which has been associated with nativelike L2 mastery in previous studies (Bongaerts, 1999).

In summary, the importance of the issue of pronunciation in our investigation has grown considerably beyond its usual level of representation in language teaching methodology. Zoltán has always wondered why he never succeeded in reaching a nativelike level in English despite his strong motivation, long-term commitment, English family relations and decades of residency in England (and even some musical training!). However, one thing definitively missing from his L2 education was *any* attention paid to improving his accent: in Hungary, focusing on improving the learners' accents tended to be rather low on most teachers' agendas. In contrast, Chapter 1 presented reports that good pronunciation can initiate a powerful positive spiral of enhanced attitudes towards the L2, also improving one's motivation and linguistic confidence (see e.g. McCrocklin & Link, 2016; Moyer, 2007). This has been affirmed by our participants' accounts of the positive feedback on pronunciation they received throughout their learning journeys, engaging them further and enduringly in the learning process. This ultimately raises the uncomfortable question as to whether ignoring pronunciation as mere decoration on the linguistic cake may be at least partly responsible for preventing many ordinary L2 learners – including ourselves – from reaching their full L2 potential.

8 Intensive Effort and Strategic Learning

Our discussion on developing nativelike pronunciation in Chapter 7 demonstrated that while certain participants achieved this exceptional result relatively easily and effortlessly, others paid conscious attention to improving their accent, sustaining their efforts over a considerable period of time. According to our data, the same pattern applies to their second language (L2) learning more generally. While it is true that certain members of our select group surprised even themselves by achieving nativelike L2 competence as a result of naturalistic communication and learning, other participants applied intensive, effortful and strategic learning in order to reach their linguistic goals. Let us start this chapter with a brief description of the former type – the effortless learners – because this will set the backdrop against which the majority of our sample's hard work will become salient in contrast.

8.1 Absorbing the Language Naturally

In our data set, we find accounts attesting to the fact that learners could acquire their special L2 competence with relative ease, in sharp contrast to the sustained and strenuous effort that most ordinary L2 learners have to exert to reach advanced levels. Theresa, for example, admits:

> I don't know, it just happened. You know, it's just natural, I think. I don't see learning a language as something I have to *do*. I think it just happens. And maybe I'm gifted that way, that I'm just able to absorb it.... I never felt as though it was a chore or a duty.

Peng also used the verb 'absorb' to characterise how he picked up vocabulary:

> I'm not a very focused student in the sense that I don't do drills, or I don't record all the new words and expressions I see in a paragraph. No. I try to read from the good authors as much as I can, and try to absorb all the good expressions and sentences and structures unconsciously. So

I just absorb those ideas, but then those structures become part of my repertoire.

Perhaps the most extreme example of a spontaneous learner in our sample is Hanna, who initially characterises herself as a 'lazy' learner. Let us take a closer look at what she actually meant by this.

HANNA: 'I'VE BEEN A "LAZY" LEARNER…'

As already mentioned in Chapter 6, Hanna found learning English in her home country, Finland, easy right from the start. However, while this early success did play a role in her ongoing motivation, the real engine of her progress was her naturalistic use of the L2 in communication with her international friends. Her hometown was too far from her upper secondary school, so at age 16 Hanna moved into student accommodation, which was also used as housing for international students. She was soon included in their social circles, and a similar situation occurred when she later attended university. She enjoyed the experience so much that she decided to switch to studying English language and literature at a university outside of Finland, in another European country. While there, she first had an American roommate and later an English one, and although she recalls her accent at the time was 'still incredibly Finnish', she found that her English on a broader level implicitly improved. In fact, she adds:

> I've always been an incredibly lazy learner… Actually, when I was at uni a professor said to me, 'Oh, Hanna, you're one of the best students I've had in terms of first-year language skills, but you are also one of the laziest students I've ever had'.

Indeed, Hanna did not go out of her way to complete her homework or do any studying beyond the minimum required for her classes, and neither does she recall being particularly strategic in her learning:

> I can't think of a time when I've specifically set myself some strategies of how I would learn something. … I can't think of times when I've been consciously looking like 'How can I learn this?'

However, although she may not have been an applied student from an external standpoint, it turns out that what Hanna really cared for was creating opportunities to use the L2: 'I've always looked for [L2] contacts, like, "How I can use the language?" or, "I'm going to watch this show" or "I want to find international friends that I can speak to"'. Language learning for her was 'not language for the language's sake, but actually using it... it is the medium of all these other things you want to do. So that's I guess how I learned'. She simply tried to live her life in English, and this became particularly true when, after graduating, she moved to England and later married an Englishman. It was there, after about three or four years, that she found that people would sometimes mistake her for a native speaker – without it ever having been an explicit goal for her.

It turns out that Hanna is not, in fact, a lazy learner; rather, she found a way to incorporate naturalistic language learning into her everyday life in such a way that she enjoyed the experience more than she felt she was exerting conscious effort. While Hanna and similar participants did not recall often 'sitting down' at a desk and doing drills – thus averting the *feeling* of effortful learning – the amount of time they invested in their nativelike L2 is huge given their heavy reliance on L2 input.

8.2 Exerting Effort

We started the discussion in this chapter by describing naturalistic and relatively painless learning, partly because this is the archetype that many would associate with the kind of exceptionally gifted L2 learners whom we investigated in our study. Our data set confirms that such fortunate individuals do indeed exist – although recall that even Hanna had to contribute to her progress by consciously and consistently immersing herself in L2 use opportunities. Nonetheless, the dominant learning pattern that emerges from our participants' accounts is not one of effortless learning. Other interviewees told us a rather different story about their L2 acquisition, one which was characterised by concentrated effort and disciplined, strategic learning, not unlike the accounts of unexceptional language learners who achieve success. Livia, for example, found her learning experience 'always really intensive' to the point that she 'just never relaxed'. For Denny, German was 'always a struggle' and 'trying to kind of get an error-free knowledge of the language is difficult'. In contrast to her effortless learning experience with English, when it came to learning German she remembers 'not particularly enjoying the actual process' and having to force herself to build studying into her routine to sustain her learning. Heidrun, too, remembers an effortful experience:

> I desperately wanted it. I desperately wanted to be good, better than the others; I really wanted it, and I put lots of effort into it and lots of language studying and lots of listening and lots of analysing. I just wanted to be good...

As we will see below, Heidrun relates her efforts in language learning to her experience with practicing a musical instrument, an analogy that Colin echoes:

> [For] both music and language... there is an absolute need for regular, regular repetition. You could not sit down and read for an hour or two about geography and think, 'Okay, I know about glaciers' or something. You have to do it daily.

Unlike our first set of learners, these reports of intensive, sustained effort recall the experiences of successful but rather ordinary language learners. Perhaps the best effort-related example of a seemingly traditional learning experience is Amelia, whose story offers a good representation of the role of intensive effort in achieving nativelike L2 competence, while also introducing some creative strategies.

AMELIA: 'VERY ENGAGED, VERY ACTIVE, VERY PERSISTENT, VERY DISCIPLINED'

As seen in previous chapters, Amelia's interest in language learning has been closely connected with her passion to travel, and indeed, her summer holidays throughout her teenage years were accordingly 'packed'. However, this international experience – and the inherent L2 exposure it offered – was also accompanied by a systematic and proactive approach to enhancing her L2 exposure. For example, this is how she remembers her first study abroad period in Germany as part of her British undergraduate degree:

> I was very engaged, very active, very persistent in and very disciplined about L2 learning.... I signed up for night classes, I went to sports things, I did everything that I could, and found myself doing all kinds of weird stuff just to meet people. I went out, I joined clubs, I did everything you could think of to speak the language and to create opportunities.... I did make a conscious effort to expose myself to the language, reading as much as I could, having the radio on, listening to the language all the time. I forced myself only to read German books, which was tough for me!... It was certainly a very intense period of time where everything was focused towards a goal: towards me improving my German.

This kind of intensive effort was not limited to that sole period in her life, and it followed her when she moved to Austria as well. Unlike Hanna, Amelia's focus was on taking any opportunity to use the L2 regardless of her interest in the activity itself, making it an effortful endeavour. In addition, Amelia's strong work ethic was not limited to seeking L2 communication opportunities but also involved paying studious attention to vocabulary and accuracy in her L2 use:

> [I spent time] learning vocabulary very, very consciously, in the old-fashioned way: sitting and just learning vocabulary.... And for me, it was a very conscious engaging with language, in that I was interested in structure and interested in words. If I saw a new word I liked, I was going to write it down. I was very conscious about trying to use new words that I liked the sound of or that I liked the look of.

Amelia also employed some creative, personalised learning strategies:

> I also had imaginary conversations in German: it makes me sound slightly loopy, but just when you're in the shower, I would think, 'What would I say if I was gonna have this conversation in German? How would that go?' So, imagining having conversations in my own head was something that I did very strongly, trying to find the language and use the language in my mind.

Amelia's story is a prime example of the majority of our participants' disciplined and intensive efforts in language learning, but her story is also valuable for our discussion regarding how this effort was deployed, that is, the learning strategies our participants used, and in particular how they were tailored to work for the individuals themselves. For example, as we saw in Chapter 6, the use of 'imaginary conversations' was a particularly effective compensatory strategy for learners like Sarah and Amelia to get communicative practice outside of social situations. Let us expand further on similar uses of strategic learning.

8.3 Strategic Learning

As discussed at the beginning of this chapter, certain participants recalled a relatively effortless learning experience; however, it turns out that this kind of experience does not preclude the use of strategic learning. Even Kristopher, whom we got to know as a highly naturalistic learner – recall that he is the unique learner who mastered Mandarin and Japanese largely through listening to people – recounts how he continuously focused on his mistakes in order to improve on his accuracy. Without corrective feedback in a formal classroom environment, he even had to devise an ingenious strategy to encourage people to overcome their politeness and correct him:

And I would tell them, 'Please correct me'. And they were reluctant; they felt it might offend me. So in order to get them going, I would correct them. If they spoke English, I would say, 'No, that's wrong', and they would get upset. And then they would correct me, and it worked! It's like if you want somebody to hit you, you hit them first, right? They realised, 'Oh, he's not offended by this!'

Kristopher was also creative in implementing a cunning memorisation strategy that fit into his communication-focused nature:

I had a funny habit, which used to annoy people. If I found a new word, I would always ask three people the same word. So I would say to Person A, 'What does this word mean, do you think?' and they would tell me. And then I'd go to Person B, and the same thing three times in a row. And they'd get upset and say, 'Well, you just asked A and B, why are you asking me?' And I said, 'Well, I like to hear it from three different people'. It's somehow different when I hear it from three people – somehow it sticks.

Such a strategy also helped him to understand and navigate the subtle nuances of language, which also contributed to his nativelike grasp of vocabulary.

Kristopher's example illustrates how even the more naturalistically inclined language learners of our pool supplemented their studies by means of conscious strategies, and applying creative learning methods was even more pronounced for our more effortful participants. Similar to Amelia, Colin has been strategic in achieving his learning goals by devising techniques for systematically speeding up the natural process of obtaining L2 input:

I would literally listen to what people said in certain circumstances. So, what did somebody say when they were embarrassed? Or what did somebody say when they knocked into someone? And so you had all these social situations, and what I was doing was like a magpie, picking out these phrases and repeating them. I remember thinking at the time, 'I will use that phrase at the next opportunity, however contrived the situation might be!' Or 'I will knock into somebody and say, "Sorry", and see what their reaction is'.

This kind of conscious attention to communicative situations – even instigating incidents for the sake of language learning – reflects a high level of dedication to the cause, and Colin's determination is perhaps best demonstrated by the fact that during his first stay in Germany, even after he had achieved nativelike proficiency in everyday conversations, he was still not fully satisfied with the direction his language had taken and pushed on:

After about Christmas, I reached a plateau. And I realised that I had to do something to go beyond that plateau of being very, very comfortable in my surroundings, daily contact... I had all this ability to blend in on a daily basis, but what I wanted was to be able to sit at a table and discuss, you know, the Suez Crisis, or 9/11, or whatever. But I didn't feel I could do that, so I had to up my game. By reading, particularly newspaper articles, and learning that vocabulary.

The conscious nature of this learning engagement is evidenced by his account of his shorter stay in France many years later:

I had arrived with 10 years of teaching and with a massive amount of knowledge, all kind of bursting, ready for me to do what I did in Germany, which was to wring out every possible chance of getting that fluency, which I was wanting to get. Thinking back on it, [my four-month stay] probably was worth a year, because I was that much more mature, much more aware of my language strategies.

We find similar details of investing creative energy in pursuing strategic learning methods and goals in virtually all of our participants' accounts. Here are some examples:

- After many years of studying German as a young student and a couple of years taking German classes at the Goethe-Institut London as an adult, Denny found herself disappointed with the time she had invested in her learning versus her resulting German proficiency. To jump-start her motivation, she decided to 'set a deadline and just really go for it'. Using her enjoyment of being in Germany as the main driving force, she decided to spend a month in Berlin and work 'intensively' to improve her proficiency, with a view to taking the highest-level proficiency exam the following year. The external goal and limited timeline helped her to conserve motivational energy by building German into her routine, so that it became 'not something that I had to think about, or motivate myself to do every day', a concept we will return to in Chapter 10.
- Although Uwe did not personally consider his nativelike oral proficiency as an 'achievement', he held his writing proficiency in a very different light, as it was an aspect of his L2 that he spent much concentrated effort on developing, something that involved what he characterises as 'the many efforts I put into monitoring myself' and that he recalls focusing on 'really consciously'.
- For an extended period soon after arriving in the UK, Ranko felt lacking in his understanding of English grammar, and he decided to watch grammar explanations on YouTube every single day to speed

up his learning: 'I remember for six months, every night, just watching YouTube about English grammar, about tenses… present simple, present continuous, present perfect'. This habit followed him even past this period, although it manifests in a more relaxed manner to reflect his proficiency progress.
- As a music teacher, Heidrun knew the value of systematic practice: 'And don't forget, I'm a musician; I'm used to practicing and disciplining myself. And I think that was also true for the language, that I actually had this discipline to keep at it and gradually improve'. This manifested, for example, in her vocabulary learning: 'When I didn't understand something, I always had my book and wrote things down and immediately learned them. I was like a detective of finding new words… I went the extra mile that others didn't'.

The systematic learning of L2 lexis by Heidrun was also displayed by other participants in varied forms. For example, Carl recalls that 'since I browse the internet so much, I get to hear and read a lot of different words. And if I'm interested in a word, I'll look it up and see what it means. And then I'll probably start using it'. Sarah echoes this approach: 'With Hungarian, it was a case of listening out for unknown vocabulary, so if I heard an interesting expression, I might write it down, and I would certainly try and use it'. Shinhye's experience was not dissimilar: 'I listened to native speakers' conversations and when I picked up an expression that I'd never used, I'd try to use that expression in a situation where I could, where it was appropriate… actually I forced myself to use it'. Such a conscious effort to activate newly learnt vocabulary was also one of Timur's core learning techniques: 'I would find these language chunks, maybe expressions like, "What skeletons do you have in your closet?" and I would write these things down. And then I would try to use them'.

8.4 Effort That Did Not Feel Like Effort

A final point we would like to emphasise about our participants' conscious engagement with the learning process concerns what the notion of 'effort' meant to them. Yes, it involved exerting conscious and deliberate energy in promoting various aspects of their L2 proficiency, but no, it did not have to be 'painful' effort! Participants were aware of what every athlete or musician knows, namely that learning a skill requires controlled practice, but certain individuals' interest in the target language and in language learning in general 'sweetened' this process for them. The following three accounts are remarkably consistent in this respect, despite being from three learners whose ages, backgrounds and learning histories vary considerably:

I'd say I'm somebody who finds focusing on things really difficult. And I'd say that I am gripped by English as a subject; I've always been interested in kind of reviewing tenses and things like that. I'll study it, and I'm not somebody who naturally studies anything. When I was 16, nobody would have thought I'd end up with a PhD. Nobody. And that's happened on the strength of how much I was interested in the subject. So it's always been really intensive [but] it never felt like a chore, coming back to it. It just felt like it was something I was exploring and I was really interested in. (Livia)

When I was very passionate about something in English, about the content or the topic, or when I was really passionate about a presentation, it hardly ever felt like effort. Because I was so happy that I could share something important for me. (Capucine)

Was it a walk in the park? I did work. I did learn English. I did learn vocabulary lists and things. But maybe because it was a quite holistic experience, it wasn't like, 'I now will learn English by learning all the vocabulary in my vocabulary notebook'. That was not me. To me, it was pleasure work.... So it's not that I didn't do anything about English, that it just sort of by *osmosis* flowed into me. That's not true. But I didn't notice it as effort.... It's this being always on alert, but in a relaxed way – 'tuning into English that is out there' is a state that I'm in. And so it doesn't fall under the category of work. But neither is it a walk in the park. (Uwe)

8.5 Discussion and Some Lessons to Draw

The overall picture emerging from this chapter will have been quite familiar to many language learners. Obviously, our exceptional participants enjoyed some unique benefits of their giftedness, but in many ways they engaged with learning their target L2 in a manner not dissimilar to how many ordinary learners would. The areas where they stood out were their determination to tackle things systematically and their strategic approach, that is, their ability to personalise the learning procedures in a way that maximised their innate learning potential. Moyer's (2021) recent overview of gifted language learners is fully in line with this conclusion. She first highlights the volitional investment that

> undergirds their painstaking efforts to refine and advance language skills over a considerable span of time. Attention to fine detail, consistent rehearsal, self-reflection – and yes, self-critique – are the hallmarks of their approach. Perhaps these elements come down to inborn traits to an extent, but all have struggled linguistically, psychologically, and socially, and none seems to have taken any shortcuts based on uncanny talent or mysterious gift. (Moyer, 2021: 48)

Moyer (2021: 48) then emphasises the strategic aspect of gifted learners' approach: 'Another striking pattern is that these L2 users make the most of the resources at hand'. This practice of tailoring one's learning strategies to suit the individual and thus maximise the learning potential is a characteristic our participants share with the proverbial 'good language learner'. The concept and study of the good language learner was introduced in the late 1970s (see e.g. Rubin, 1975; Stern, 1975), focusing on relatively ordinary successful learners who made good use of learning strategies to capitalise on their language learning endeavours. These studies sought to identify the constellations of learner characteristics and strategies that distinguished successful language learners from their less effective counterparts (see also Griffiths, 2008; Norton & Toohey, 2001). As part of their legacy, there is a solid body of recent work in the SLA literature focusing on learning strategies (e.g. Cohen & Henry, 2019; Griffiths, 2018; Oxford & Amerstorfer, 2018).

Ultimately, there are many different strategies and approaches that can lead to successful learning, provided that one takes a flexible approach. As Griffiths (2015: 432) puts it, 'Strategies are not the whole answer, and the strategies that are chosen and which are effective depend on the context, the learning goal, and the learner's own unique set of individual characteristics'. This is consistent not only with our participants' accounts but also with reports about other nativelike learners. For example, Leaver and Campbell (2014: 7) conclude about superior-level learners that 'there was no clear path to the top. Students made it in their own way, on their own schedule, and meeting their own interests'. Interestingly, they also point out that polyglots often acquire each foreign language in a different way as an adaptation to the specific nature of the language, to the learner's background with a related language or to the opportunities that were available to the learner.

In summary, this chapter has not revealed anything earth-shatteringly new for ordinary language learners, but confirmed that engaging with L2 learning in a disciplined and creative manner is a prerequisite for becoming a successful L2 speaker, as it also characterises the exceptionally gifted. One important takeaway is, though, that strategic and disciplined learning can be an enjoyable process – and perhaps finding ways to enjoy the process is strategic in itself, conserving and rationing long-term motivation for intensive effort (a theme we will return to in Chapter 10). Nonetheless, although the required effort does not have to be painful, the overall lesson for ordinary learners and exceptional learners alike is that there are no real shortcuts. Finally, it is appropriate to conclude this chapter with an excerpt from Moyer's overview, as it captures the key themes discussed above:

> Gifted L2 learners do not awaken one day, surprised at their own accomplishment. Their abiding efforts have brought their goals to fruition.... A multitude of factors influences the outcome, and many changes will mark the process. Those in it for the long haul must be able to shift strategies with changing learning conditions. (Moyer, 2021: 153)

9 Reinforcing Relationships and Social Expectations

A unique aspect of language as a subject matter, one that distinguishes it from most school subjects, is that it is inherently a *social entity*. After all, communication by definition involves multiple parties, and therefore learning a second language (L2) is inevitably influenced by the learner's social relationships and perceptions. This was duly recognised in Gardner's (1985) famous theory of language learning motivation, and his summary is still one of the clearest manifestos of the social dimension of language learning:

> The words, sounds, grammatical principles and the like that the language teacher tries to present are more than aspects of some linguistic code; they are integral parts of another culture. As a result, students' attitudes toward the specific language group are bound to influence how successful they will be in incorporating aspects of that language.... As long as language programmes require students to make the other language part of their behavioural repertoire, it seems reasonable to hypothesize that such attitudes will influence the relative degree of success with which this can be achieved. (Gardner, 1985: 6–7)

This social understanding has fundamentally shaped all subsequent research on identifying the driving forces of language learning, and in our current investigation social influences have also emerged as decisive factors, particularly in two areas. The first area is in the *impact of specific L2 speakers* on our learners' progress, particularly from a motivational perspective (hence the 'reinforcing relationships' phrase in the chapter title). The second area concerns the *overall influence of the L2 community* on the participants' L2 learning through mediated social expectations and participants' desire to blend in with their surrounding communities (hence the 'social expectations' part of our title). In order to offer a concrete illustration of the nature of these seemingly abstract social forces, let us consider Colin's story, in which these elements are particularly salient.

COLIN: THE 'CRITICAL' ROLE OF RELATIONSHIPS

Colin is a retired language teacher whose remarkable qualities are not only demonstrated by having mastered two foreign languages – German and French – at a nativelike level, but also by the fact that he helped launch the exceptional L2 learning journeys of two other participants in our sample, Lisa and Sarah, as their secondary school language teacher (although with Sarah, it was another L2, Hungarian, that she finally excelled in, but the language learning bug was sown in those early years). Colin's own L2 learning history is fairly 'conventional': he started learning French in school at the age of 11 and added German at 13, taking both languages for his A levels and studying them afterwards at university. Here, we focus on his 'stronger' language, German – Colin claims that his French is 'weaker', as a result of which sometimes in France he is taken for a Belgian rather than a local.

Colin's learning motivation was characterised primarily by his strong desire to integrate into the community of L2 speakers. He reflects now:

> There was this kind of feeling that I want to pass off myself, I want to blend in completely, I want to be completely part of that culture, language, country.... When I was in Germany with twenty German people, I think I just became German. I did not see myself as the English person there. It's the fact that you can, almost like a chameleon, blend in completely… so I certainly didn't feel like an outsider whatsoever.

However, the key for Colin was the way in which this sense of social motivation was complemented by the relationships he developed throughout his learning journey, enabling him to exceed the limits of his conventional learning background. Although he enjoyed the process of language learning right from the beginning and made good progress, the first real difference in his development came when he went on his first school exchange to Germany. He spent two weeks in Münster, and it was there at the school's music lessons that he found a true and lifelong friend, Ulrich:

> I think that was absolutely critical for my learning. Because all of a sudden, I had a friend in Germany who was incredibly keen on English and learning English. And we were very, very good at telling each other what our mistakes were.... [Ulrich and his parents] were absolutely obsessed by teaching me as much as I could possibly learn. And I think this was really critical, because I went to them year after year, visiting them as an exchange.

The second big push in his development came years afterwards, during his university studies. Colin studied abroad in Germany in his third year, and towards the latter half of the year, he met a young woman, Jutta, whom he soon began dating:

> This was fantastic for me, because I'd never had a girlfriend before.... With her, I was going through these emotions, which I'd never ever had in English. And I think that was amazing; it was like, I suppose, the closest I would ever come to having a first language experience [in German], because I had to find words, and to express feelings that I'd never had to ever say in English.... That relationship gave me an edge; it really is no question.

It was after this year that he started to pass for a German, and looking back he has no doubt that it was his relationships with Ulrich and Jutta that played a critical role in reinforcing and furthering his language development.

While we have seen in previous chapters that Colin's L2 learning success also relied on other components (e.g. his mimicry ability), the social underpinnings of his learning were indispensable, and it is unlikely that he would have reached the same zenith without the additional push generated by his German relationships. Colin is not alone in this respect, as other participants' accounts also contain direct references to social motives anchored in relationships with specific individuals as well as with the host community in general. Let us survey these social motives starting with the smallest social unit, the nuclear family, and then expanding the circle gradually towards the community at large.

9.1 Family Members

It does not require much justification to state that close family members can exert a great deal of positive (and also negative) influence on someone's standards, norms and attitudes in all areas of living, including language learning. Indeed, we find clear illustrations of this normative force in our data. Starting with the siblings Capucine and Lou, both of them recount that they were keen to learn English partly to impress their parents, and Capucine also recalls the profound impact that her sibling had on her:

> Lou is three years older than me and never actually lived in an English-speaking country, yet their English accent has always been praised by anyone who's had the opportunity to talk to them in English, especially by their English teachers. Growing up, I was quite proud of Lou, but I also remember feeling frustrated because the teachers we had in common

never stopped talking about them and sometimes called me by their name because Lou left such a big impression on them! That really motivated me and triggered an interest in language.... Looking back, I know that Lou's amazing skills in English are what actually led me on to love this language as much as I love it today, and that perhaps the sort of intimacy that I share with English stemmed from my strong relationship with Lou.

Interestingly, Capucine also summarised very clearly one of the key themes of this chapter when she stated that the bulk of her learning 'was at that time when you grow up and you have these people that you admire so much in your life around you. And these people can have a great influence on the decisions you're making'. This is corroborated by Kristin, who also attributes some of her L2 learning success to her older sister:

Whenever she did her English homework, I would just like be in the room and listen. And I think that helped, because we are a bit competitive, and so I'd be like, 'Ooh, what's something you've learned that I haven't learned yet?'... I think just having an older sister that was good at everything made me want to be good at it as well.

We saw in Chapter 4 how family influences could provide learners with a favourable set-up that gave them a head start in their language learning motivation. Indeed, in some sense, Capucine and Kristin's elder siblings contributed to their respective head starts in a similar way to their parents. However, sibling relationships also had the benefit of providing an ongoing and more particular effect – that of role modelling – for these participants, which was in turn reinforced by their close relationships with each other and others' perceptions of these relationships. It thus appears that sibling comparisons and competition act as a potent source of ongoing motivation; we briefly saw similar utility from competitiveness in Chapter 6, and we will return to this concept in Chapter 10.

9.2 The Language Teacher

Again, little needs to be said to justify that teachers can also have a lasting influence on students, and this is mentioned repeatedly in our data set. Recall, for example, that Colin was the German teacher of Lisa, who also reached nativelike proficiency in that language, and Shinhye recounts that her first interest in English was inspired by her second teacher and how she had 'a big, huge crush on him, I mean, as a teenage girl'. His pronunciation was 'a totally different sound to me. So I wished that I would be able to speak like him… and that was my huge motivation in learning and studying English'. In this sense, Shinhye's teacher acted as a linguistic role model for her. Kerry was equally lucky to have 'this amazing instructor and his vocabulary… he had the most elegant vocabulary. And I would just write down all the words that he used… It's like, "Wow, I want to speak like that"'.

The teachers of our data set also contributed to our participants' success by creating positive environments. As we saw in Chapter 7, Capucine's teacher was careful to ensure that the classroom was a safe space for students to focus on their learning rather than their peers' disapproval. Hanna, in turn, describes a former teacher as 'amazing' and 'so cool', as she remembers her classes with her: 'It was one of the best bits in school.... You wouldn't necessarily be always so motivated to learn [on a daily basis], but it's actually just fun to go to her classes. That was quite motivating, looking back'.

Finally, let us cite one more example because it describes a teacher who went beyond merely acting as a powerful role model or creating a positive environment by also setting high expectations tailored specifically for Carl. As he explains, in ninth grade, he found himself well ahead of his peers and the curriculum expectations:

> You aren't expected to be fully fluent. But I talked to the teacher and she set those [high] expectations on me. So I had to work a lot.... I was happy that she did; I got to finally show my ability to speak English.... The teachers definitely helped, especially with the teachers who gave me extra assignments to actually give me a chance where I could grow.

The concept of teachers' roles in their students' language learning extending beyond teaching material is not a new one. Nonetheless, we would like to reiterate from our data set that teachers are able to serve a unique, multifaceted role for their pupils – not only as teachers, but also as motivators, creators of positive environments and especially as role models themselves.

9.3 Friendships

Colin's account presented earlier shows what a difference even a single friend can make, and other participants had similar stories to share. Amelia highlights the positive role of a German penfriend with whom she started corresponding when she was 15, and every summer they would spend a week in each other's homes. Lisa, too, had a similar friend from her exchanges with whom she continues to meet up several times a year, even today:

> We used to sit in the cinema together, and obviously, she would show me what she's learning, which books she's reading in class. And I used to then buy them and also read them. So it was [a] very positive [effect], because then I had somebody who was encouraging me to learn the language.

The effectiveness of the friends above as role models may have been reinforced by the fact that they too were language learners themselves, putting them in the same boat as our participants. However, being a peer language learner was not a prerequisite for having a pivotal effect on our participants. For example, Lesley recounts that during her university studies she met two young Austrian men with whom she became close friends; at the end of the programme, the three made a bet that the next time they saw each other, she would speak German with them instead of English. Although this was not the primary or even secondary reason for Lesley's move to Germany post-graduation, it was the last push to seal the deal and reignite her desire to learn German.

Finally, particularly when a learner resides within the L2 community, the motivational power of friendship can extend beyond one individual to a more general group of people. Recall, for example, that Hanna placed a lot of her learning motivation and efforts on her ability to communicate with her group of international friends, as early as secondary school but even on through university as she expanded her social circles internationally. Ira's explanation summarises perfectly the power of friendship groups:

> For me, coming here [to the UK] and getting a really tight-knit friendship group has really motivated me, because you want to be on the same level with language as they are, because you want to feel like you're part of the group.

Friends can thus contribute to learner motivation in a variety of ways: as role models and learning peers, as well as simply providing the motivation for the end goal of language learning: social interaction.

9.4 Significant Others and Spouses

Given the intense emotional involvement in the L2 that participants could have, it may not be surprising that these emotional waves overlapped on the personal relationship level. When she learnt English, Capucine dated a young man who was half-French and half-English, and as she recalls: 'It's not that I liked English because I liked him. It's more the other way around; I think I liked him because he was a little bit English'. Her relationship with him not only reinforced her love for English, but it also facilitated her language development on a practical level: the two spoke English together, which turned English 'into something that was part of my daily life'. This is a benefit that all of our participants with L2 significant others were able to take advantage of, sometimes to an extreme extent as we saw with Colin and his 'first language experience' with Jutta.

Capucine's story also recalls another incidental benefit of having a relationship with an L2 speaker: that of positive emotionality, in the way that she had similar positive feelings towards both the language and her partner. Heidrun is another example of this: while Heidrun was soaking up the English language and culture in the UK, she also met her now-husband, an Englishman, who followed her home to Austria. She finds that speaking English at home has kept her proficiency 'fresh', but notes that even without him, she 'would have clung to an English person, because I just love using the language, and I love the culture so much'. In this sense, relationships with L2 speakers and with the L2 itself can be mutually reinforcing, contributing to a sense of sustained positive emotionality, which as we will see in Chapter 10 acts as fuel for sustaining long-term motivation.

Other members of our sample also married a speaker of their nativelike L2 (e.g. Theresa, Lesley and Marjan) and were able, like Heidrun, to take advantage of the associated benefits. For participants like Sarah and Joy, their romantic relationships were in fact so powerfully motivating that they were the initial spark for our participants to begin learning the L2 in question at all. As Sarah recalls, 'I wanted us to have Hungarian friends and to be able to speak to Zoltán's family and to be able to invite them round. So that was a motivation'. Kristopher's story is particularly telling in this respect, because his pronunciation and grammar were almost flawless by the time he met his wife, but his marriage paved the way for full nativelikeness:

> So my Japanese was really good. But when I look back at it, there were very small mistakes that I would make when we got married. And I told my wife, 'Look, if I make any mistakes, you've got to tell me... any small thing, tell me', and so she would. And that was really helpful, because that allowed me to correct all those teeny tiny things... [and] the cultural things that would be very hard to grasp otherwise.

While of course it should be clarified that none of our participants was so calculating as to date or marry their partners for the sake of their language learning, it is clear from our data set that these relationships nevertheless contributed significantly to these participants' language learning motivation and linguistic development.

9.5 Other Role Models

We have seen above that family members, teachers and friends can all perform potent role modelling functions, but the scope of this robust form of social motivation is even wider. Our data shows that participants could also be deeply impacted by certain attributes of the people around them who did not fall under the above categories, and it is interesting to consider the kinds of people and the particular aspects of their respective L2 speech they chose to imitate. Sarah, for example, found non-native-speaking role models inspiring in her mastering Hungarian:

> My role models are actually often non-Hungarians who have learned really good Hungarian, because I think they're more realistic role models in a way. They're non-native speakers like me, and I think, 'If they can do it, I can do it. I want what they have'.

This is in line with the importance attached to *near peer role models* in the literature (see Muir *et al.*, 2019), and as Sarah recalls a specific example, the power of such modelling comes through clearly:

> One of [my classmates in Hungary] was really good.... That was again a bit of a 'Petula Clark moment' (see Sarah's story in Chapter 6), where I wanted what she had. I knew I probably couldn't be like the teacher, but I wanted to be like the Bulgarian classmate who was so good at Hungarian that she could get by in any situation and translate anything.

Kerry instead was impressed with the grammatical sophistication of her roommate and the lexical sophistication of her friend (who in turn picked that up from another roommate):

> My roommate's grammar was really, really good. And I started really listening to the way she used grammar and saying, 'I gotta sound like that, because she sounds much more intelligent'.... My friend Rebecca had a roommate when she lived in Italy who used that kind of language [like my instructor's] – very elegant – and Rebecca picked it up. And I would learn from her; I always admired her Italian so much. She used beautiful words. I remember for 'roommate', she used the word *coinquilina*. And it's like, 'Ahh!! That word! It just sounds so much better'... I would like to be more like Rebecca; I'd love to have and use some more of those words that she used.

As we have seen in Chapter 7, certain learners in our study had accent-related role models; here we see that their choice of role models could also be based on other kinds of specific linguistic characteristics that they admired or wanted to improve.

9.6 The Workplace

In previous chapters, we have discussed the work-related motivation of four of our participants, Lesley, Lisa, Marjan and Rianne, but here we will dive more specifically into two of the avenues by which the workplace can affect learners' motivation. First, we will reiterate perhaps the most obvious avenue: the way in which L2-related expectations stemming from the workplace can cause an intense surge in one's commitment to improve their L2 proficiency. Lisa, for example, reached her outstanding level of German competence after she got a job where she was expected to improve her technical L2 proficiency to pass her initial probation. Rianne similarly started to seriously focus on her German when she was told in Austria, where she was doing a PhD in physics, that she would need to start teaching classes in that L2 from the subsequent year onwards. Sometimes, these workplace expectations are less direct and emerge more implicitly; for example, Lesley 'always' had 'a worry that I would lose my job because my German skills weren't 100%. I worked really hard and tried to get my language skills up to a level that meant that my job wasn't in danger'. These expectations can also be internally accompanied by a sense of competition or keeping up, as in the case of Lisa: 'I think it's partly a matter of pride. I want to be able to do everything in German as much as my colleagues are'. Similarly, Rianne derived motivation through observing her colleagues: 'They all come from different countries, and all of them are just doing [it]. You want to get there as well, and you don't want to lag behind'.

Luckily, the case of workplace-driven motivation in our data set is not all doom and gloom, with work environments meting out strict linguistic criteria with little reserve. Alongside broader workplace expectations, specific individuals within the workplace also contributed to our participants' motivation and learning, facilitating their improvement in more tangible, supportive ways. For example, Rianne recalls that one of the ways that helped her pick up German so quickly was that her supervisor 'tried to speak as much German as he could to me'. Similarly, Lisa sought support from her colleagues via corrective feedback in her written reports, which she found doubled both as practical help as well as a kind of progress check – one of the keys for sustained long-term motivation, as we will see in Chapter 10. Lesley received similar corrective feedback from her colleagues, which she found helped her to correct her mistakes and build her confidence in the workplace.

Perhaps the best representation of the positive effects that both the workplace environment and individuals in the workplace can have when merged together is Marjan's story. As we saw earlier, her desire to be a successful working professional in England drove her to push her learning past its previous limits. This was, in part, because of her desire to 'be part of the community', but she adds:

> [The things I did to improve my English] were required by the job, really.... As a professional, you feel you want to justify to your patient – and to yourself as well – that you're doing a good job, and you keep up to date with the new developments and the new treatments. And you want to learn as much as possible.

What helped facilitate this desire (and requirement) was that early on in her career, Marjan recalls an 'absolutely fantastic' supervisor who adjusted her rotation schedule to give her time to 'really build up my expertise and my language skills', and she encountered a variety of people over the years who extended similar support. These colleagues gave Marjan the time, space and encouragement she needed to take on new challenges – paving the way for her to achieve nativelike proficiency.

9.7 The L2 Community

As we began to see with work-related motivation, the social motivation to improve one's L2 proficiency can derive not only from relationships with individual L2 speakers but also from relating to the L2 community at large. Recall Colin's story from the beginning of this chapter, in which he describes himself as wanting to be a linguistic 'chameleon'. Others in our data set echo this sentiment, for example Kristin when she explains, 'I wanted to blend in, and that's why I wanted to have better pronunciation and intonation', and Joy makes the belonging aspect of such a 'blending in' explicit:

> I wanted to be part of the community; Iceland was my home. Icelanders were my people – they were my husband's people, so they were my people.... The goal was to be like an Icelander, belonging and being part of a bigger way of life and using this language as part of the way of life. So, that's what would trigger that desire to stop and to drill down.

She also describes a powerful mediating process whereby this social motivation, the desire to avoid being seen as a foreigner, exerts its impact: 'The thing that frustrated me most was if I felt that I didn't have the grammatical repertoire at my disposal when I needed it. I suppose in retrospect it was because it made me look like a bumbling foreigner'. Kristin similarly expresses the desire to avoid sounding 'really "international"', and Judith concurs regarding her Norwegian proficiency:

> You learn one Scandinavian language, but you spend a lot of time in all of the Scandinavian countries and you start speaking what they call *skandinaviska*, which is a kind of mishmash of all the Scandinavian languages. And I know a lot of non-Scandinavians who do that, and I've worked quite hard to resist that, because then that marks you out as a foreigner.

Others did not use the term 'foreigner' as the target to avoid, but instead referred to something very similar when they expressed that they wanted to avoid 'standing out' (Sara). Lesley addresses this point head-on: 'I was so determined to learn the language properly, so that I could just fit in! Because if you've got an accent and struggle to speak or express yourself properly, you stand out, and I didn't really want to stand out'. Later when she reiterates this point, she links it to being 'foreign':

I think nativelikeness means that you don't stand out from the crowd anymore; you start to fit in. People don't make exceptions for you anymore. You are able to take part in normal life without it being extremely obvious that you're not German. It makes life much easier for you... and makes you feel more at ease. You feel more at home in the country, too, because you're not obviously foreign.

In this sense, and as we saw in Chapter 6, integrativeness for certain participants acts not solely as an appreciation for the target language and its corresponding culture(s), but also as a more direct desire to align with – and to integrate into – a specific L2 community.

9.8 Discussion and Some Lessons to Draw

We began this chapter by highlighting the fact that language learning is inherently a social enterprise and therefore social factors rooted in relationships and the learners' perceived social identities are expected to play a decisive role in shaping the learning process. We will revisit the notion of language identity in more detail in the final chapter of this book, so here we would like to merely summarise the more social-specific details that have emerged from our investigation with respect to the former.

Consistent with the traditional principles of L2 motivation research (e.g. Dörnyei & Ushioda, 2021; Gardner, 1985), we have found ample evidence in our data that social links and attitudes made a tangible difference in our participants' pursuit of their language learning goals. Specific manifestations of such driving forces in their accounts were linked to family members, friendships and influential language teachers, as well as significant others and spouses – most often enduring relationships that were able to influence participants over a long period of time. When these individuals were speakers of the L2, they often represented for our learners the specific community with whom they desired to communicate – the closer the individual to the learner, the more pressing the need and the more rewarding the outcome. Others were L2 learners themselves, such as participants' friends, peers and teachers, and they acted as role models against whom our participants would compare themselves, also driving motivation. Additionally, in some cases our participants had relationships with native speakers of the L2 who were also language learners themselves, thereby doubling as communicative motivation and role models, and role models were also mentioned from other contexts, further confirming Muir *et al.*'s (2019) findings. The takeaway for the ordinary learner here is to work towards creating bonds with L2 speakers and fellow learners, and to recognise and nurture these relationships where they already exist. While forging relationships with L2 speakers can be difficult in a foreign language learning context, fortunately modern technology now provides ample opportunities for connecting people internationally, as we saw in Chapter 4.

As expected, the workplace also constitutes a powerful normative force, not only on a broader level in terms of the linguistic expectations of different work environments but also on the individual level in terms of both interpersonal encouragement and tangible learning support. While the vast majority of studies in L2 motivation have tended to focus on learners in secondary and tertiary education (Boo *et al.*, 2015), our data set suggests that highly advanced levels of L2 attainment extend beyond formal education, both linguistically and temporally. Indeed, certain learners in our participant pool did not achieve nativelike proficiency until years after they finished their formal education – necessarily entailing at least some influence of their workplace on their L2 development. Further investigation into L2 speaker motivation in the workplace might look towards the relationship between workplace expectations and when these are too high – as in the case of native-speakerism – and when these intertwine constructively to support L2 learners/speakers rather than exclude them, as they have with our participants.

Finally, the broadest social impact of our participants' accounts originated in their desire to align as closely as possible to the social standards, practices and expectations of the L2 community, that is, to 'blend in' and avoid 'standing out'. We opened this chapter with Gardner's theory of language learning motivation and the concept of *integrativeness*, which entails positive attitudes towards the L2 community and its constituents. However, the manifestations of integrativeness we discovered in our data set could also extend beyond positive attitudes to a more expansive desire to, in some senses of the word, assimilate. This alternative sense of integrativeness has appeared in the literature before: Graham (1984: 76) proposed the concept of *assimilative* motivation, which he describes as a peer-group phenomenon that learners may or may not be aware of, in which the learner 'desires to become an indistinguishable member of the target speech community'. Our participants' accounts diverged from the concept of assimilative motivation in two important ways. First, Graham claimed that the desire to assimilate generally dissipates by the end of adolescence, which might in turn explain the low instances of nativelikeness in adult learners. However, various learners in our study who expressed the desire to blend in were well past adolescence, pointing to the need for further quantitative investigation to determine the usefulness of this construct across different age groups. Secondly, while assimilation in Graham's interpretation and in the general sense of the term entails learners' rejection of their heritage language and/or culture, our participants did not tend to recount such feelings. Simply put, our participants were able to assimilate *without* forsaking their first languages and identities, which we will discuss in more detail in Chapter 12.

10 Sources of Persistence

Our investigation has made it clear that even for exceptional learners, the process to reach a nativelike level of proficiency took an extended period of time. This also applied to those participants who appeared to pick up their selected second language (L2) relatively effortlessly and largely naturalistically – their journeys, too, were long and involved various twists and turns and sometimes ups and downs. This confirms the age-old observation that a prerequisite to success in L2 learning is the ability to *persist*, and our research shows that not even gifted learners are exempt from this. But what exactly does the required 'persistence' involve? What were the sources of our participants' tenacity, and how did they sustain their commitment over the course of several years? In other words, how can we characterise the long-term motivational endurance of our participant sample? This chapter aims to address these questions. In order to offer an initial taste of the issues involved, let us take a closer look at Marjan's learning history. Her journey towards reaching nativelike proficiency in English was a gradual process involving various stages, with her persistence bearing fruit incrementally as we will see below:

MARJAN: 'IT WAS TURNING UP EACH DAY…'

Although young Marjan had a good start at language learning, she chose to pursue a profession in physiotherapy. While studying to this effect, she went on holiday and met her now-husband, Art, a Spanish and English teacher from England. Their mutual love for international culture soon turned into a budding relationship conducted primarily in English, resulting in Marjan's proficiency 'really picking up'. After graduating, Marjan relocated to England and found employment in a hospital. At the time, her English proficiency was excellent for a 'day-to-day basis', but far from it in a professional capacity, which brings us to the period in her life that is instructional for our current discussion: when Marjan was able to build on her solid L2 foundations and ultimately reach nativelikeness. Her progress was fuelled by several ingredients:

(a) *A vision of becoming an English-speaking professional.* Marjan didn't learn the L2 for its own sake but rather to achieve her vision of becoming a high-functioning English-speaking professional. As she states, 'I don't think I would have been necessarily unhappy if I wasn't very fluent at the end of even now, if I felt I achieved what I wanted to achieve'.

(b) *Stepwise progression.* She set herself realistic goals and expectations, accepting increasing professional responsibilities and ending up as a university lecturer.

> I took on more things, I just pushed myself to do more. I set myself new tasks, more challenging scenarios and challenging situations.... [This] forced me to be better at [English], because the situations I've forced myself to be in pushed me in many ways to develop and scale up my English in lots of different areas.

She came to terms with the gradual nature of L2 learning, focusing on one step at a time:

> It was turning up each day, and I knew that after each day, it consecutively became easier to speak the language. So though it was hard, I knew at the end of the month, or the end of two months, three months, six months, I knew that my language improved, and I got better and more confident.

(c) *Satisfaction from peer comparisons.* 'I also felt I wasn't that bad compared to other people. You know, you sort of compare and think "Well actually, I sounded alright"'.

(d) *Enjoyment of L2 use.* 'I was keen on speaking a foreign language – I really quite enjoyed it, which I think makes a difference'.

(e) *Accumulated self-confidence.* Marjan recalls that although her parents were not particularly proficient in foreign languages, they were confident and were always happy 'to have a go'. They inspired in Marjan a good deal of initial communicative confidence, which she then augmented with a confidence in herself as an English-speaking professional and as someone embedded in an English-speaking social environment:

> I was quite reasonably confident language-wise. I would have a go and if it wasn't quite right, it didn't really worry me too much.... I think what helped me was the confidence within

> myself in what I did, what I was. I felt more and more confident about my job, my personal situation and the friendships I developed. I became confident in *me* really, with who I was, where I was, what I was doing.... I think it's my self-confidence that allowed me to acquire the language, rather than necessarily anything else.

Significantly, her confidence was nurtured not only by professional accomplishments but also positive feedback from her community: 'People around me were complimentary about my English all the time. I felt grounded really... so my confidence grew, I think, because of all of that feedback'. We will return to this last topic in Chapter 11.

We have selected Marjan's story as an illustration as it contains a broad variety of relevant themes, but other participants' accounts were similar to Marjan's in that their L2 learning also involved a prolonged process that required long-term effort to maintain their progress, as we will see below. Because of the prominence of this aspect for second language acquisition (SLA) in general, the study of long-term motivation has become an established topic in the field, and research findings confirm Marjan's experience, namely that persistence is a multicomponent construct. That is, L2 learners can sustain their goal-directed behaviour in several ways, drawing on a variety of resources and being empowered by a variety of factors, ranging from an innate faculty of grit to the application of conscious self-regulatory strategies. The most elaborate conception of the long-term motivation construct to date has been Zoltán's extended framework (Dörnyei, 2020; Dörnyei & Henry, in press), which describes sustained and enduring motivation in terms of a strong initial goal/vision; an effective action plan that includes energy-saving, energy-regenerating and energy-amplifying features; and the requisite amount of self-regulation needed for encountering setbacks and difficulties. To elucidate the construct, Zoltán likened a learner's sustained motivated behaviour to embarking on a long car journey, and specified the following five factors as major contributors to achieving an extended driving range:

(a) a full tank of high-octane fuel: having a strong, self-concordant vision;
(b) fuel economy: having a range of habitually employed actions;
(c) a hybrid engine that performs fuel regeneration: experiencing satisfaction generated through progress checks and affirmative feedback;
(d) regular opportunities to refuel: passion and a positive emotional tenor; and
(e) effective breakdown cover: having the capacity and skills for self-control.

Let us take a closer look at these components and consider how they are represented in our participants' accounts.

10.1 High-Octane Fuel: A Self-Concordant Vision

Human action is goal directed; therefore, achieving a goal has traditionally been seen in psychology as a principal driving force of action. Sustained, ongoing behaviour obviously requires long-lasting fuel, that is, a fortified goal, and psychological research has identified two potent amplifying factors in this respect: *vision* and *self-concordance*. Regarding the first, adding an imagery dimension to a goal (i.e. imagining the outcome vividly and seeing oneself achieving the goal 'in the mind's eye') can considerably increase the pulling power of the desired target. This impact is further augmented if the envisaged goal is self-concordant, that is, it corresponds to the learner's personality and identity; a self-concordant goal can therefore be described as representing a person's enduring interests and passions, as well as their central values, beliefs and convictions (see also Dörnyei & Kubanyiova, 2014). The fusion of vision and self-concordance – that is, having a *self-concordant vision* – offers a particularly compelling motivational force suitable for energising long-term action, and Peng's reflection is consistent with this:

> When I was in high school, I studied English because I had a whole new vision ahead of me... there was a possibility of finding an English-speaking lifestyle or to be able to move to America. I think ideals are beautiful, visions are beautiful... they will reign over your energies or your desires, so they propel you to move forward.

As we saw earlier, Marjan's vision was to become an English-speaking healthcare professional, and Heidrun talks about her 'dream' when she refers to her self-concordant L2 vision: 'Nativelikeness was definitely something I wanted to achieve. Because I'm ambitious, and that was my dream'. Interestingly, Rianne, who managed to acquire two languages at a nativelike level, created a mental 'divide' between her perception of her L2 English and German: English 'was something I needed for my job later on, and to stay internationally oriented', while German was 'the way to experience [Austria], to be also part of the community there. German was the thing that I needed for more social life, and also the teaching part, where you could make the connection with students'. All of these forms of self-concordant visions acted as enduring goals that provided our participants with the long-term driving force to pursue and persist in their language learning over the course of many years.

10.1.1 'Use it or lose it' and the question of fossilisation

A well-known aspect of L2 proficiency is *attrition*, that is, the fact that one's linguistic competence deteriorates over time in the absence of regular use (hence the saying, 'use it or lose it'). This has obvious implications for long-term motivation because situations in which one needs to engage with the L2 – most commonly when living in an L2-speaking country or having an L2-speaking partner – will automatically act as a motivation-sustaining factor. Lisa expresses this very clearly: 'It's also just from living here. Really, I think the motivation comes from [this], obviously wanting to talk to my neighbours, watching the news, watching comedy programs in German, as unfunny as they can be'.

However, the picture may not be as simple as that, because many expats living in a foreign country do not acquire a very high level of L2 proficiency or soon become fossilised. Recall, for example, what Joy stated in this respect: 'There were plenty of examples of people around me who had fossilised. But that was never an option for me. I didn't want that for myself'. When asked why, she answered, 'Because I didn't see myself as needing to fossilise. Why would you? Why would I stop if I could communicate in a way that was effortless, and that would not cause misunderstandings?' This is an excellent example of the fact that even when learners are embedded in an L2 environment, they need to 'see themselves' being able to make progress, that is, they need to have a progressive vision. Unlike her peers, Joy continually envisioned her linguistic abilities improving, thus fuelling her motivation to continue putting in effort. Colin's account illustrates this point well, because as he recounts about his stay in Germany, he only reached his more broadly nativelike level of proficiency once he consciously 'upped his game':

> When I was in Germany, I made massive progress. But then after about Christmas, I reached a plateau. And I realised that I had to do something to go beyond that plateau of being very, very comfortable in my surroundings, daily contact… I had all of this ability to blend in on a daily basis, but what I wanted was to be able to sit at a table and discuss the Suez Crisis, or 9/11, or whatever. But I didn't feel I could do that. So I had to up my game…

This sense of progressively adjusting one's goals allows learners like Colin to continually re-evaluate the effectiveness of their learning strategies and effort output, which appears to be particularly key for avoiding fossilisation. The use of 'moving goalposts' in maintaining a self-concordant vision is therefore reflective of the dynamic nature of long-term motivation: if a self-concordant goal is said to represent an individual in some way, it must also shift to represent changes to that individual over time.

10.2 Fuel Economy: Habitual Actions

One way of making the initial fuel last longer is to economise on the motivational energy that one exerts to power one's learning, particularly on a day-to-day basis. An established way of conserving such volitional energy is the employment of *habitual actions*. A habit is a behaviour pattern that has become (semi-)automatic in the sense that it is performed almost involuntarily, and its motivational significance lies in the fact that it is not initiated by volitional decisions (e.g. in the morning most people do not conduct cost–benefit calculations before brushing their teeth, but simply do it as part of their daily routine). Therefore, if we set up constructive, goal-specific habits, in effect we go on 'motivational autopilot' and the execution of these habitual actions does not incur any significant volitional costs.

Denny especially was explicit about such routines: 'Studying German had to be something that was built into my routine, not something that I had to think about or motivate myself to do every day'. One such example was listening to German audio during her daily commute: 'I always had 40 minutes every day of input, just by virtue of getting on my bike and cycling to work. And that would have been dead time'. In the previous chapters, we have described more than once how principled certain participants were about performing learning behaviours regularly (e.g. Ranko watching instructional videos about English grammar every evening for some six months), and the recurring nature of many of these tasks acted as a sustaining factor.

Another example is the daily habit Kerry picked up while studying in Italy:

> In Italy, you don't just shop once a week; you go out every morning to the bakery, and then you go buy *formaggio* [cheese], and then you go from store to store, and in every store you have a conversation. And so I would get into these long conversations about 'What's in this bread?' and you know, 'blah, blah, blah'... and I did a lot of learning that way.

Kerry's daily conversations about produce introduced regular speaking and listening practice into her routine, helping her to join her local community while also saving her the motivational energy it might otherwise take to find language partners. This may not be possible in contexts where the L2 is not spoken, but almost any L2-related habit can take the motivational pressure off regular 'studying'. For example, Capucine, Peng and Shinhye all incorporated their L2s into their writing routines, in either diaries or their creative writing. Timur found he struggled with memorising vocabulary and thus began using spaced repetition software on a regular basis. Finally, Carl's example presents perhaps the most 'fun' – and effective – way to economise on motivation, capitalising on the habitual nature of an activity he enjoys: 'One thing that I strongly recommend is constantly speaking the language. That's how I learned it, at least. Every day I play video games with English friends, and that really just helped "cheat" my language [improvement]'.

10.3 Fuel Regeneration: Progress Checks and Positive Feedback

Earlier we discussed the power of overarching, long-term goals/visions, but there is more to goals with regard to long-term motivation: it is a well-established fact in motivational psychology that setting *short-term, incremental goals* tends to provide extra energy, because it gives learners specific, reachable targets for which to aim. Significantly, such short-term targets also function as *progress checks* by making visible one's advances towards the desired target. The satisfaction gained from such a tangible sense of progress (e.g. when a weightlifter exceeds their personal best) has a potent energy-yielding capacity that can regenerate some of the used-up motivational fuel, based on the principle that success breeds success. Let us first consider the setting of goals in our sample.

10.3.1 Goal-setting

Ira was fully aware of the useful role that carefully devised subgoals can play in motivating the language learning process:

> One of the main things is setting goals that aren't too far away from you. So if you've never really encountered that language before, it can be really demotivating to be like, 'Oh, I want to be able to speak to everyone for five hours in a row', because you feel you're not going to achieve it. I think I have reached nativelike speech because I've reached all these small goals, which has kind of *led* me to this place where I'm at right now.

However, Amelia rightly points out that within the very long-term enterprise of language learning, establishing such subgoals is not entirely straightforward:

> I don't know what those goals are for language learning or how you measure you've achieved your goals. Because I think goals in language learning are so much more difficult to articulate.... And if you say you want to excel at language, what does that even mean? How do you know when you've reached that level?

One obvious answer to this dilemma in goal-setting is to take exams (where possible), which has been, for example, Denny's strategy:

> The thing that helped me the most is having those exams that cost money.... I basically booked myself onto a course that would eventually lead to the final proficiency exams of the Goethe-Institut. So I was like, 'Right, I just need to give myself a deadline. I've invested all this time and money'.

Sara talks about similar external subgoals in terms of 'new challenges', emphasising their strategic function in her persistence:

I think a big part of my long-term motivation has to do with that there were always some new challenges that came along the way. Like in primary school, at the beginning, it was songs and stories, and then slowly we started taking tests. Then we got to high school, and we knew, 'Huh, now the level's going to be higher than in primary school. Okay, great'. Then it was the final exam at the end of high school. And then I was like, 'Oh now I'm going to *study* English [at university]', and then, 'Oh, now, I'm going to be an English teacher' – so again, it adds another layer to it. And then I decided to get my MA from an international university, that was another [challenge]. So all along, externally there have been things that have challenged me and pushed me and provided some of the motivation.

For those skilled in goal-setting – and who are mindful of their own limits and expectations – short-term goals are an obvious and easy step to promoting the mileage of a long-term goal. For others, while externally defined subgoals such as exams or formal educational targets do have their drawbacks and may not work for every learner, such incremental goals can be a useful tool to split the overarching dream into motivational bite-sized chunks.

10.3.2 Positive feedback and perceivable progress

Positive feedback – especially if it focuses on progress rather than the general 'Good job!' kind of praise – functions similarly to achieving a subgoal in that it provides a tangible record of having improved. This being the case, it also constitutes a type of progress check, and the motivational power of such progress checks has been underlined by our participants. For example, Kristin explains, 'I think it's important to feel you're mastering it and that people tell you, "Yeah, you're good at it!"… [to] have that motivation as well'. Livia reflected on the sense of progress gained from meeting personal linguistic targets: 'It felt like [the more] you were achieving all these little targets along the way, the more you could get an insight into different facets of the culture', and Lisa specifically mentioned the progress element:

> I did keep track of my progress, because I had to permanently see how many mistakes I was making in my reports and so on for work. So every time I wrote anything, I'd see how many comments came back. And it's got to the point now where I have maybe one or two small errors, which is the same as if I were writing anything in [my L1] English.

Along these lines, Hanna's comment is particularly revealing regarding the satisfaction one can gain through feelings of progress: 'The feeling of success you get in language [study] just feels amazing.... Like, if you decide, "I want to run a 10k", once you get to 10k, that's going to feel amazing, because you've achieved it'. While as Amelia brought up, language learning does not necessarily have the easily measurable benchmarks of foot races, it appears that both positive feedback and self-perceived progress can act just as well in place of a stopwatch or finish line.

Finally, returning to Marjan's story, we see the power and sense of regular, more general progress checks in language learning: progress checks were implicitly built into her job, both through a personal learning development log and through periodic case conferences in which she had to explain her medical decisions to her team and 'be quite confident in your language to really explain to others what you were doing'. Over time, describing her medical practice to others both in written and spoken formats became easier, and Marjan was able to see this progress looking back over her old logs and from her peers' feedback, helping her to feel confident in taking on new challenges. Marjan's story thus brings to the fore the way that successful progress checks can also build up one's confidence, with past successes encouraging future ones. This is a critical factor in language learning, because, quite frankly, we are not overly exaggerating by saying that linguistic success is largely a confidence issue. We discuss this question in Chapter 11.

10.3.3 Competitiveness

While, as Amelia so aptly points out, setting short-term subgoals in language learning can be difficult due to the flexible nature of language, one way our participants used to circumvent such problems is through defining their own progress against that of other language users – that is, through comparison. Traditionally, competition has been regarded in educational psychology as less effective than cooperation in terms of general achievement outcomes (e.g. Johnson *et al.*, 1981), but recent studies have found that, if managed well, competitiveness may correlate with academic achievement on an individual level (see e.g. Baumann & Harvey, 2018, 2021; Hwang & Arbaugh, 2009). This is in line with the fact that, as we saw in Chapter 6, our participants highlighted the topic's importance in sustaining their motivation. Being competitive means that a person sets a goal of being better than some peers, and in this sense it also belongs to the broader rubric of 'progress check' as it offers a satisfying comparison through which one's qualities become visible. Even if the comparison is unfavourable, competition can still be motivating, driving the wish to avoid the frustration of not living up to one's own expectations. Colin could not have been any clearer about the beneficial impact of such comparisons – along with the benefits of positive feedback – when he talks about his 'weaker' nativelike language, French, which 'wasn't anywhere near as good as my German':

> When I would come across other colleagues who only taught French, I thought, 'Well, my French is better than theirs'. And I could compare it. And we had French exchanges, and we went to France. And people said, 'Oh, how fantastic your French is'.

Rianne is equally explicit about the motivational power of gauging oneself against others:

> Sometimes you're just like, 'Okay, I'm never going to master it', or 'I'll never be at the point of being completely satisfied with it'. But then you realise how far you've come towards others. There were constantly new researchers coming into the Institute, so I was constantly confronted with people who were at the stage where I was two years ago. And that puts you in the contrast of 'Oh wait, so I really did learn something!' Compared to that level, that is quite motivating.

Similar references occur across our data set; we have already seen an example in Marjan's story, and William specifically admits to having a competitive streak: 'My goals have usually been just to be like, better than everyone else. Whenever other people have been better than me at it, I've been kind of trying to succeed more at it'. Heidrun concurs, 'And then of course, when you get good, and when you have good results, that's very motivating. And I think I was the best in my class, so I liked that'. On the other hand, Peng offers an example of the motivating force of an unfavourable comparison: 'When I arrived in Shanghai, I realised they started learning English from kindergarten. So their English was so much better than mine. So I was motivated out of nowhere'. We should note here, however, that social comparison is a potentially dangerous tool, as it involves both winners and losers, and not every loser is as invigorated by negative comparison as young Peng.

10.4 Additional Fuel: Positive Emotionality and Passion

Although research into the role of affect in language learning concerning emotions other than anxiety has largely been overlooked in the past (for an overview, see Oxford, 2022), in the last decade the topic has begun to flourish as researchers, teachers and learners alike begin to see the value in positive emotions (MacIntyre *et al.*, 2016; Martínez Agudo, 2018; Simons & Smits, 2021). Emotions have the capability to sustain and amplify existing motivation, and therefore a steady *positive emotionality* is potentially an ideal foundation for supplying additional fuel during sustained learning (see also Mercer & MacIntyre, 2014). In fact, certain participants made a point of emphasising the importance of having ongoing positive emotional experiences during their goal pursuit. We have already seen above one source of positive affect – reaching one's goals – and Joy further emphasises the positive sentiment coming from successfully approaching the desired target: 'For me, it has a lot to do with how language has connected to things that are just enjoyable... I guess it's running towards something that is a pleasurable goal I wanted'. Lesley offers a perfect summary of the motivational power of the enjoyment of successfully using a language:

> I've always enjoyed languages... when you actually have a conversation with somebody and you can understand everything! It's amazing! It just gives you a buzz. You realise that all that hard work is starting to pay off. That was always motivating, it gives you a boost to keep learning.... You can actually feel that you've improved, which is good. It makes you want to keep trying and working on it.

A telling piece of indirect evidence for the significance of positive emotionality is offered by accounts when our participants who succeeded in their primary language failed in another one due to negative feelings attached to the latter. Hanna still vehemently declares, 'I hated Swedish. It took so much time away from other [languages],... I was really bitter that I had to do Swedish instead of like, French or Spanish'. Kerry says about her French, 'I never really got inspired because I never had [a good experience]; I had a lot of really bad French teachers', and fellow Canadian Joy shares the feeling about her French learning: 'Let's just say that it didn't go well as compared to my other language experiences.... it was so boring, to sit there and learn these little dialogues or learn this grammar rule'. Interestingly, we also have accounts when learning a language got off to a good start, but then it lost its appeal: when Dutch Ira was 17, she was given the option to take the higher-level French class due to her previous high performance, but she was not met with the same measure of success in the class as with her English. Although previously she had been 'really good' at French, she lost her positive emotionality and found that this course 'just crashed and burned'. She found the course too demanding and the grading very harsh, eventually dropping the language.

Finally, a particularly good illustration of the issue comes from Lou, because it actually concerns the language (English) that they managed to master at a nativelike level:

> I tried to do the exam that gives you officially a very good level of English, so I did some classes, but I didn't go through with it because it was really specific English, talking about like charts, and I didn't really understand because it was so super academic.... That's when I realised I was not interested in English in terms of learning academically. What I like about English is the fact that it's a language where you can communicate with so many people in the world. So that's what I wanted to keep, and that was the only thing that interested me.

Despite the poor experience they describe, Lou managed to preserve their positive emotionality with English and continue on to nativelikeness by identifying what it was they valued in the language and doing what Uwe now recommends: 'follow the light, and just be drawn in, and it'll work out by itself'.

10.5 Breakdown Cover: Self-Control Skills and Capacity

The end of Section 10.4 already touched upon demotivating experiences that took the pleasure out of L2 learning. Such experiences can be caused by a variety of factors related to the teacher, the course or the L2 learning environment, but learners may also encounter low moments when suffering setbacks – or when they simply get tired of learning. Realistically, in any long-term action there will inevitably be stumbling blocks, and learners will encounter obstacles one way or another. Therefore, the final ingredient of long-term motivation is the capacity to resist discouragement when problems occur, rather than giving up. Research has found that learners differ considerably in this respect: some appear to be able to bounce back relatively easily from failures, whereas others are more inclined to give up when facing discouraging or disrupting impulses. The precious potential for persistence has been examined under many different names in the literature (e.g. grit, resilience, self-control, coping capacity, stamina, hardiness, buoyancy, mental toughness and self-regulation), but the diversely labelled constructs tend to show considerable overlap.

What is important for us to note here is that while our exceptional participants seemed to possess a high degree of this resilience when learning their chosen language, they, too, were subject to the detrimental effects of demotivating factors with other languages they learnt. For example, William told us that 'just not giving up if you fail at something is the most important part; not feeling sorry for yourself for things that you shouldn't feel sorry for', and yet we also saw in Chapter 6 that at the time of being interviewed, William was seriously considering dropping French as a school subject, because he found it too hard. It seems, therefore, that the inner recourses that our participants employed to combat negative influences were often specifically activated for their preferred language(s) only. Let us look at how some of our participants reflected on the topic of resilience.

Amelia suggests that 'you've got to be able to cope with mistakes, have the courage to put yourself out there and be willing to be judged'. Sarah agrees that language learners need to be 'thick-skinned', and as she reflects on this matter she admits, 'I was quite sensitive to bad experiences with the language and being disapproved of.... But I was in a Hungarian environment, and so I couldn't let a few setbacks put me off, even if sometimes I really just wanted to hide at home'. That is, for her it was the daily necessity that activated her grit, and she overcame bad experiences by cognitively processing them with a growth mindset:

> You have highs and lows, and sometimes you reach a plateau. But you do push beyond it. I think you just have to not be too hard on yourself, and know that some days it just doesn't go as well as others. I think you just have to put it down to a bad day.

Like William, Sarah made use of a growth mindset that allowed her to see her linguistic shortcomings as temporary – and surmountable – setbacks (see also Dweck, 2008; Lou & Noels, 2019). Sarah adds that she also used a technique from her singing practice: 'If I have a bad day with my singing voice, doing some exercises does loosen it. So, going back and looking up that vital word that you couldn't remember is a really good idea'. This is not unlike the folk wisdom that if you fall off a horse, you have to get straight back on! Slovenian Sara also relied on exercising a form of thought control, offering the following example:

> Just a couple of weeks ago, I received some feedback on some of my reports and it wasn't good. I had a really hard time with that.... [An experience like this] usually takes me back: I'm a little bit sad about it, and it maybe bums me out a little bit. But at the end of the day, I get over it because it's not something *big*, and I remember, 'Oh, no, actually I still really like English. And I enjoy this. And I've chosen this for a reason'. That's kind of how it usually goes.

Joy instead applies a spiritual strategy of cognitive resilience: 'For me, personally, my first recourse is always to pray... that's my first line of [defence]; I ask God for understanding, and I ask Him to help me carry on and to not give up'. Joy also alludes to how this strategy helps her to 'live my life here in light of a bigger picture', something Capucine also relates to: 'Sometimes you get negative reactions or really inappropriate ones, but it's not the majority, because for each person that was rude to me, there were probably two others being nice about it'.

Other times, participants displayed a more psychologically assertive way of responding to negative setbacks through instances of *psychological reactance*. Psychological reactance occurs when learners feel a surge of motivation as a result of negative experiences (e.g. being told you cannot do something), usually for the sake of proving someone wrong or preventing the same experience from reoccurring (see e.g. Brehm, 1966; Thompson, 2017). A prime example of this is Lesley's story in Chapter 6, but similar accounts from other participants provide further evidence of this as effective motivational breakdown cover. Amelia, for example, was treated negatively because of her first language (L1) accent and responded accordingly, an attitude that followed her to her L2:

> [That] made me dig my heels in even more. But that's also part of my personality, that I thought, 'Right, well now I'm really gonna keep my accent, because if that's how you're gonna judge me, then let me show you, prove you wrong in a different way [by exceeding your expectations]'.

Sarah, too, responded to many negative experiences in a similar way: 'I think [negative experiences] probably hurt me, but because of that, I would want to make sure that I didn't get into that position again' – turning an initially demotivating experience into a doubly motivating one.

In summary, a key to establishing an effective 'breakdown cover' is to adopt a *can-do* attitude. Timur captures this process as 'you kind of programme your brain to believe what you can or cannot do', and elaborates on this as follows:

> Is there an underlying limitation in your brain? Or is it something that we tell ourselves: 'Oh, well, I can't do it'. *Then* it's a self-fulfilling prophecy, right? So, this is something I tell myself: 'It's doable. You *can*. You *can* do it. And so just do it'. I know that learning a language is not easy. It's difficult, but it *is* attainable.

10.6 Discussion and Some Lessons to Draw

Several lessons are emerging from our analysis regarding persistence. First, the broad rubric of our participants' persistence involved multiple and varied factors and practices, such as a strong initial vision, the employment of habitual actions and an action plan with incremental subgoals that allow for regular progress checks, as well as sustaining positive emotionality and exercising conscious self-control. As such, Dörnyei's (2020; Dörnyei & Henry, in press) extended model offered a good overall fit with our participants' trajectories of long-term learning and corresponding motivation. It was reassuring to see, for example, that the participants' accounts supported the notions of a self-concordant vision and stepwise goals as progress checks.

Second, our results confirm that even the most gifted and motivated L2 learners will occasionally experience self-doubt and periods of reduced interest (see also Beltman & Volet, 2007), and at times like this they, too, need to find inner resources to bounce back. In this they were generally successful in their primary L2. As we saw throughout the chapter, these resources can include but are not limited to a growth mindset, self-affirmations, positive external feedback and even psychological reactance – all of which can benefit any learner, exceptional or not.

Third, some learners are undoubtedly better at displaying persistence than others, and in everyday parlance we often refer to them as having 'grit' or some similar notion. However, upon a closer analysis of our participants' accounts, their grit turns out to manifest in a combination of various strategic actions and reactions – both mental and behavioural – rather than merely being an innate faculty to be drawn upon. A compelling piece of evidence to support such an understanding is that certain participants showed different levels of resilience with different languages and situations, which we would not expect if their resilience was part of their inherent genetic or personality makeup. The question of whether resilience is a personality trait or a skill has divided psychologists over the past decades (see e.g. Leys *et al.*, 2020), but in light of our findings we would lean towards the latter, skill-based conception. This would point to potentially good news, that grit and resilience may be trainable skills that all learners are able to acquire in order to unlock their sustained learning potential.

Fourth, competitiveness turned out to be a more salient issue in our sample than how it is typically represented in the motivation literature. Although competition and competitiveness are known to be highly motivating on a general level, there is curiously little written on this subject in the language learning motivation literature. Nonetheless, as we saw in Chapter 6, competitiveness and classroom competition appeared to have a strong and ongoing motivational effect among our participants. Building on this in the current chapter, we have explored how this effect manifests both as a learning subgoal and as a kind of progress check, both of which are important parts of the 'fuel regeneration' process that helps sustain long-term motivation. Thus, it seems that certain participants were not unlike elite athletes in the sense that their competitiveness pushed them in the long run to achieve the ultimate. As such, implementing competition into the everyday language learner's routine may be beneficial for sustained learning; however, as is the case in sports as well, caution must be taken when straddling the line between competition that helps the learner to persist and competition that pushes the learner too far.

Finally, we also established that some of the strategies and mechanisms that aided in persistence also contributed to developing an overall sense of confidence, which in turn is a crucial component of persistence, and we address this topic in detail in Chapter 11.

11 Second Language Confidence, Comfort and Ownership

This chapter is the first of two addressing the final stage of our participants' learning histories, describing what it meant for them to reach their destination. In this chapter, we scrutinise what this destination actually involves, and the final chapter will then explore how getting to this destination has affected, or even changed, the participants. At the beginning of the book (in the Introduction and Chapter 1), we argued that no matter how 'nativelike' a second language (L2) learner's proficiency is, it will never be fully equivalent to that of a native speaker. Indeed, all of our participants agreed that if they are pushed too hard, sooner or later they will display linguistic markers that are not compatible with genuine native-speaking standards, both from the mythological and realistic perspectives of the native speaker. Accordingly, the selection criteria for our participants included not that they should possess laboratory 'nativelike' proficiency (e.g. verified by tests), but rather that they should be able to pass for a native speaker for at least a short while in a communicative situation. We conveniently referred to this level of competence as 'nativelike' throughout this book, but it begs the question what this level of accomplishment really means in our participants' case. While we explored some of the linguistic and social aspects of this level of attainment in Chapter 3, in this chapter we will turn to the affective – and perhaps more desirable – side of nativelikeness for our learners. We saw in Chapter 10 that our participants were able to sustain their long-term motivation in part due to their positive emotionality throughout the learning process, but how does the end state – achieving nativelikeness – affect their emotional states and relationships with their L2s?

In the Introduction, we offered a tentative answer to this question when we suggested that our selected interviewees have achieved a highly *confident* ability to use the L2, which allowed them a great deal of leeway in *comfortably* crafting their own authentic *L2 voices* and establishing an *ownership of the L2* in a way that most other language learners can only aspire to. Indeed, most 'ordinary' language learners learn to live with their linguistic limitations and to operate using an often extensive but still limited L2 code, whereas our select few gained the possibility to form their L2 identities with relatively few constraints. While the role of positive emotions has recently been gaining traction in the field of second language acquisition (SLA) (see e.g. MacIntyre *et al.*, 2016), we know very little about what kinds of emotions play a role at the end state of language learning, particularly when it involves nativelikeness. In this chapter, we further discuss aspects of our participants' nativelikeness along these lines, from three intertwining perspectives: (a) *confidence*, (b) a *comfortable L2 voice* and (c) *ownership of the L2*.

11.1 Confidence

Marjan's story in Chapter 10 highlighted the utmost importance of confidence in learning and using an L2: recall that she concluded, 'I think it's my self-confidence that allowed me to acquire the language, rather than necessarily anything else', and later she reiterated, 'Confidence is quite a big, big thing'. Does this apply to all of our participants? Are they all linguistically highly confident individuals? If we examine this matter more closely, the picture turns out to be less straightforward than Marjan's account. For example, Timur stated the following:

> I'm a perfectionist, and maybe because of that, I also have a bit of a low self-esteem. So when people tell me that I'm nativelike, I don't know if I believe them. It's like, 'Oh, maybe we're just sitting in a cafe and there's lots of noises'.

In our data set, issues about confidence were perhaps most vividly expressed by Italian-born Livia, so let us begin the discussion by presenting her story.

LIVIA: 'IT WAS ABOUT MY CONFIDENCE MORE THAN ANYTHING ELSE...'

Livia loved the English language right from the start and made such good progress with it during her school years that she chose to study it at university. At the age of 20, she moved to London and has been there ever since. In the years following, she completed a BA in English literature and an MA in creative writing, became a published author (in English) as well as a translator, and most recently completed her PhD in creative writing. This may sound like an unqualified language learning success story, yet not everything went as smoothly as it sounds. After arriving in England, Livia underwent a massive linguistic confidence crisis:

> In the first few years, it was about my confidence more than anything else. So for instance, I wouldn't go out very much because I

was really stressed that if I'd had like a couple of drinks, I wouldn't be able to speak to people. Confidence in my work was also a real issue, because I felt that I was struggling more [than my peers], but I was concealing a lot of that insecurity.

Although Livia's English was admittedly 'really good', she did not accept it: 'I wasn't aware that I spoke English really well.... I kind of continued on this route of battling my own self imposter syndrome'. This evaluation captures her situation fittingly, because the essence of imposter syndrome is that people continue to doubt their own talent and feel like a fraud, no matter how high achieving they are – Livia, too, found it difficult to accept her already outstanding L2 accomplishments.

The real breakthrough for Livia occurred when she started to find herself in the multicultural milieu of various contexts, such as working in London's Camden Market. As she recalls, 'Those multilingual contexts were more productive. They were enabling because they allowed me to cultivate the fact that I had a different cultural background, which could exist in that context', which in turn helped her to take a different perspective on her language. As a result, she eventually succeeded in coming to terms with her limitations and adopted a more forbearing attitude towards herself:

> I think that my confidence comes out of the fact that I have accepted that certain things will stay hard for me. You know, I am a slower reader, and that's fine. And I'll be more open about the difficulties, and that helps me actually not to put incredibly exacting standards on myself. In a sense, it frees me to speak with less tension, and it makes me a better speaker in turn, if that makes sense.

As a result of her transformed mindset, she has finally assumed her nativelike persona fully:

> Once you feel legitimised in who you are, I think a lot of the tension falls off.... I find that now that I'm willing to acknowledge the fact that I exist between two worlds.... I'm more confident in English.

Livia's intriguing insights corroborate the oft-cited truism that 'language performance is largely a confidence game': even though she already had an undoubtedly high level of English competence, she was unable to operate at peak capacity until she solidified her confidence through adopting a more realistic stance. Denny also picks up on the theme of being more forbearing with oneself:

I still very much feel that I have a lot to learn with English, and I do see the limitations of [my] language; I am using English at quite an advanced level anyway, even for a native speaker, so I do give myself a bit of a break, even though I am aware of my limitations.

The confidence that our participants speak of appears to be drawn from two dimensions: on the one hand, it is largely about their knowledge and command of the L2; on the other hand, it also comprises their ability and agency in deploying this knowledge in a variety of contexts, which is often more of a social than a linguistic question. Marjan further explains that the confidence required for her unhindered L2 performance involves two separate but interrelated aspects: 'I feel confident in myself and confident in being part of my community'. In Livia's case, too, the two components had a dynamic relationship with each other: first she developed her L2 abilities but was unable to feel confident in herself and her L2 competence, then she gained some confidence as a member of various international communities in London, which in turn helped prepare the ground for her realistically appraising her L2 proficiency and performing more naturally. Colin's experience with French shows how this relationship can also work in the opposite way. From a community perspective, he recalls receiving a lot of external affirmation, and 'people said, "Oh how fantastic your French is"', but this was not enough for Colin's confidence in his linguistic abilities:

I still had this nagging doubt... I really never met any English person in my acquaintanceship where I thought 'God, their French is just fantastic'. So I was therefore aware that my French was very, very good. But personally, I needed to have that immersion. As a kind of confidence thing.

In contrast to Livia's experience, Colin felt externally affirmed as a speaker first – in part as a result of positive feedback and the comparisons he himself was drawing – before he finished developing the L2 abilities that allowed him to have his now-unwavering L2 confidence.

Perhaps the most relieving takeaway from our participants' accounts of confidence is that it was not something they possessed from the beginning, but rather something they built up gradually. Rianne, for example, recalled:

I felt, most of the time in the beginning – especially with German and teaching [in German] – that I was just stumbling and rumbling around. And I felt like this kind of car that was going on this very bumpy road, and I was just trying to go straight somehow and hoping it somehow worked.

She continues, 'But it always worked out somehow', and as teaching in German became progressively easier, her confidence increased. The gradual build-up of confidence was also transferable across specific L2 skills for learners, feeding back into their general upward trajectory over time. As Sara explains:

> I think it gave me a bit more confidence that I was like, 'Oh yeah, like, my pronunciation is pretty good. And I don't struggle with English generally as much'. So that gave me more confidence. And then if there were problems that I stumbled upon in English, it didn't take all of the motivation out of me.

Finally, the level of confidence certain individuals among our participants described went beyond simply trusting in their L2 abilities, instead extending to them considering the L2 as something they could rely on even in especially confidence-demanding situations. Shinhye's account is particularly relevant in this respect, because she explains that she managed to build up *more* confidence in her L2 use than in her native tongue, Korean:

> I never wanted to be put on the spot or to speak in front of other people. But when it comes to English, I can do it better. I feel more confident, I feel like I can do this, and I don't mind asking questions when there are hundreds and thousands of people. I still feel nervous, like my hands get sweaty and all of that, but I think I can do it more *willingly* in English than in Korean.

Let us conclude with an insightful interview extract concerning the depth of the L2 community's relationship with confidence in our data set. Denny elaborates on the role of nativelikeness on her membership in the L2 community:

> Being unmarked, being recognised as nativelike, has given me the kind of confidence to just go about my life and not really worry about what people might think of me, because I'm enough like them to not be a threat and to be accepted.

In Chapter 9, we explored how certain participants expressed the desire to integrate seamlessly into their L2 communities and be perceived as socially belonging within them; here we see the kind of confidence and mental freedom that achieving this goal might present.

11.2 A Comfortable L2 Voice

One of the fundamental success criteria in any communication – whether in a first language (L1) or an L2 – is that the speaker should adopt a comfortable, authentic voice. Pairing with this, it is generally assumed that the voice a speaker uses is concordant with them, their personality, beliefs and identities. For most native speakers this develops naturally over time, but even they might run into trouble in this respect, for example when faced with a new sociocultural situation (e.g. an unfamiliar level of formality or genre) – this is when people would remark, 'This didn't sound like her'. For language learners, the added difficulty in developing their own L2 voice is that they operate with a limited L2 code, which for beginner and intermediate learners can sometimes make them think something along the lines of 'Oh dear, I sound like a child!' Even for upper advanced learners, these difficulties can lead to frequent frustration and searches for reassurance in finding the precise nuance necessary to maintain a self-concordant L2 voice.

The identity-related role of one's L2 voice will be addressed in Chapter 12, but the important point for the current discussion is that this is an area where our exceptional participants have a real advantage: they may not be perfect in every aspect of the L2, but they feel relaxed and comfortable using the language and expressing themselves how they would like to be presented. As there has been little research thus far into the affective states that arise from being nativelike, this concept of comfort with regard to constructing one's L2 voice has been heretofore unexamined, but our data suggest it is an altogether different condition than the L2 confidence addressed in Section 11.1. Our best example of this sense of ease is Uwe and how he describes his L2 ability in 'high-stakes' lectures or presentations: 'My English ability props me up and allows me that sort of flexibility and psychological calm that I think I need in such situations'. Peng describes the feeling of 'progressing in my competence and in my confidence as well', and explains that nativelikeness means that 'I'm able to move beyond my weaknesses and my advantages as I speak English, and then move more into the thought'. He finds that even beyond confidence, 'nativelikeness gives yourself more voice, and then you just have more efficacy in expressing yourself'. Kristin even specifically uses the word 'comfort' to describe her state: 'It's like some sort of comfort to know that I've become nativelike'.

Shinhye expresses the same sentiment, describing how she felt after she had become nativelike in her sojourn in the United States: 'I felt comfortable using English, and I also felt comfortable around people who use English mainly'. She elaborates:

> I felt a little more relaxed, because I knew what was going on. It was not necessarily because I could pick up everything or I could understand 100% of what the teachers said, but I had become familiar with how the class is structured, how people interact in class, and when to speak or not to speak. And I knew everybody in the class, so I didn't really feel the anxiety that I felt in the first semester.

Shinhye's earlier confidence meant that she knew she could rely on her English ability; here, her comfort meant that she felt more at ease expressing herself in English language situations because of it. As with confidence, we also see here a dynamic relationship with the same two elements: being comfortable with one's L2 ability (and in this case, voice) and also with operating within one's environment. This latter aspect was highlighted by Judith, who explained that being nativelike allows her to feel 'completely at home' in Norway, particularly because she is not marked out as a foreigner as some of her colleagues might be. Lesley concurs:

> [Nativelikeness] makes life much easier for you... It's just more comfortable... and makes you feel more at ease. You feel more at home in the country, too, because you're not obviously foreign. I think it just makes life in general much nicer. And life becomes less complicated, maybe even less frustrating.... People don't treat you differently. You know, they just treat you the same as everyone else.

In sum, the comfort we found in our data set subsumes the sense of confidence discussed above, and as such, affects learners' relationships with their L2 communities and is, in turn, affected by them. Where comfort diverges from confidence, instead, is that it also entails a certain ease and lack of strain when learners express themselves in the L2, often allowing them to relax and feel at home in their L2 communities. However, we believe that more investigation is necessary to better understand the depth to which this comfort extends. For example, while Uwe talks about the 'psychological calm' and 'flexibility' he gains from his L2 ability, he draws a line between this and the ease he feels when speaking his L1 German:

> Like when I'm in Germany, and you just talk to somebody without thinking at all... I can feel myself sort of loosening up literally – I miss that. That brings with it a certain sense of – I'm not sure what that is; not even 'belonging' is the right word – comfort, a complete ease.

Nonetheless, from our participants' accounts we can agree that even if the comfort they feel in the L2 is slightly different from its L1 counterpart, it is still something that most ordinary learners can only aspire to.

11.3 Ownership of the L2

So far, we have used two descriptors – confident and comfortable – to characterise the special affective state of our participants, and these adjectives appear to capture the natural ease with which our interviewees approach using their L2. However, as we further analysed the data – particularly Denny and Uwe's accounts – a third notion also emerged in this respect: having *ownership* of the L2. This is admittedly related to confidence and comfort – such as with Livia's statement of how her feelings of legitimacy helped her to overcome the tension she felt as an L2 speaker – yet it also highlights an additional 'intimacy with the language' (Denny) that allows for flexible and creative L2 use. This is undoubtedly connected to having formed a unique bond with the language (discussed in Chapter 5), as explained by Denny in relation to her formative sojourn in Berlin:

> I suppose the element of ownership [with the language] is kind of coming back in the way that I would have felt about Berlin as a place, that this [language] was something that belonged to me. And I think that is probably still there, even though I don't necessarily speak German as well or use it as much now. But I still feel that this is something *of* me, and that *I* am of.... That has probably been the most fulfilling thing out of all of it.

Later, she tries to capture the essence of the notion using the metaphor of 'home':

> The language itself is a home for me. I don't know how to describe it. There is an element of just feeling really, really safe and secure in having had that experience, that richness of the country, of places, of books as well. And I feel that that home is still there, that sense of belonging is still very much there.

The sense of 'home' that Denny speaks about here goes beyond simply blending in with the L2 community; rather, she speaks about the language itself belonging to her. Recall also that Capucine similarly referred to her L2 English as 'a shelter, a safe space'. Uwe focuses on the implications of this ownership:

> There is so much more that you can do [with language], and with my language competence, I can do it myself. I can invent phrases that maybe professional speakers of English don't use. But if I like them, they will have a similar effect. And that's what I feel I do these days; I feel quite comfortable playing around with things.

L2 ownership thus means that rather than conforming flawlessly (but rigidly) to a set of standard linguistic rules, learners feel an extra sense of flexibility and creativity; they know the spoken and unspoken rules, and feel confident and comfortable using them to such an extent that they feel free to bend or flout them to further express their L2 voice. Timur equates this with having a broad overview of every aspect of the L2:

> It's the awareness of what language is and what it isn't. And also, what is your style? What do you need to do [to learn it]? I think in the beginning,

> I had a lot of misconceptions about what it takes to speak English, and what is English and whatnot.... And I have more awareness of that now.

Importantly, while this sense of ownership can be internal, the linguistic flexibility it allows for is, like confidence and comfort, mediated by the social nature of language. For example, Theresa describes making the language her own through comedy:

> I think as a language speaker, you learn words, and you start playing around with them; and then you try and be funny and say something wrong intentionally. And then they bloody correct you. Really?! I always find that hugely annoying when they know I'm German, and they just [do that]. Pff.

On the other hand, she notes here that when her interlocutors assume her to be a native speaker, such 'play' hits the listener as comedically intended. Comedy is thus the perfect demonstration of the way native-likeness and the ownership that comes with it play out: in order for a joke to work, the speaker must first understand all of the listener's linguistic and cultural rules, and the listener in turn must be able to quickly understand that the speaker is purposefully flouting one of these rules for comedic effect. If the listener instead believes that the speaker made a mistake, the joke does not work. In this sense, ownership, too, represents both an individual and a social issue: the speaker implicitly claims ownership over the language, but the listener must also believe this claim. As such, a non-nativelike individual might feel ownership of a language, but they may not have, as Uwe puts it, 'a similar effect' on their interlocutors. It is this two-way street that perhaps best represents the essence of being nativelike.

Still, as is the case with all of our data set, there is always an exception to the rule. While participants like Denny and Uwe claim intimacy with – and ultimately ownership of – their L2s as something that belongs to them but also that they belong to, others like Thamarasie feel differently:

> I don't think I ever thought of making English mine. For me, that language was a very good tool, which helped me in my studies, and then on to my job, *et cetera*. For me, it was a tool. I never thought of claiming ownership of it.

Thamarasie might instead be considered a 'language technician': the L2 is a tool that she is a master at using. Rather than valuing her language abilities for the flexibility and creativity they allow her, Thamarasie focuses instead on her command of the language: 'For me, if you use it, use it properly. So for me, the grammar has to be correct. And then that's it'. Although she may not feel a sense of ownership over her L2 as such, she describes a similar sense of linguistic agency when working with native speakers:

> For me, it was comfortable. Because I know that my grammar is correct. I don't have a problem. In my last duty station, in Rome, there was an Irish girl. Now to me, I would think Irish – they're native English speakers, no? But I remember, I would edit *her* writing as well. And she didn't mind, and I didn't mind.

11.4 Discussion and Some Lessons to Draw

The starting point of the discussion in this chapter was that no matter how excellent and 'nativelike' the proficiency of our participants, it will never match a (monolingual) native speaker's competence in every respect. Yet, we have consistently argued throughout this book that being linguistically perfect is not really the key issue, and therefore studies that compare the various linguistic features of near-native L2 speakers to native-speaking standards do not clarify the situation beyond confirming that there are indeed differences. Yet, despite not being 'perfect', the exceptional L2 learners whom we have investigated stand a class apart from their more 'ordinary' learning counterparts, and this chapter set out to capture the essence of their unique competence. Three terms emerged from the interviews as descriptors of our participants' unique linguistic state of being: confidence, comfort and having ownership of the language. Of these, confidence has a rich history both in SLA and in mainstream psychology, so let us start with this concept.

Linguistic self-confidence was first introduced in the L2 literature by Clément et al. (1977) to describe a powerful mediating process in multi-ethnic settings that affects a person's motivation to learn and use the language of the other speech community (for a review, see Clément & Gardner, 2001). While confidence more generally refers to the belief that a person has the ability to produce results and accomplish goals competently, Clément and colleagues explored it primarily as a socially defined construct that determines a learner's future desire for intercultural communication. Clément et al. (1994) extended the applicability of this self-confidence construct by showing that it is also a significant motivational subsystem in foreign language learning situations in which there is little direct contact with L2 community members but considerable indirect contact with the L2 culture through the media. On the other hand, psychology has taken a more cognitive conception of self-confidence, typically referred to as *self-efficacy* after Albert Bandura's (1977) seminal work on the subject. Self-efficacy refers to people's judgment of their capabilities to carry out specific tasks, and Bandura argued that such perceived competence is a powerful motivational factor because it determines the choice of activities attempted, along with the level of aspiration, the amount of effort exerted and the persistence displayed (for a recent review, see Irie, 2022). Our findings presented in this chapter support the validity of both conceptualisations – not only as a motivational factor that can greatly affect learner aspirations, effort output and persistence, but also as a socially mediated construct.

Unlike the notion of self-confidence/efficacy, the other terms highlighted in this chapter – a comfortable L2 voice and ownership of the L2 – have not been used widely in the psychological or SLA literature, except for the former in a research strand on learners' *personal voice*, which subsumes their unique sound, manner and style of speaking/writing, and in some interpretations, their social positioning as well (Tardy, 2012). Regarding the latter, Kramsch (2003: 134) defines voice as something that develops as the outcome of learners 'mediating between different, often conflicting, historicities and collectivities' in order to express their identity through language, and as such some studies have approached the topic from a sociolinguistic perspective (e.g. Magnusson & Stroud, 2012). Although there have been attempts to relate the notions of voice and voice construction more closely to L2 learner identities and L2 learning, respectively (e.g. Canagarajah, 2015; Nasrollahi Shahri, 2018), the discussion so far has largely remained on an abstract level. Our participants' accounts suggest that voice should indeed, as Tardy (2012) helpfully summarises, be treated as a dialogue between the individual and social dimensions of expression, but also that adequate attention needs to be paid to the individual dimension and the learners' relationship with the L2. It also remains to be seen whether the comfort with which our participants constructed their L2 voices is attainable for the ordinary learner, or whether it is a property unique to nativelikeness. Further investigation should therefore look towards more robustly examining what this construct might entail and if it is an affective state achievable for the ordinary learner. Ultimately, our participants recognised the notions of comfort and L2 voice as useful concepts when discussing their nativelikeness, which suggests that there is much further mileage in this line of inquiry.

Lastly, the concept of language ownership has been largely used with a broader social connotation, for example to refer to speech communities 'owning' a language or language variety (e.g. Nic Fhlannchadha & Hickey, 2018; Norton, 1997; Widdowson, 1994). Higgins (2003: 615) defined speakers' ownership as 'the degree to which they project themselves as legitimate speakers with authority over the language', and we can see from cases such as Theresa's and Thamarasie's that the notion of ownership occurring in our data set is to some extent a social entity entailing that self-same authority and legitimacy. However, the concept also emerged as an individual-level construct, involving the scope of the use of the L2 that a person felt intimacy with, as with Uwe's interpretation. This recalls Chapter 5, in which we discussed the unique bond our learners developed with their L2(s) usually quite early in their trajectories;

we might thus consider ownership to be the mature manifestation of this bond and consequently a key element of L2 mastery and nativelikeness alongside confidence and comfort. While this interpretation of ownership has some overlap with the notion of learner and speaker identity (to be discussed in Chapter 12), we believe that future research can usefully adopt this category as an important aspect of the L2 learner's relationship with their target language(s).

12 The Question of L2 Identities

In the previous chapters, we have described many different aspects of our participants' journeys towards their exceptional language learning success. In this final chapter, we shall conclude by considering the 'arrival' stage, that is, what membership in the highly selective club of nativelike second language (L2) speakers means to our participants and how it has affected their self-conceptions. Let us begin by taking a look at two relevant interview extracts:

> To summarise my feelings [on nativelikeness], I feel good, because to the extent that it's possible, I've achieved my goal. And then secondly, it's become less of a prominent thing for me, which is also a good thing. In a group of people who all speak English, I just want to be sort of unmarked. (Timur)

> What does it mean to me to understand that I'm approaching a nativelike level, or to realise that I've achieved it? Everything and absolutely nothing at the same time. (Denny)

Even from these two extracts, we can see that our question of meaning is not at all straightforward and indeed has multiple layers to it.

In order to uncover the various layers involved, we shall explore our participants' language identity from a number of different vantage points. A wide range of different notions exists related to identity that are relevant for the case of nativelike L2 learners/speakers; for example, the role of *imagined communities* in the process of becoming nativelike (Norton & Pavlenko, 2019), and Norton's theory of *investment*, which looks at the relationships between identity, ideology and capital, particularly for the end-state of nativelikeness (Darvin & Norton, 2015; Norton Peirce, 1995). However, as the narratives that we collected take place over an exceedingly wide range of temporospatial contexts (e.g. study abroad, adult migrant, foreign language and even internet-based community contexts, over several decades), we focus our attention here on a more general conception of our nativelike learners' identities – that of Block's (2007) *language identity* – in hopes of providing a broad overview upon which future research can expand.

Block (2007: 40) defines language identity as 'the assumed and/or attributed relationship between one's sense of self and a means of communication which might be known as a language'. Drawing from Harris and Rampton's (2002) analysis on cultural processes within creole (socio)linguistics, Block breaks this down into three types of relationships an individual can have with a language: *language expertise*, *language affiliation* and *language inheritance*. Starting with the last, language inheritance refers to being born or raised in a community setting associated with a particular language; the learners of our study by nature do not have inheritance relationships with their L2s, although it is often assumed by their interlocutors that they do. Language expertise, on the other hand, involves the individual's proficiency and expertise in the language, and particularly for our participants' cases, their ability to pass for a native speaker in the L2. Finally, language affiliation refers to an individual's attitudes towards and affective relationship with the language, alongside 'the extent to which a person identifies with and feels attached to a particular form of communication' (Block, 2007: 40). Nativelikeness thus brings to the table interesting possibilities for this sense of language identity, in that while our participants did not inherit their languages, they nonetheless had the language expertise usually associated with first language (L1) speakers of the language. As such, our question is then how this in turn affected their conceptualisations of their affiliation with their nativelike L2s, and in turn their language identities on the whole. As we shall see, not all of the accounts in our participant pool will be compatible with each other, but with a complex issue such as language identity it might be unrealistic to expect the emergence of a uniform picture. In order to illustrate this further, let us consider Uwe's perspective on the topic, as he expresses the complex subtleties particularly vividly.

UWE: 'MY IDENTITY IS MORE LIKE A RUBIK'S CUBE'

Uwe's language learning history was one of the main sources of inspiration for us to write this book. Having grown up in what was previously East Germany, Uwe managed to develop a level of English that was, according to everyone who knows him, indistinguishable from native-speaking standards – except for a variety of cultural references he had no access to in the isolation of his communist homeland. He later moved to Hungary to teach English and applied linguistics in higher education, married a Hungarian colleague and created his trilingual family in which both parents speak to their daughter in their respective L1s and with each other in English. It is therefore no wonder that when asked to describe his language identity, Uwe responded:

> I don't know what metaphor I would use for my identity. It's more like a Rubik's Cube... I can move around, and I foreground and I background things. And there's a core – I don't know what that core is, but maybe that core is my professional self. And that I feel that psychologically my life is in order. There are things to improve, for sure, but there's a very solid, healthy core that allows me to use language truly as a tool in situations.

As he further explains, this solid psychological core helps him to avoid 'language uncertainty', that is, 'a sense of "Why am I?" "Where am I?" "Why am I not someone else?" I'm basically pretty anchored as a person'. It is then intriguing to hear how he conceives language in relation to this core, backtracking on referring to language as a tool, which he finds 'rather utilitarian', and presenting his language identity as a kind of wardrobe: 'And language has become like a garment that allows me to dress for the occasion to best express what it is that's inside, whatever there is inside'. He elaborates on this metaphor as follows:

> I think I like the garment idea. It's more like it's a facet of who I am. And because there're several sides to me, I have become comfortable with changing them. And it's not just like I change and I lose my sense of self; it's a change that's recurrent. So here's my English pullover, and there're my German trousers. And it's always the same trousers and the same pullover; it's not like I'm getting lost in translation sort of thing.

Uwe's account not only demonstrates the multifaceted nature of language identity, but it also highlights some key issues that we shall explore further in this chapter, most notably the question of 'personal core', the association of specific self-conceptions (such as a professional identity) with this core and the relationship of language expertise to participants' language affiliations and, by extension, personal identities. Let us start with the last point.

12.1 The Fusion of Language Expertise and Personal Identity

In previous chapters, we have discussed our participants developing what we have termed a 'unique bond' with the L2. Part and parcel of this is that in certain interviews, we encounter clear expressions of the fact that the participant's relationship with their L2 became a core component of their personal identity. In other words, their language affiliation with their L2 grew to an extreme extent, in a wholly positive way that matched their expertise with the language. Denny could not have expressed this more explicitly concerning her command of English (which she mastered at a nativelike level prior to German, but before our 18-year-old threshold criterion):

> I absolutely loved English from the word go. I think that had a lot to do with the first kind of initial positive learning experience of it, and then really quickly building confidence in it and it becoming part of me, becoming who I was. I was somebody who spoke and knew English well.

She relates this sense back to her experience with German, describing the relatively longer journey to feeling a similar sense of German-speaking identity, and explaining that 'it eventually kind of becomes part of who you are'.

For Shinhye, English has been something that she has had a strong relationship with for the better part of her life: 'English is something, I think, that defines me, that I want to be identified with.... I think my English is something that makes me more distinguishable? Or stronger?' In Thamarasie's case, her affiliation with English has also become closely associated with her spiritual identity:

> My mother tongue is Sinhalese, but I felt more comfortable with English. When I pray, I pray in English in my mind. I cannot pray in Sinhalese, because I've never done it. I feel it's strange if I have to address God in my language. I know He would understand, but I feel very uncomfortable.

Her preference for English has also progressed onto other aspects of her life: 'I feel I can appreciate things better in English.... The appreciation of the world is clearer to me in English than in Sinhalese'.

Thus far, we have seen participants' L2 expertise affecting their language affiliations and therefore their identities *as L2 speakers*, that is, learners identifying strongly with their ability to speak the L2; however, the extent of their L2 identity's influence was not limited to this. Capucine's experience with her L2 is very close to Denny's, but she adds a further element to the language-related dimension of her identity, a kind of wanderlust: 'I was always really interested in the English language and English culture. I think I was always that French girl who was thinking in English and sort of thinking about what life could be somewhere else'. Even Shinhye, who in the end returned to South Korea after her sojourn in the United States, admits that at one point she was considering staying there: 'The reason that I wanted to stay in the USA is mainly because of the opportunity, the fact that I could use English.

English is something that can represent me very strongly'. In certain participants such as Peng, the longing to be elsewhere was particularly pronounced and was one of the main precursors to his motivation to learn English:

> I always felt I was someone different; I had a different identity growing up. I always wanted to go somewhere else, you know, to try to always seek some alternative perspective on things.... That's why I tried to study English: I wanted to study abroad and eventually live abroad, so that I could have my own lifestyle.

In Chapter 6, we discussed the significance of a cosmopolitan outlook in certain participants' lives, and this aspect of their language learning motivation appears to affect not only their relationships with their L2s but also its overlap with their personal identities. As we can see above, learners' identities as L2 speakers and other major parts of their identities could be inextricably intertwined, mutually reinforcing one another.

Additionally, it appears that our nativelike learners' language identities could also influence even their sense of (inter)national identity. Lou argues that this has always been part of their personality: 'I never really cared so much about having a national identity.... I was always internationally orientated', and this is what drove Lou to pursue their L2 English and is now reinforced by it. In Sarah, as we saw in Chapter 6, the yearning to become international was particularly strong, and she is clear about the fusion of this cosmopolitan outlook with both her language and national identities:

> I don't really have a bilingual identity as such. At least it doesn't have much bearing on my life at present. But being an international person who speaks languages, certainly still does. I'm always aware of it.... When I lived in Hungary I felt like an international person, which I was happy with because that was the identity that I wanted. And then in a way, I feel like an international person back in the UK as well.

Finally, for Judith her Norwegian competence buttressed what she calls her 'European identity':

> For me, personally, it reinforced my identity as a European: someone who feels at home in different parts of Europe, which I do.... I have been to very many different parts of Europe, and wherever I go, I kind of feel European. So Norwegian is an added aspect of that...

However, while Lou, Sarah and Judith describe their identities as L2 speakers as reinforcing their international self-conceptions, sometimes this relationship resulted in more complex outcomes, as we shall see below.

12.2 A Separation of L1 and L2 Identities?

As we saw above, for certain participants – particularly for some of the more cosmopolitan ones like Peng – the international dimension of their language learning motivation and identities merged seamlessly with their core personality. For others, the coexistence of their native and cosmopolitan personas resulted instead in what they described as separate L1 and L2 identities. In fact, for English Colin, such a division is a prerequisite to becoming nativelike in an L2:

> You have to become somebody else. You can't stay yourself; you can't stay English if you're going to speak a foreign language. You have to give that up. The more I think about it, the more extraordinary it is really... you become somebody else. You can't stay the same.

He illustrates this vividly with his experiences of speaking his L2s:

> I've got a German inside me. And a French person inside me. I know that if I'm in France with French friends, then I am a different Colin than I am in German with German friends in Germany. I think part and parcel of that is that you adopt a different voice.

Interestingly, Colin can also trace back the separation of his English and German identities to early on in his language learning history:

> I had a lovely German teacher, who immediately – I think this was quite critical, really – gave every boy a German name. I was Werner. Suddenly, you felt you're a different person. When I went into the classroom, I was suddenly Werner, and I was a different boy. You could become that little bubble when you walked into the class.

Colin's interpretation of his L2 identities is perhaps the most compatible with the experience of being taken for a native speaker, namely because he is taken to be a member of a community with which he identifies strongly. In other words, Colin's language expertise and affiliation aligned, and thus when his language inheritance was assumed, it was not a problem for him but rather a wanted outcome. This is not always the case, as we will see later in this chapter.

Denny, whose English expertise was largely merged with her language affiliation and personal identity as we saw above, offers some further evidence of the complex, layer-like aspect of one's language-related identity:

> I feel like I'm a slightly different person when I speak the different languages. At my core, I am the same person, but I feel I become someone else when I open my mouth and start speaking German. I'm recognisably

me, but there's another dimension to me. I don't know, extension? Dimension?

However, she offers a slightly more nuanced perspective than Colin's as she further elaborates on how best to understand this extension/dimension:

> I would stop short of saying you're enacting a different version of yourself. It's not like an act that you put on, but a part of yourself that you don't activate because there are certain expectations and certain communication demands that are just not there in the other language.... The context of that other culture just allows you to talk about various other different topics that you wouldn't normally enter, to build relationships in a different way.

In this, Denny's conception of her L2 identities seems to coincide more closely with Uwe's conception of linguistic garments, albeit with a more cultural and therefore socially embedded focus. Slovenian Sara illustrates this different culture-bound behaviour with regard to humour:

> When I speak English, I'm just way funnier! Because most of the humour, most of the jokes that I pick up on are from TV shows from English American TV shows. And so then I'm not as funny in Slovene. I'm not! I think some of those things don't transfer; they stay within the same language.

Similar to Denny, however, Sara also questions whether the difference amounts to two separate identities:

> With my identity, I do notice there're slight differences between a Slovene Sara and an English-speaking Sara. But then I try not to think of those as two separate things. At the end of the day, I know I'm still Sara. It's the same person, it's just different languages... it's just two sides of the same coin.

To demonstrate that it is difficult to draw firm conclusions in this matter, let us cite Lou, who also talks about humour – stand-up comedy – but for Lou, their L2 performance and identity is far enough from their personal identity that they describe it as a kind of acting:

> When I'm writing for comedy, I can sometimes take a step back, do it in English, and then everything is clearer. It's like you can talk to another person.... I always thought that sounding native was like learning a play, or something theatre-like. So it's like an option: you have a character.

Part of the ambiguity surrounding how participants conceptualise language identity as either an extension of their core personality or two separate identities (i.e. L1 and L2 related) stems from the fact that different languages allow for expressing certain communicative content in a different way. This is an established academic principle that has been researched under the rubric of *linguistic relativity* (see e.g. Lucy, 2016), also known as the weak version of the Sapir–Whorf hypothesis. Our participants were, by and large, aware of this phenomenon; for example, Sara explained:

> So even if we're talking in Slovene most of the time, there might still be certain phrases and things, or sentences that come out in English because I'm like, 'Oh this just sounds better, and it captures my feeling and what I'm actually trying to say.… It's better in English, so I'm just gonna say it in English right now'.

This linguistic allowance of certain communicative content in one language but not in another also extends to the *manner* of speaking, as illustrated by Shinhye:

> I am not an outgoing person. I never really raised my hand or asked questions in my entire life, especially in Korea. I never wanted to be put on the spot or to speak in front of other people. But when it comes to English, I can do it better. I feel more confident, I feel like I can do this, and I don't mind asking questions when there are hundreds and thousands of people.… But my Korean, the Korean me is a lot less confident, kind of timid, so I try not to speak so much.

In Shinhye's case, we should also note that her acknowledgement of the different allowances of her languages also reflects a closer sense of affiliation with her L2 than her L1.

A further behavioural implication of the L1–L2 contrast is that languages differ in their politeness rules and degree of *directness*, which is inevitably reflected in how speakers use them and thus how they appear when using them. Rianne outlines this very clearly:

> I have the feeling that in Dutch I'm more direct in the way I say things. While in English, I have a tendency to be more like… it's not called sugar-coating, but… waffling a bit more than I would do. And in German, I would also be more direct. So you do have a feeling that depending on the language you're using, you need to say things differently in order to make the same argument.

Peng further underlines the role of the *pitch* differences characterising different languages, reflecting on the difficulty of how to interpret this phenomenon in relation to how it projects his personality:

> When I speak English, definitely I sound different. I speak more calmly and with a lower pitch when I speak Mandarin, but when I speak English, I use a higher pitch.... It's definitely a very interesting personality. At least, it's a personality; at most, it's a self-identity, a self-concept.

Finally, perhaps Kerry illustrates best the ambiguous nature of L2-related behavioural differences when she describes more recently attending a local Italian literary talk and uses the phrases 'Italian mode' and 'Italian personality' together: 'I met all these people, and we just got into a conversation, we're yakking in Italian together, and [my friend] was like, "Kerry, it's like you never left!" I just went into my Italian mode and personality'.

12.3 Identity Erasure and Resistance to Mislabelling

In Sections 12.1 and 12.2, we first saw some arguments made by our participants that their L2 expertise was an integral part of their notion of personal identity, even extending to their perceptions of national identity. We also saw that even if one has the feeling that their L2 identities substantially differ from their L1 counterpart(s), this may not necessarily mean for everyone that the two are fully separate. However, our data also contain a further identity-related option that is particularly relevant for nativelike L2 speakers: namely that a person may not *want* to be identified as a member of the L2 community, and their language identities had significantly less overlap with their personal identities.

Participants like Colin did not differentiate between being German as a speaker versus being part of the German community, but others certainly did. For example, we saw that Sara compares 'Slovene Sara' with 'English-*speaking* Sara' (emphasis ours), demarcating a difference between her language and community-based identities. While as we saw above, there is a great deal of overlap between the two, for certain participants the distinction was vital to how they preferred to be identified by others. This manifests in our data set with participants who reject entirely the idea of being assumed to have L2 inheritance and being taken for a member of the L2 community, despite having nativelike expertise. Finnish Hanna has been one of the most outspoken in this respect:

> I never feel British. Never. Obviously, it's a massive compliment if somebody thinks that you're a native speaker. Like, it feels really good, but I am also very quick to remind people that I'm not. I'm really proud to be Finnish, and if I had a strong [Finnish] accent, I wouldn't mind, I think, because it's part of me. I'm a Finnish speaker, not a native English speaker.

Such a position starkly contrasts with the desire to blend in, which we have seen represented in other participants in previous chapters. Hanna's is not, however, an extreme stance, because British Lisa for example represents a very similar approach: she likes it when people mistake her for a German 'because that must mean that my language skills are good', but on the other hand, she has no specific desire to sound German and not British. As she explains, despite living in Germany and having a German passport:

> I would say that I still feel British, and I think that it will always stay this way. I don't feel particularly German – it's not that I reject everything that is German, but from an identity point of view, I don't feel particularly German.

In a similar vein, German Theresa also finds it flattering to be taken for a native speaker in terms of what it suggests about her proficiency, but it also incurs in her a feeling of 'absolute horror': 'because I'm not British, and I will never be British. It's not who I am, so I think there's a loss of identity – not gaining identity, it's actually losing the identity'. In this sense, the spillover of Theresa's projected language identity onto her sense of national identity became a directly unwanted outcome. Denny further elaborates on this ambiguous feeling:

> Nativelikeness is something that can be very problematic, and it's something that is very disturbing sometimes because I've been in situations, especially in the context of Brexit, where people have tried to claim me as their own.... And it's like, 'No, no, no! I *am* Bulgarian, I feel Bulgarian, I'm Bulgarian to my core'. I'm always going to be a little bit odd and strange in the local or native context, and I've grown to accept that.

These instances of participants' resistance to passing raise several questions. First, through what mechanisms do linguistic and community-based identities overlap for nativelike L2 speakers, and in what ways are they able to play an agentive role in this interaction? We saw earlier Denny recalling that she 'absolutely loved English from the word go' and that English 'became part of me', reflecting a strong linguistic affiliation alongside her language expertise, yet this perspective presents a stark contrast to her 'disturbing' and 'problematic' interpretation of certain instances of passing. Second, we have seen that certain learners (e.g. Timur or Heidrun) expressed a marked preference for their L2 identity. This raises the question of how one's evaluation of their language identity is also dependent on their attitudes towards both their L1 and L2 identities, which is inevitably affected by the social environment's appraisal of the respective cultures/communities. We find hints of this in Lesley's account:

> I still don't feel German. If you asked me, 'What's your nationality?' I would reply, 'Well, Scottish'.... Saying you're Scottish always seems to get a positive reaction from people.... When I was working in France, for example, this happened quite regularly: I mentioned that I was Scottish, and all of a sudden people were nicer to me. Scotland's got a good reputation for some reason.

Finally, there is also the question of the danger of falling through the cracks in this identity maze and ending up with no prominent language identity, the prospect of which Dutch Ira, for example, finds alarming:

> I ran into a Dutch person, and they'd been here for six years, and they had an English accent in Dutch. And it just really scared me.... So, if I have an accent in English but I don't speak Dutch very well, then you're always kind of in between. So, in my head, you're not really at home in either country that way... I think if both languages don't seem like your native language, you don't really feel like you're from anywhere.

Block (2007: 20–21) refers to such a state as *ambivalence*, or 'the uncertainty of feeling a part and feeling apart', in which an individuals' conceptions of 'a stable self are upset and... they enter a period of struggle to reach a balance'. Yet interestingly, it is not Ira's L2 competence itself that causes her to lose touch with her L1 identity: 'I don't really think [being nativelike in English reduces my Dutch identity]. Just because for me, English and Dutch are kind of separated in my mind'; rather it is more the result of living abroad. Uwe concurs, suggesting that this feeling of in-betweenness is part and parcel of being an immigrant:

> There's a term in psychology, anomie? So it's like a no-man's land: you're neither here nor there. And a great many people, when they move away, particularly when they're older, and they move into a different cultural surrounding, when they plateau after a certain time, in terms of acculturation – they get stuck. Because you no longer know who you are culturally speaking; you're not here and you're no longer there. Or you break through that in some form, either in an integrated way, or in an assimilated [way], or whatever.

Of course, this then raises the question of what it means to be 'in between' and whether this is necessarily an undesirable outcome. Block (2007: 22) suggests this ambivalence is indeed unwelcome; he refers to it as a 'conflict' and argues that 'individuals strive for a coherent life narrative, seeking to resolve conflicts and assuage their ambivalent feelings'. However, while other participants did experience some form of L1 attrition – a shift in language expertise that usually occurred after having spent a substantial period within predominantly L2 communities – the accompanying identity shift, if it was interpreted as such, was less pronounced than Ira fears. Of those who largely avoided experiencing anomie or ambivalence, participants like Hanna, Theresa and Denny made a point to foreground their L1-related identities in interactions where they might otherwise be 'incognito'. Others, however, explicitly desired the addition of their L2 identities and often did not see this as a loss of their L1 counterparts, also avoiding periods of ambivalence. Joy's experience perhaps best summarises this approach:

> I don't see [nativelikeness] as an erasure. I think of it as an addition. And you know, all of those other [cultural] things that I just mentioned, for me are very intimately and intricately intertwined with language… so it's very much an integrated part of the experience. And for me, I never saw it as a loss of part of me; I saw it as a choice that I was adding. And so it was expanding who I was; it wasn't shrinking, or diminishing.

Others still experienced periods of ambivalence, but ultimately arrived on the other side of the identity maze through other paths, as we shall see below.

12.4 Family-Related and Professional Identities

While Ira expressed her apprehension about the potential of being left without a solid language identity, for others like Joy, being ambivalent and 'in between' might be less of a problem. For example, Kristopher admits, 'I don't see myself as Canadian. But I don't see myself as Japanese either, you see. So, I don't see myself as belonging to any country. But to be honest, that doesn't bother me in the least'. In his case, Kristopher's core identity is scaffolded by his *family* rather than his national identity: 'Maybe because of that, my connection with my wife and children is very strong. I feel like that's my identity: my family. My wife and children. That is where I feel I belong'. We thus find that Kristopher's language identities support his core identity rather than infringing upon it as it might have if he were to have a stronger sense of national identity. Timur has also found solid grounding in his family in the midst of his identity turmoil, replacing his national identity with an ethnic/familial one that is further substantiated by his language identities:

> I would describe my identity in one word: messed-up. But in a way, it's a good kind of messed-up…. Throughout my life I went back and forth between 'I'm Russian, I'm not Russian'. But now I have a bit of a more nuanced sort of view of that, when it comes to languages at least. We have two kids, a five-year-old and a three-year-old, and one expecting… having children helped me in a way to ground myself a little bit too, because I speak to them exclusively in Russian, and they speak back to

me relatively okay in Russian. So I have that as part of my anchor identity as well. But there's also English, a lot more English, because my wife and I speak English.

Timur talks about the need for an 'anchor identity', and it turns out that one's *professional identity* can also potentially fulfil this purpose. We have seen this explicitly expressed in Uwe's story described at the beginning of the chapter with his 'professional core', and we also find that Rianne too derives her identity anchor from the professional realm: 'Because I always work with people from multiple countries, I never really cared so much about having an identity in that [national] sense'. She adds:

> I'm not looking just within the Netherlands for a job, but I'm looking for like [anywhere] in Europe, or I can see myself kind of everywhere, so to speak.... And that is really what [nativelikeness] brought me, this kind of open, international view, because you just know you can identify with multiple languages, and thereby with multiple identities.

In this sense, although we saw earlier that Rianne acknowledges that her L1 and L2 identities are different in some tangible way, at her core she sees herself as an international European researcher, which is reinforced by her multitudinous linguistic identities. Livia, too, finds being 'in between' a welcome state despite her previous struggles for legitimacy as someone who writes in her L2. She now views her professional writer self as a 'bridge' between her merged L1 and L2 identities and their respective peoples:

> If [nativelikeness] happens to you like it's happened to me, it makes you very conscious of being a bridge, and that's quite lovely.... It's always about connecting one point or another.... If you assume that you exist as a bridge between people, then I think that's a lovely spot to be in. It makes your work harder, because you've got no centre, but I don't know, I wouldn't have it any other way really.

The relationship between professional and language identities can also work in the opposite way. Shinhye, who ultimately was unable to stay in the United States to fulfil her dream of living entirely in her L2 English, instead found that she 'had to *create* opportunities to use English' back in South Korea, which she did through her job:

> When I got a job at my current position, I was not necessarily asked to teach in English, but I did. I think I enjoyed the reputation of being a professor who taught courses in English... being noticed as someone who speaks fluent English meant more to me [than some others' criticism].

In this way, Shinhye was able to affirm her language identity through her profession. Finally, Judith also explains in this respect that

> being nativelike reinforces my professional identity. And this is perhaps not something I aimed for – or it didn't so much happen at the beginning – but is still important now.... I'm able to speak in an academic context in Norwegian, and also write in Norwegian. I'm quite proud of that aspect of my identity.

12.5 Discussion and Some Lessons to Draw

The issue of language identity is unquestionably a complex and multifaceted subject; although definitions and foci differ, conceptualisations of identity in recent research in second language acquisition are generally understood to be multitudinal, dynamic and socially embedded (Duff, 2012; Miller & Kubota, 2013; Norton, 2013; Norton & Pavlenko, 2019; Ushioda, 2009). Constructs of identity within applied linguistics are most commonly used to explore multilingual individuals' experiences within society without focusing on their experiences as learners specifically (e.g. Duff, 2015; Kramsch & Whiteside, 2008), although aspects of identity have also been extended to language learning specifically, for example in Bonny Norton's previous work on identity and investment (see e.g. Norton, 2013; Norton Peirce, 1995) and in the notion of future self-guides in Dörnyei's (2005, 2009a) L2 Motivational Self System (see also Block, 2007; Henry, 2017). The question of nativelikeness introduces a unique issue in this respect, as it places speakers at the intersection of their personal identities and their identities related to being L2 speakers, as well as their L1- and L2-related national, ethnic and community-based identities. Our findings well reflect this inherent intricacy: certain participants talked about identity-related issues at some length and yet no uniform picture has emerged from their accumulated accounts.

It appears reasonably certain that there are some elemental differences in how advanced learners communicate in their L2(s) relative to their L1 communication patterns, but the question remains open regarding the distinctness of their language-related identities and the level of integration they have with one's core personal identity. It is certainly an attractive proposal that the amalgam of L2 nativelikeness, the speaker's personality and the host culture's affordances results in a unique and distinct package that is divergent enough from the individual's similar L1-related package to be considered separate, as with Colin's case. We find clear support for such a division in our data, but there is also evidence that other participants did not feel entirely comfortable with such a black-and-white split. They instead used varied metaphors for the division that converged on the idea that their various language identities are linked together through one's personal core, which makes it difficult to decide how such linked entities are represented in one's self-concept.

Along similar lines, Pavlenko (2006) conducted a survey of bi-/multilinguals regarding the degree to which respondents experienced the phenomenon of language identity division, occasionally referred to as 'linguistic schizophrenia'. Our results corroborate with Pavlenko's regarding the diversity of participants' identity approaches; she, too, found that many survey participants recounted a sharp difference between their L1 and L2 identities, and also that some others displayed more integrated approaches. One of her respondents, Bertha, even recalls being able to anchor her linguistic identity through her children (Pavlenko, 2006: 26), a phenomenon we observed with participants like Timur and Kristopher. Notably, Pavlenko concludes that some of these issues, particularly those concerning 'sharp' identity separation and ambivalence, are more relevant for individuals living in *monolingual* contexts, and we find this to be the case with our nativelike participants.

Beyond Pavlenko's research, our own study further begs the question of how nativelikeness might actually complicate the process of identity formation, given the sense of identity erasure that participants like Theresa and Denny experienced as a result of their advanced L2 expertise. Moyer (2013: 178) suggested that it might be inevitable that, due to the close relation of accent and identity, some gifted learners experience feelings of Uwe's anomie – or ambivalence – at some point in their learning experience before settling into what she calls 'a comfortable L2 identity'. We certainly observed this in *certain* participants, but curiously not with all, which raises the question of how some learners were able to maintain a positive emotionality and avoid this psychologically taxing experience. Ultimately, the answer will depend on the learner's context, their individual identities not limited solely to their language identities, and more specifically, how identity is thought to interact with individual differences in people's linguistic affiliations as well as their attitudes towards the L1- and L2-related cultures where relevant. While we have largely focused on the 'late' state of learners' L2 identities, that is, how they conceived themselves after having achieved nativelikeness, further investigation into the *process* of language identity formation and navigation of nativelikeness-related identity shifts could produce useful evidence regarding the evolving structures of L1 and L2 identity at the intersection of self- and group-based perceptions. Additionally, research into the power relations behind nativelikeness through frameworks such as investment would be further illuminating for the issue. We can thus foresee fruitful future research examining this topic further, because a valid conceptualisation of the nature and formation of one's L2 identity as it relates to nativelikeness would have considerable theoretical and practical implications.

Conclusion

This project has grown out of an initial research idea that turned out to be irresistible: a little over a year ago we realised that the autobiographical accounts of exceptional language learners constitute a treasure trove of insights and possible lessons that has not been sufficiently explored to date. As we started to make tentative moves towards preparing a proper research project, we received such encouragement and support both from our publisher, Multilingual Matters, and from several would-be participants, that before we knew it we had the process well under way. It has undeniably taken up a massive amount of energy and time – after all, gathering and analysing a qualitative corpus of over 460,000 words is, by definition, hugely demanding – but we never considered the investigation 'hard work'. Rather, it felt like a 'heart project' right from the start, displaying the electrifying and engaging nature of what should characterise every interesting research project but which, unfortunately, is so often lost in the paperwork of the surrounding world and its prevailing 'publish or perish' culture. Having said that, it is admittedly with some relief that we can now conclude the process, because all of the other aspects of our lives that have been pushed aside by our ongoing fascination with this cohort of language learners are increasingly beckoning.

The subtitle of this book – *Motivation, Cognition and Identity* – is undeniably a broad one, and the reason for such a specification is that our project has progressed in a manner not unlike some of the early qualitative studies of the 1960s and 1970s in that it addressed some fundamental questions of the field of second language acquisition (SLA) that could only be answered by drawing on a broad spectrum of relevant factors. The success of our exceptional research participants involved a combination of motivational and cognitive considerations, and it soon became clear to us that identity-related issues also played a major role in how our interviewees succeeded in achieving their extraordinary outcomes. In presenting our findings, we found we had to make a special effort not to get *too* lost in the richness of the details, thus we focused primarily on the novel results that have emerged from our data set. We also made the decision to process and interpret the data relatively 'lightly' so as to lessen the force of our preconceived ideas and beliefs on the bottom-up insights, which otherwise would have resulted in a more reductionist picture. Thus, although Zoltán has done extensive work on individual second language (L2) learner differences in the past, we kept an open mind – for example, some of his best-known theoretical tenets (e.g. the L2 Motivational Self System; see Dörnyei, 2005, 2009a) do not feature in this book at all, because our data gave us little reason to include it. Our goal instead was to amplify any fresh and potentially cutting-edge insights that emerged in the motivational, cognitive and identity domains.

The presentation of our findings in the current volume has followed a fairly elaborate organisational framework, comprising nine analytical chapters, and this division helped us to report the results in a fairly orderly manner, beginning with the initial conditions of learning and then proceeding through various aspects of the learning process until we reached the final destination, nativelike L2 proficiency. Because the material in each chapter is summarised in a concluding discussion section, we will not repeat those overviews here; instead, we would like to spend the remainder of this Conclusion highlighting eight selected points that we have found most memorable and forward-facing:

(1) *The absence of a 'silver bullet'.* In his overview of polyglots, Kenneth Hyltenstam (2021: 70) concludes that these gifted learners' outstanding achievement is underpinned by 'a synergy of factors, each of which independently enhances language learning, but which together have added value'. This was also true of our participants, with an important addition to Hyltenstam's conclusion: the synergy of factors often displayed patterns that deviated considerably from each other, thereby evidencing that there are *multiple pathways* to accomplishing exceptional L2 learning success. Individual variables in isolation did not have sufficient explanatory power, and it was rather telling that even when we identified an issue that appeared to concern a large proportion of our participants (e.g. the link between some aspect of musicality and L2 learning success), there were always individuals who did not fit the particular mould or even displayed the opposite pattern (e.g. 10% of our sample were not only unmusical but were also outright musically inept). Our data set proved the popular adage 'for every rule there is an exception', with the caveat that we have not yet found the rule.

(2) *A dynamic combination of factors.* Besides the absence of a single silver bullet, it also became obvious from our interviews that what really mattered was the *dynamic combination* of various attributes and factors that had the potency to launch someone on a positive upwards learning spiral. There was no single factor that could be said of every single one of our participants, nor did any of the factors play out in

equivalent or even predictably systematic ways. The importance of various factors and even various combinations of factors waxed and waned throughout participants' lives in demonstrably diverse ways, suggesting that not only are there multiple pathways to L2 learning success, but also that the pathways themselves are neither linear nor fully predictable.

(3) *Motivation–cognition interaction.* Arguably, the theoretically most intriguing combination of factors emerged with respect to *motivational* and *cognitive* variables. Only such a combination can explain, for example, the fact that a learner pursuing a language at an admittedly average level and without any special flair suddenly switched to a cognitive hyperdrive with the same language after a motivational transformation – resulting in their learning not only improving dramatically but also taking them to a stratospheric echelon. It is clear that in such cases the added motivational control somehow amplified or intensified the learners' cognitive functioning, but further research is needed to identify the mechanisms underlying such an interaction.

(4) *The motivational implications of the unique bond with the L2.* Virtually all of our exceptional learners were found to have formed a *unique bond with the L2*, linking it in some powerful way to their personal identities. In Chapter 5, we argued that this intimate relationship went beyond the disposition captured by the notion of L2 'attitudes', because it constitutes a deeper, chronically accessible connection with strong links to learners' identities. If future research confirms the validity of such a special bond, this will have important implications for motivation theory both in terms of theoretical models that incorporate this entity and practical approaches that are geared towards generating such a bond.

(5) *Mimicry ability and musicality.* In terms of cognitive factors and processes in adult L2 learning, the main addition to our understanding has been the highlighted importance of the interrelated factors of *mimicry ability* and *musicality*. Our data suggest that the capability to imitate pronunciation and accent is not restricted to L2 learning, because certain participants described this capacity also being used in mimicking first language (L1) accents (and in Colin's case, even birds in the Amazon rainforest). Additionally, while musicality has been connected in the past – although mostly anecdotally – to language learning success, in our study it has emerged as a prominent cognitive companion to learners' language aptitude. Both mimicry ability and musicality will require further theoretical clarification and empirical validation before being potentially integrated into SLA theory, but based on our research findings we predict that such explorations will be productive.

(6) *The significance of increased attention to pronunciation.* Following from the fact that pronunciation/accent is a core area of linguistic

self-representation both in one's L1s and L2s, it stands to reason that our participants assigned unique importance to the matter. Nonetheless, contemporary language teaching methodology in many countries has by and large failed to attach a similar significance to teaching pronunciation, partly due to disputes over what model to follow and also because it may be argued that from a communicative language teaching perspective, a less-than-perfect but still clearly understandable accent is not disruptive. Such a position, however, neglects learners' pronunciation-related learning goals as well as their pronunciation potential, leading to increased fossilisation of a non-native accent in learners who might desire otherwise. This, in turn, prevents those learners from experiencing the rise of a *powerful positive spiral* of learning commitment that authentic pronunciation and the ensuing positive linguistic self-image can generate.

(7) *A comfortable L2 voice and ownership of the L2*. Our findings highlighted the importance of two success criteria of L2 learning not commonly mentioned in the SLA literature: the establishment of an L2 voice that the learner considered fully *comfortable*, and the development of a subjective-personal *ownership of the L2*. The former is distinct from being nativelike (or even from being highly advanced) in the sense that its main characteristic is that it should be self-concordant and aligned with the person's own language identity – in fact, certain participants were known to feel uncomfortable sounding fully nativelike in an L2 either because of the fear of losing their own ethnocultural identity or because of the possibility of being mixed up with a speech community from which they would like to remain distinguished. Although nativelikeness is certainly not an absolute requirement for developing a self-concordant L2 voice, our data suggests that nativelikeness facilitates the ease with which learners do so. Additionally, the related concept of *L2 ownership* goes beyond being merely comfortable or linguistically confident, and also beyond the development of a unique bond with the L2, as it also involves the creative adaptation of the L2 code towards achieving one's varied communicative purposes and L2 voice. We foresee further investigation into the process of developing both a comfortable L2 voice and L2 ownership – as well as into how integral nativelikeness is to the mix – proving fruitful for facilitating advanced L2 learner development.

(8) *The relationship between L1 and L2 identities*. The final chapter addressed a fundamental issue regarding language identity, the question as to whether nativelike learners' L1- and L2-related personas are perceived as *fully* independent and separate from each other, or whether they are better seen as fused aspects of the same linguistic extension of personal identity. For a long time, scholars

have sensed that individuals adopt different communicative features when operating in an L2 (see e.g. Dörnyei & Kormos, 2000), and while there has been much research on the social identities of multilinguals and the social factors leading to the adoption of these features (see e.g. Norton & McKinney, 2011; Ohara, 2001), there has been no systematic research examining the implications of nativelikeness on such a difference. That is, how do learners' expertise in and relationships with their L1s and L2s, both interactionally and internally, reflect the makeup and structure of how they form, perceive and perform their identities? This issue was a central topic discussed by our participants, which warrants further research to determine the structure of L2 identity and the various internal and external factors that contribute to the variance in its conception.

In summary, investigating exceptional language learners has taught us a variety of valuable lessons about what really mattered to them in their journey of SLA, and the insights gained from our study carry special importance by virtue of these learners' extraordinary ultimate attainment. We do realise that not everything presented in their accounts is directly transferrable to other, more 'ordinary' learners' practices – for example, not every learner can afford to dedicate significant periods of their lives to language learning like so many of our participants did – but we were pleased to see that a great deal does have the potential to be applicable. While this is yet a first foray into the psychological experiences of exceptional language learners, we believe we have at least begun to pull back the curtain on advanced ultimate attainment for the benefit of learners, teachers and researchers alike, and we hope to have sparked enough curiosity in the topic to inspire further research. Ultimately, to reiterate what we said in the Introduction, our adventure into nativelikeness has not disappointed, and we have been genuinely pleased to share some of the sources of excitement that we encountered upon exploring our interviewees' vibrant and captivating stories.

Appendix

Interview Schedule

A. Introductions

- Please feel welcome to skip any question or section if at any point you wish to do so. We can also stop or pause the interview at any time with no problem.
- Do you have any questions before we begin?
- Ask if it's okay to start recording.

B. Introducing the Format

- Describe the two parts: Initial storytelling in which participants lead the interview, and then some follow-up questions if there's anything on the checklist that may not have been mentioned.

C. Story

First off, what languages have you learned in your life (first, second, third, etc.), and which ones can you pass for (or have previously passed for) a native in?

- What kinds of instances have you been taken as a native speaker?
  - How long do you think you could 'fool' someone?
  - In what way do you think you would give yourself away?
- How on earth did you manage to achieve such an exceptional thing; can you tell me a bit of your story?
  - [Interviewer can ask for elaboration/clarification, but this should be largely participant led]

D. Additional Questions/Checklist

[Check these off as/if they are mentioned throughout Section C]

- ☐ Learning process/strategies (particular, special tricks?)
- ☐ Is there an aspect of language which has been particularly important to you? (If they need clarification: for example, grammar, vocabulary, pronunciation, formulaic language, or fluency.)
    - Were there things which you found particularly difficult?
- ☐ Dialect/varieties
    - When we talk about language proficiency, we tend to assume that language is a uniform thing, but of course there are different varieties/dialects. When you were learning, did you intentionally choose a specific dialect or variety?
- ☐ Language dominance (and L1 maintenance/loss)
    - Specific situations in which you are more or less confident?
- ☐ Identity regarding different language(s), and possible change over time
- ☐ Sustaining long-term motivation
    - You've come this far, do you feel that you're still learning that language?
- ☐ Any particularly intensive periods
- ☐ Significant relationships (friend, significant other, mentor, etc.)
- ☐ Role model(s)
- ☐ Family support (childhood, travelling, international connections, etc.)
- ☐ Passions? (hobbies/sports, reading, etc.)
    - What is it that you like about language learning? Is there anything important that you get from language learning that you don't get elsewhere?
- ☐ Musical training
- ☐ Thoughts on nativeness (or on the native/non-native debate, if aware)

E. Reflections

- What has the concept of becoming nativelike in your proficiency meant to you throughout your life (i.e. earlier on, but also after achieving it and up to now)?
- Is there anything else that comes to mind that you would recommend us to look into for our project?
- You should receive a draft in the next few weeks. Would it be okay if something new or interesting comes up, to run it past you? An email, or a quick chat if you prefer?
- Thank you from the both of us; you'll hear from us soon!

References

Abrahamsson, N. and Hyltenstam, K. (2008) The robustness of aptitude effects in near-native second language acquisition. *Studies in Second Language Acquisition* 30 (4), 481–509.

Abrahamsson, N., Hyltenstam, K. and Bylund, E. (2018) Age effects on language acquisition, retention and loss: Key hypotheses and findings. In K. Hyltenstam, I. Bartning and L. Fant (eds) *High-Level Language Proficiency in Second Language and Multilingual Contexts* (pp. 16–49). Cambridge: Cambridge University Press.

Ahn, A.S. and Bong, M. (2019) Self-efficacy in learning: Past, present, and future. In S. Hidi and K.A. Renninger (eds) *The Cambridge Handbook of Motivation and Learning* (pp. 63–86). Cambridge: Cambridge University Press.

Al-Hoorie, A.H. and MacIntyre, P.D. (eds) (2020) *Contemporary Language Motivation Theory: 60 Years Since Gardner and Lambert (1959)*. Bristol: Multilingual Matters.

Amorati, R. (2020) Accessing a global community through L2 learning: A comparative study on the relevance of international posture to EFL and LOTE students. *Journal of Multilingual and Multicultural Development*. Advance online publication.

Andringa, S. (2014) The use of native speaker norms in critical period hypothesis research. *Studies in Second Language Acquisition* 36 (3), 565–596.

Bandura, A. (1977) Self-efficacy: Toward a unifying theory of behavioral change. *Psychological Review* 84 (2), 191–215.

Baran-Łucarz, M. (2012) Ego boundaries and attainments in FL pronunciation. *Studies in Second Language Learning and Teaching* 2 (1), 45–66.

Baran-Łucarz, M. (2014) The link between pronunciation anxiety and willingness to communicate in the foreign-language classroom: The Polish EFL context. *The Canadian Modern Language Review* 70 (4), 445–473.

Barkhuizen, G.P. (ed.) (2013) *Narrative Research in Applied Linguistics*. Cambridge: Cambridge University Press.

Baumann, C. and Harvey, M. (2018) Competitiveness vis-à-vis motivation and personality as drivers of academic performance: Introducing the MCP model. *International Journal of Educational Management* 32 (1), 185–202.

Baumann, C. and Harvey, M. (2021) What is unique about high performing students? Exploring personality, motivation and competitiveness. *Assessment & Evaluation in Higher Education* 46 (8), 1314–1326.

Beltman, S. and Volet, S. (2007) Exploring the complex and dynamic nature of sustained motivation. *European Psychologist* 12 (4), 314–323.

Benson, P., Brown, J., Bodycott, P. and Barkhuizen, G. (2013) *Second Language Identity in Narratives of Study Abroad*. Basingstoke: Palgrave Macmillan.

Besson, M., Barbaroux, M. and Dittinger, E. (2017) Music in the brain. In R. Ashley and R. Timmers (eds) *The Routledge Companion to Music Cognition* (pp. 37–48). New York: Routledge.

Biedroń, A. (2011a) Near-nativeness as a function of cognitive and personality factors: Three case studies of highly able foreign language learners. In M. Pawlak, E. Waniek-Klimczak and J. Majer (eds) *Speaking and Instructed Foreign Language Acquisition* (pp. 99–116). Bristol: Multilingual Matters.

Biedroń, A. (2011b) Personality factors as predictors of foreign language aptitude. *Studies in Second Language Learning and Teaching* 1 (4), 467–489.

Biedroń, A. and Pawlak, M. (2016) New conceptualizations of linguistic giftedness. *Language Teaching* 49 (2), 151–185.

Bijvoet, E. and Fraurud, K. (2012) Studying high-level (L1-L2) development and use among young people in multilingual Stockholm: The role of perceptions of ambient sociolinguistic variation. *Studies in Second Language Acquisition* 34 (2), 291–319.

Bijvoet, E. and Fraurud, K. (2016) What's the target? A folk linguistic study of young Stockholmers' constructions of linguistic norm and variation. *Language Awareness* 25 (1–2), 17–39.

Birdsong, D. (2004) Second language acquisition and ultimate attainment. In A. Davies and C. Elder (eds) *The Handbook of Applied Linguistics* (pp. 82–105). Oxford: Blackwell.

Birdsong, D. (2005) Nativelikeness and non-nativelikeness in L2A research. *IRAL – International Review of Applied Linguistics in Language Teaching* 43 (4), 319–328.

Birdsong, D. (2007) Nativelike pronunciation among late learners of French as a second language. In O.-S. Bohn and M.J. Munro (eds) *Language Experience in Second Language Speech Learning* (pp. 99–116). Amsterdam: John Benjamins.

Birdsong, D. (2014) The critical period hypothesis for second language acquisition: Tailoring the coat of many colors. In M. Pawlak and L. Aronin (eds) *Essential Topics in Applied Linguistics and Multilingualism* (pp. 43–50). Cham: Springer.

Block, D. (2007) *Second Language Identities*. London: Continuum.

Bolton, K. (2016) Linguistic outsourcing and native-like performance in international call centres: An overview. In K. Hyltenstam (ed.) *Advanced Proficiency and Exceptional Ability in Second Languages* (pp. 185–214). Boston, MA: De Gruyter Mouton.

Bongaerts, T. (1999) Ultimate attainment in L2 pronunciation: The case of very advanced late L2 learners. In D. Birdsong (ed.) *Second Language Acquisition and the Critical Period Hypothesis* (pp. 133–160). Mahwah, NJ: Lawrence Erlbaum.

Boo, Z., Dörnyei, Z. and Ryan, S. (2015) L2 motivation research 2005–2014: Understanding a publication surge and a changing landscape. *System* 55, 145–157.

Botes, E., Gottschling, J., Stadler, M. and Greiff, S. (2020) A systematic narrative review of international posture: What is known and what still needs to be uncovered. *System* 90, Art. 102232.

Braun, V. and Clarke, V. (2006) Using thematic analysis in psychology. *Qualitative Research in Psychology* 3 (2), 77–101.

Braun, V. and Clarke, V. (2013) *Successful Qualitative Research: A Practical Guide for Beginners*. Los Angeles: SAGE.

Braun, V. and Clarke, V. (2021) One size fits all? What counts as quality practice in (reflexive) thematic analysis? *Qualitative Research in Psychology* 18 (3), 328–352.

Braver, T.S. (ed.) (2016) *Motivation and Cognitive Control*. New York: Routledge.

Braver, T.S., Krug, M.K., Chiew, K.S., Kool, W., Westbrook, J.A., Clement, N.J., Adcock, R.A., Barch, D.M., Botvinick, M.M., Carver, C.S., Cools, R., Custers, R., Dickinson, A., Dweck, C.S., Fishbach, A., Gollwitzer, P.M., Hess, T.M., Isaacowitz, D.M., Mather, M. ... Somerville, L.H. (2014) Mechanisms of motivation–cognition interaction: Challenges and opportunities. *Cognitive, Affective, & Behavioral Neuroscience* 14 (2), 443–472.

Brehm, J. W. (1966) *A Theory of Psychological Reactance*. Oxford: Academic Press.

Brendel, B. and Ackermann, H. (2009) Foreign accent syndrome FAS: An incidental 'speech talent' following acquired brain damage. In G. Dogil and S.M. Reiterer (eds)

Language Talent and Brain Activity (pp. 193–212). Berlin/New York: De Gruyter Mouton.

Busse, V. (2017) Plurilingualism in Europe: Exploring attitudes toward English and other European languages among adolescents in Bulgaria, Germany, the Netherlands, and Spain. *The Modern Language Journal* 101 (3), 566–582.

Canagarajah, A.S. (2013) *Translingual Practice: Global Englishes and Cosmopolitan Relations*. Abingdon/Oxford/New York: Routledge.

Canagarajah, A.S. (2015) 'Blessed in my own way': Pedagogical affordances for dialogical voice construction in multilingual student writing. *Journal of Second Language Writing* 27, 122–139.

Carroll, J.B. (1973) Implications of aptitude test research and psycholinguistic theory for foreign-language teaching. *Linguistics* 11 (112), 5–14.

Carroll, J.B. (1981) Twenty-five years of research on foreign language aptitude. In K.C. Diller (ed.) *Individual Differences & Universals in Language Learning Aptitude* (pp. 83–118). Rowley, MA: Newbury House.

Carroll, J.B. and Sapon, S.M. (1959) *The Modern Language Aptitude Test*. San Antonio, TX: Psychological Corporation.

Celce-Murcia, M., Brinton, D. and Goodwin, J.M. (2010) *Teaching Pronunciation: A Course Cook and Reference Guide* (2nd edn). Cambridge: Cambridge University Press.

Cheng, C.M. and Chartrand, T.L. (2003) Self-monitoring without awareness: Using mimicry as a nonconscious affiliation strategy. *Journal of Personality and Social Psychology* 85 (6), 1170–1179.

Chik, A. (2018) Beliefs and practices of foreign language learning: A visual analysis. *Applied Linguistics Review* 9 (2–3), 307–331.

Christiner, M. and Reiterer, S.M. (2015) A Mozart is not a Pavarotti: Singers outperform instrumentalists on foreign accent imitation. *Frontiers in Human Neuroscience* 9, Art. 482.

Clément, R. and Gardner, R.C. (2001) Second language mastery. In W.P. Robinson and H. Giles (eds) *The New Handbook of Language and Social Psychology* (pp. 489–504). Chichester: John Wiley & Sons.

Clément, R., Gardner, R.C. and Smythe, P.C. (1977) Motivational variables in second language acquisition: A study of Francophones learning English. *Canadian Journal of Behavioural Science/Revue Canadienne Des Sciences Du Comportement* 9 (2), 123–133.

Clément, R., Dörnyei, Z. and Noels, K.A. (1994) Motivation, self-confidence, and group cohesion in the foreign language classroom. *Language Learning* 44 (3), 417–448.

Cohen, A.D. and Henry, A. (2019) Focus on the language learner: Styles, strategies and motivation. In N. Schmitt and M.P.H. Rodgers (eds) *An Introduction to Applied Linguistics* (3rd edn, pp. 165–189). London/New York: Routledge.

Cook, V. (1999) Going beyond the native speaker in language teaching. *TESOL Quarterly* 33 (2), 185–209.

Cook, V. (ed.) (2002) *Portraits of the L2 User*. Clevedon: Multilingual Matters.

Cook, V. (2016) Premises of multi-competence. In V. Cook and L. Wei (eds) *The Cambridge Handbook of Linguistic Multi-Competence* (pp. 1–25). Cambridge: Cambridge University Press.

Costa, P.T. and McCrae, R.R. (1992) *Revised NEO Personality Inventory (NEO-PI-R) and NEO Five-Factor Inventory (NEO-FFI) Professional Manual*. Odessa, FL: Psychological Assessment Resources.

Costa, P.T. and McCrae, R.R. (2008) The revised NEO personality inventory (NEO-PI-R). In G.J. Boyle, G. Matthews and D.H. Saklofske (eds) *The SAGE Handbook of Personality Theory and Assessment* (pp. 179–199). Los Angeles, CA: SAGE Publications.

Cutler, C. (2014) Accentedness, 'passing' and crossing. In J.M. Levis and A. Moyer (eds) *Social Dynamics in Second Language Accent* (pp. 145–167). Berlin/Boston, MA: De Gruyter Mouton.

Darvin, R. and Norton, B. (2015) Identity and a model of investment in applied linguistics. *Annual Review of Applied Linguistics* 35, 36–56.

Davies, A. (2003) *The Native Speaker: Myth and Reality* (2nd edn). Clevedon: Multilingual Matters.

De Costa, P.I., Randez, R.A., Her, L. and Green-Eneix, C.A. (2021) Navigating ethical challenges in second language narrative inquiry research. *System* 102, Art. 102599.

De Wilde, V., Brysbaert, M. and Eyckmans, J. (2020) Learning English through out-of-school exposure. Which levels of language proficiency are attained and which types of input are important? *Bilingualism: Language and Cognition* 23 (1), 171–185.

Derwing, T.M. and Munro, M.J. (2009) Putting accent in its place: Rethinking obstacles to communication. *Language Teaching* 42 (4), 476–490.

Derwing, T.M., Fraser, H., Kang, O. and Thomson, R.I. (2014) L2 accent and ethics: Issues that merit attention. In A. Mahboob and L. Barratt (eds) *Englishes in Multilingual Contexts: Language Variation and Education* (pp. 63–80). Dordrecht: Springer.

Dewaele, J.-M. (2018) Why the dichotomy 'L1 versus LX user' is better than 'native versus non-native speaker'. *Applied Linguistics* 39 (2), 236–240.

Dewaele, J.-M., Bak, T.H. and Ortega, L. (2021) Why the mythical 'native speaker' has mud on its face. In N. Slavkov, S.M. Pfeifer and N. Kerschhofer-Puhalo (eds) *The Changing Face of the 'Native Speaker': Perspectives from Multilingualism and Globalization* (pp. 25–46). Berlin: De Gruyter Mouton.

Dogil, G. and Reiterer, S.M. (eds) (2009) *Language Talent and Brain Activity*. Berlin/New York: De Gruyter Mouton.

Dörnyei, Z. (2001) *Motivational Strategies in the Language Classroom*. Cambridge: Cambridge University Press.

Dörnyei, Z. (2005) *The Psychology of the Language Learner: Individual Differences in Second Language Acquisition*. Mahwah, NJ: Lawrence Erlbaum.

Dörnyei, Z. (2007) *Research Methods in Applied Linguistics: Quantitative, Qualitative, and Mixed Methodologies*. Oxford: Oxford University Press.

Dörnyei, Z. (2009a) The L2 motivational self system. In Z. Dörnyei and E. Ushioda (eds) *Motivation, Language Identity and the L2 Self* (pp. 9–42). Bristol: Multilingual Matters.

Dörnyei, Z. (2009b) *The Psychology of Second Language Acquisition*. Oxford: Oxford University Press.

Dörnyei, Z. (2020) *Innovations and Challenges in Language Learning Motivation*. New York: Routledge.

Dörnyei, Z. and Kormos, J. (2000) The role of individual and social variables in oral task performance. *Language Teaching Research* 4 (3), 275–300.

Dörnyei, Z. and Kubanyiova, M. (2014) *Motivating Learners, Motivating Teachers: Building Vision in Language Education*. Cambridge: Cambridge University Press.

Dörnyei, Z. and Ryan, S. (2015) *The Psychology of the Language Learner Revisited*. New York/London: Routledge.

Dörnyei, Z. and Muir, C. (2019) Creating a motivating classroom environment. In X. Gao (ed.) *Second Handbook of English Language Teaching* (Vol. 2, pp. 719–736). Cham: Springer.

Dörnyei, Z. and Ushioda, E. (2021) *Teaching and Researching Motivation* (3rd edn). New York: Routledge.

Dörnyei, Z. and Henry, A. (in press) Accounting for long-term motivation and sustained motivated learning: Motivational currents, self-concordant vision, and persistence in language learning. In A.J. Elliot (ed.) *Advances in Motivation Science* (Vol. 9). Cambridge, MA: Academic Press.

Dörnyei, Z., Henry, A. and Muir, C. (2016) *Motivational Currents in Language Learning: Frameworks for Focused Interventions*. New York/London: Routledge.

Doughty, C.J. and Mackey, A. (2021) Language aptitude: Multiple perspectives. *Annual Review of Applied Linguistics* 41, 1–5.

Duff, P.A. (2012) Identity, agency, and second language acquisition. In S.M. Gass and A. Mackey (eds) *The Routledge Handbook of Second Language Acquisition* (pp. 410–426). Abingdon/New York: Routledge.

Duff, P.A. (2015) Transnationalism, multilingualism, and identity. *Annual Review of Applied Linguistics* 35, 57–80.

Dweck, C.S. (2008) *Mindset: The New Psychology of Success* (Ballantine Books trade pbk. ed). New York: Ballantine Books.

Ehrman, M. (1999) Ego boundaries and tolerance of ambiguity in second language learning. In J. Arnold (ed.) *Affect in Language Learning* (pp. 68–86). Cambridge: Cambridge University Press.

Eisenberg, J. and Thompson, W.F. (2011) The effects of competition on improvisers' motivation, stress, and creative performance. *Creativity Research Journal* 23 (2), 129–136.

Ferdinand, N.K. and Czernochowski, D. (2018) Motivational influences on performance monitoring and cognitive control across the adult lifespan. *Frontiers in Psychology* 9, Art. 1018.

Field, J. (2003) Promoting perception: Lexical segmentation in L2 listening. *ELT Journal* 57 (4), 325–334.

Flege, J.E. (1984) The detection of French accent by American listeners. *The Journal of the Acoustical Society of America* 76 (3), 692–707.

Fonseca-Mora, M.C. and Machancoses, F.H. (2016) Music and language learning: Emotions and engaging memory pathways. In P.D. MacIntyre, T. Gregersen and S. Mercer (eds) *Positive Psychology in SLA* (pp. 359–373). Bristol: Multilingual Matters.

Foote, J.A., Trofimovich, P., Collins, L. and Urzúa, F.S. (2016) Pronunciation teaching practices in communicative second language classes. *The Language Learning Journal* 44 (2), 181–196.

Galmiche, D. (2018) The role of shame in language learning. *Journal of Languages, Texts, and Society* 2, 99–129.

Gardner, R.C. (1985) *Social Psychology and Second Language Learning: The Role of Attitudes and Motivation*. London: Edward Arnold.

Gardner, R.C. (2019) Looking back and looking forward. In A.H. Al-Hoorie and P.D. MacIntyre (eds) *Contemporary Language Motivation Theory: 60 Years Since Gardner and Lambert (1959)* (pp. 5–14). Bristol: Multilingual Matters.

Gardner, R.C. and MacIntyre, P.D. (1991) An instrumental motivation in language study: Who says it isn't effective? *Studies in Second Language Acquisition* 13 (1), 57–72.

Giles, H. (ed.) (2016) *Communication Accommodation Theory: Negotiating Personal Relationships and Social Identities Across Contexts*. Cambridge: Cambridge University Press.

Gluszek, A. and Dovidio, J.F. (2010) The way they speak: A social psychological perspective on the stigma of nonnative accents in communication. *Personality and Social Psychology Review* 14 (2), 214–237.

Gnevsheva, K. (2017) Within-speaker variation in passing for a native speaker. *International Journal of Bilingualism* 21 (2), 213–227.

Graddol, D. (2006) *English Next: Why Global English May Mean the End of 'English as a Foreign Language'*. London: British Council.

Graham, C.R. (1984) Beyond integrative motivation: The development and influence of assimilative motivation. *On TESOL '84. A Brave New World for TESOL. Selected Papers from the Annual Convention of the Teachers of English to Speakers of Other Languages*, 75–87.

Granena, G. (2019) Language aptitudes in L2 acquisition. In J.W. Schwieter and A. Benati (eds) *The Cambridge Handbook of Language Learning* (pp. 390–408). Cambridge: Cambridge University Press.

Granena, G. and Long, M.H. (eds) (2013) *Sensitive Periods, Language Aptitude, and Ultimate L2 Attainment.* Amsterdam/Philadelphia, PA: John Benjamins.

Griffiths, C. (ed.) (2008) *Lessons from Good Language Learners.* Cambridge: Cambridge University Press.

Griffiths, C. (2015) What have we learnt from 'good language learners'? *ELT Journal* 69 (4), 425–433.

Griffiths, C. (2018) *The Strategy Factor in Successful Language Learning: The Tornado Effect* (2nd edn). Bristol: Multilingual Matters.

Guiora, A.Z. (1972) Construct validity and transpositional research: Toward an empirical study of psychoanalytic concepts. *Comprehensive Psychiatry* 13 (2), 139–150.

Guiora, A.Z. (1994) The two faces of language ego. *Psychologica Belgica* 34 (2–3), 83–97.

Guiora, A.Z. and Acton, W.R. (1979) Personality and language behavior: A restatement. *Language Learning* 29 (1), 193–204.

Guiora, A.Z., Beit-Hallahmi, B., Brannon, R.C.L., Dull, C.Y. and Scovel, T. (1972) The effects of experimentally induced changes in ego states on pronunciation ability in a second language: An exploratory study. *Comprehensive Psychiatry* 13 (5), 421–428.

Hall-McMaster, S., Muhle-Karbe, P.S., Myers, N.E. and Stokes, M.G. (2019) Reward boosts neural coding of task rules to optimize cognitive flexibility. *The Journal of Neuroscience* 39 (43), 8549–8561.

Hamada, Y. (2019) Shadowing: What is it? How to use it. Where will it go? *RELC Journal* 50 (3), 386–393.

Hammarberg, B. (2010) The languages of the multilingual: Some conceptual and terminological issues. *IRAL – International Review of Applied Linguistics in Language Teaching* 48 (2–3), 91–104.

Harris, R. and Rampton, B. (2002) Creole metaphors in cultural analysis: On the limits and possibilities of (socio-)linguistics. *Critique of Anthropology* 22 (1), 31–51.

Hartshorne, J.K., Tenenbaum, J.B. and Pinker, S. (2018) A critical period for second language acquisition: Evidence from 2/3 million English speakers. *Cognition* 177, 263–277.

Hendriks, B., van Meurs, F. and Usmany, N. (2021) The effects of lecturers' non-native accent strength in English on intelligibility and attitudinal evaluations by native and non-native English students. *Language Teaching Research*. Advance online publication.

Henry, A. (2017) L2 motivation and multilingual identities. *The Modern Language Journal* 101 (3), 548–565.

Higgins, C. (2003) 'Ownership' of English in the Outer Circle: An alternative to the NS-NNS dichotomy. *TESOL Quarterly* 37 (4), 615–644.

Hinton, M. (2013) An aptitude for speech: The importance of mimicry ability in foreign language pronunciation. In E. Waniek-Klimczak and L.R. Shockey (eds) *Teaching and Researching English Accents in Native and Non-Native Speakers* (pp. 103–111). Berlin/Heidelberg: Springer.

Holliday, A. (2005) *The Struggle to Teach English as an International Language.* Oxford: Oxford University Press.

Hollien, H.F. (2002) *Forensic Voice Identification.* San Diego, CA: Academic Press.

Houghton, S.A. and Rivers, D.J. (eds) (2013) *Native-Speakerism in Japan: Intergroup Dynamics in Foreign Language Education.* Bristol: Multilingual Matters.

Houghton, S.A. and Bouchard, J. (eds) (2020) *Native-Speakerism: Its Resilience and Undoing.* Singapore: Springer.

Hu, X. and Reiterer, S.M. (2009) Personality and pronunciation talent. In G. Dogil and S.M. Reiterer (eds) *Language Talent and Brain Activity* (pp. 97–130). Berlin/New York: De Gruyter Mouton.

Hughes, B.L. and Zaki, J. (2015) The neuroscience of motivated cognition. *Trends in Cognitive Sciences* 19 (2), 62–64.

Hwang, A. and Arbaugh, J.B. (2009) Seeking feedback in blended learning: Competitive versus cooperative student attitudes and their links to learning outcome. *Journal of Computer Assisted Learning* 25 (3), 280–293.

Hyltenstam, K. (ed.) (2016) *Advanced Proficiency and Exceptional Ability in Second Languages*. Boston, MA: De Gruyter Mouton.

Hyltenstam, K. (2021) Language aptitude and language awareness: Polyglot perspectives. *Annual Review of Applied Linguistics* 41, 55–75.

Hyltenstam, K. and Abrahamsson, N. (2001) Age and L2 learning: The hazards of matching practical 'implications' with theoretical 'facts' (Comments on Stefka, H. Marinova-Todd, D. Bradford Marshall, and Catherine E. Snow's 'Three Misconceptions about Age and L2 Learning'). *TESOL Quarterly* 35 (1), 151–170.

Hyltenstam, K. and Abrahamsson, N. (2003) Maturational constraints in SLA. In C.J. Doughty and M.H. Long (eds) *The Handbook of Second Language Acquisition* (pp. 539–588). Oxford: John Wiley & Sons.

Hyltenstam, K., Bartning, I. and Fant, L. (eds) (2018) *High-Level Language Proficiency in Second Language and Multilingual Contexts*. Cambridge: Cambridge University Press.

Ioup, G., Boustagui, E., El Tigi, M. and Moselle, M. (1994) Reexamining the critical period hypothesis: A case study of successful adult SLA in a naturalistic environment. *Studies in Second Language Acquisition* 16 (1), 73–98.

Irie, K. (2022) Self-efficacy. In T. Gregersen and S. Mercer (eds) *The Routledge Handbook of the Psychology of Language Learning and Teaching* (pp. 100–111). New York/Abingdon: Routledge.

Jilka, M. (2009) Talent and language proficiency. In G. Dogil and S.M. Reiterer (eds) *Language Talent and Brain Activity* (pp. 1–16). Berlin/New York: De Gruyter Mouton.

Johnson, D.W., Maruyama, G., Johnson, R., Nelson, D. and Skon, L. (1981) Effects of cooperative, competitive, and individualistic goal structures on achievement: A meta-analysis. *Psychological Bulletin* 89 (1), 47–62.

Jouravlev, O., Mineroff, Z., Blank, I.A. and Fedorenko, E. (2021) The small and efficient language network of polyglots and hyper-polyglots. *Cerebral Cortex* 31 (1), 62–76.

Kachlicka, M., Saito, K. and Tierney, A. (2019) Successful second language learning is tied to robust domain-general auditory processing and stable neural representation of sound. *Brain and Language* 192, 15–24.

Kadota, S. (2019) *Shadowing as a Practice in Second Language Acquisition: Connecting Inputs and Outputs*. New York: Routledge.

Kang, O., Rubin, D. and Pickering, L. (2010) Suprasegmental measures of accentedness and judgments of language learner proficiency in oral English. *The Modern Language Journal* 94 (4), 554–566.

Kinzler, K.D. (2020) *How You Say It: Why You Talk the Way You Do and What It Says About You*. Boston, MA: Houghton Mifflin Harcourt.

Kinzler, K.D. (2021) Language as a social cue. *Annual Review of Psychology* 72 (1), 241–264.

Knudsen, E.I. (2004) Sensitive periods in the development of the brain and behavior. *Journal of Cognitive Neuroscience* 16 (8), 1412–1425.

Kormos, J. (1999) Monitoring and self-repair in L2. *Language Learning* 49 (2), 303–342.

Kormos, J. (2013) New conceptualizations of language aptitude in second language attainment. In G. Granena and M.H. Long (eds) *Sensitive Periods, Language Aptitude, and Ultimate L2 Attainment* (pp. 131–152). Amsterdam/Philadelphia, PA: John Benjamins.

Kramsch, C. (2003) Identity, role and voice in cross-cultural (mis)communication. In J. House, G. Kasper and S. Ross (eds) *Misunderstanding in Social Life: Discourse*

Approaches to Problematic Talk (pp. 129–153). Abingdon/Oxford/New York: Routledge.

Kramsch, C. and Whiteside, A. (2008) Language ecology in multilingual settings: Towards a theory of symbolic competence. *Applied Linguistics* 29 (4), 645–671.

Kramsch, C. and Zhang, L. (2018) *The Multilingual Instructor: What Foreign Language Teachers Say About Their Experience and Why It Matters*. Oxford: Oxford University Press.

Krashen, S. (1978) Individual variation in the use of the monitor. In W.C. Ritchie (ed.) *Principles of Second Language Learning* (pp. 175–183). New York: Academic Press.

Kunschak, C. and Kono, N. (2020) Post-native-speakerism and the multilingual subject: Language policy, practice, and pedagogy. In S.A. Houghton and J. Bouchard (eds) *Native-Speakerism: Its Resilience and Undoing* (pp. 213–242). Singapore: Springer.

Kuppens, A.H. (2010) Incidental foreign language acquisition from media exposure. *Learning, Media and Technology* 35 (1), 65–85.

Lamb, M. (2019) Motivational teaching strategies. In M. Lamb, K. Csizér, A. Henry and S. Ryan (eds) *The Palgrave Handbook of Motivation for Language Learning* (pp. 287–305). Cham: Palgrave Macmillan.

Lamb, M., Csizér, K., Henry, A. and Ryan, S. (2019) *The Palgrave Handbook of Motivation for Language Learning*. Cham: Palgrave Macmillan.

Lantolf, J.P. (2006) Sociocultural theory and L2: State of the art. *Studies in Second Language Acquisition* 28 (1), 67–109.

Lantolf, J.P. (2012) Sociocultural theory. In S.M. Gass and A. Mackey (eds) *The Routledge Handbook of Second Language Acquisition* (pp. 57–72). London: Routledge.

Lanvers, U. and Chambers, G. (2019) In the shadow of global English? Comparing language learner motivation in Germany and the United Kingdom. In M. Lamb, K. Csizér, A. Henry and S. Ryan (eds) *The Palgrave Handbook of Motivation for Language Learning* (pp. 429–448). Cham: Palgrave Macmillan.

Leather, J. (1999) Second-language speech research: An introduction. *Language Learning* 49 (s1), 1–56.

Leaver, B.L. and Shekhtman, B. (eds) (2002) *Developing Professional-Level Language Proficiency*. Cambridge: Cambridge University Press.

Leaver, B.L. and Campbell, C. (2014) Experience with higher levels of proficiency. In T. Brown and J. Bown (eds) *To Advanced Proficiency and Beyond: Theory and Methods for Developing Superior Second Language Ability* (pp. 3–22). Georgetown, Washington, DC: Georgetown University Press.

Lee, J., Jang, J. and Plonsky, L. (2015) The effectiveness of second language pronunciation instruction: A meta-analysis. *Applied Linguistics* 36 (3), 345–366.

LeVelle, K. and Levis, J. (2014) Understanding the impact of social factors on L2 pronunciation: Insights from learners. In J.M. Levis and A. Moyer (eds) *Social Dynamics in Second Language Accent* (pp. 97–118). Berlin/Boston, MA: De Gruyter Mouton.

Lewandowski, N. (2009) Sociolinguistic factors in language proficiency: Phonetic convergence as a signature of pronunciation talent. In G. Dogil and S.M. Reiterer (eds) *Language Talent and Brain Activity* (pp. 257–278). Berlin/New York: De Gruyter Mouton.

Lewandowski, N. and Jilka, M. (2019) Phonetic convergence, language talent, personality and attention. *Frontiers in Communication* 4, Art. 18.

Leys, C., Arnal, C., Wollast, R., Rolin, H., Kotsou, I. and Fossion, P. (2020) Perspectives on resilience: Personality Trait or Skill? *European Journal of Trauma & Dissociation* 4 (2), Art. 100074.

Li, S. and Zhao, H. (2021) The methodology of the research on language aptitude: A systematic review. *Annual Review of Applied Linguistics*, 1–30.

Liddicoat, A.J. (2016) Native and non-native speaker identities in interaction: Trajectories of power. *Applied Linguistics Review* 7 (4), 409–429.

Lindemann, S. and Campbell, M.-A. (2017) Attitudes towards non-native pronunciation. In O. Kang, R.I. Thomson and J.M. Murphy (eds) *The Routledge Handbook of Contemporary English Pronunciation* (pp. 399–412). Abingdon/New York: Routledge.

Lippi-Green, R. (2012) *English with an Accent: Language, Ideology and Discrimination in the United States* (2nd edn). London: Routledge.

Long, M.H. and Granena, G. (2018) Sensitive periods and language aptitude in second language acquisition. *Bilingualism: Language and Cognition* 21 (5), 926–927.

Lou, N.M. and Noels, K.A. (2019) Promoting growth in foreign and second language education: A research agenda for mindsets in language learning and teaching. *System* 86, Art. 102126.

Lucy, J.A. (2016) Recent advances in the study of linguistic relativity in historical context: A critical assessment. *Language Learning* 66 (3), 487–515.

MacIntyre, P.D., Gregersen, T. and Mercer, S. (eds) (2016) *Positive Psychology in SLA*. Bristol: Multilingual Matters.

Magnusson, J.E. and Stroud, C. (2012) High proficiency in markets of performance: A sociocultural approach to nativelikeness. *Studies in Second Language Acquisition* 34 (2), 321–345.

Major, R.C. (2007) Identifying a foreign accent in an unfamiliar language. *Studies in Second Language Acquisition* 29 (4), 539–556.

Martínez Agudo, J. de D. (ed) (2018) *Emotions in Second Language Teaching: Theory, Research and Teacher Education*. Cham: Springer.

Marx, N. (2002) Never quite a 'native speaker': Accent and identity in the L2 and the L1. *The Canadian Modern Language Review* 59 (2), 264–281.

Mayberry, R.I. and Kluender, R. (2018) Rethinking the critical period for language: New insights into an old question from American Sign Language. *Bilingualism: Language and Cognition* 21 (5), 886–905.

McCrocklin, S. and Link, S. (2016) Accent, identity, and a fear of loss? ESL students' perspectives. *Canadian Modern Language Review* 72 (1), 122–148.

Mercer, S. (2012) Dispelling the myth of the natural-born linguist. *ELT Journal* 66 (1), 22–29.

Mercer, S. and MacIntyre, P.D. (2014) Introducing positive psychology to SLA. *Studies in Second Language Learning and Teaching* 4 (2), 153–172.

Miller, E.R. and Kubota, R. (2013) Second language identity construction. In J.R. Herschensohn and M. Young-Scholten (eds) *The Cambridge Handbook of Second Language Acquisition* (pp. 230–250). Cambridge: Cambridge University Press.

Miyahara, M. (2015) *Emerging Self-Identities and Emotion in Foreign Language Learning: A Narrative-Oriented Approach*. Bristol: Multilingual Matters.

Moyer, A. (2007) Do language attitudes determine accent? A study of bilinguals in the USA. *Journal of Multilingual and Multicultural Development* 28 (6), 502–518.

Moyer, A. (2013) *Foreign Accent: The Phenomenon of Non-Native Speech*. Cambridge: Cambridge University Press.

Moyer, A. (2014) What's age got to do with it? Accounting for individual factors in second language accent. *Studies in Second Language Learning and Teaching* 3, 443–464.

Moyer, A. (2021) *The Gifted Language Learner: A Case of Nature or Nurture*. Cambridge: Cambridge University Press.

Muir, C. (2020) *Directed Motivational Currents and Language Education: Exploring Implications for Pedagogy*. Bristol: Multilingual Matters.

Muir, C. (2021) Motivation. In T. Gregersen and S. Mercer (eds) *The Routledge Handbook of the Psychology of Language Learning and Teaching* (pp. 124–136). New York: Routledge.

Muir, C., Dörnyei, Z. and Adolphs, S. (2019) Role models in language learning: Results of a large-scale international survey. *Applied Linguistics* 42 (1), 1–23.

Muñoz, C., Pujadas, G. and Pattemore, A. (2021) Audio-visual input for learning L2 vocabulary and grammatical constructions. *Second Language Research*.

Munro, M.J., Derwing, T.M. and Burgess, C.S. (2010) Detection of nonnative speaker status from content-masked speech. *Speech Communication* 52 (7–8), 626–637.

Murphy, J.M. (2020) *Teaching Pronunciation, Revised*. Alexandria, VA: TESOL Press.

Nagle, C.L., Trofimovich, P., O'Brien, M.G. and Kennedy, S. (2021) Beyond linguistic features: Exploring behavioral and affective correlates of comprehensible second language speech. *Studies in Second Language Acquisition* 44 (1), 255–270.

Nardo, D. and Reiterer, S.M. (2009) Musicality and phonetic language aptitude. In G. Dogil and S.M. Reiterer (eds) *Language Talent and Brain Activity* (pp. 213–256). Berlin/New York: De Gruyter Mouton.

Nasrollahi Shahri, M.N. (2018) Constructing a voice in English as a foreign language: Identity and engagement. *TESOL Quarterly* 52 (1), 85–109.

Nic Fhlannchadha, S. and Hickey, T.M. (2018) Minority language ownership and authority: Perspectives of native speakers and new speakers. *International Journal of Bilingual Education and Bilingualism* 21 (1), 38–53.

Nikolov, M. (2000) The critical period hypothesis reconsidered: Successful adult learners of Hungarian and English. *International Review of Applied Linguistics in Language Teaching* 38 (2), 109–124.

Norton, B. (1997) Language, identity, and the ownership of English. *TESOL Quarterly* 31 (3), 409–429.

Norton, B. (2013) *Identity and Language Learning: Extending the Conversation* (2nd edn). Bristol: Multilingual Matters.

Norton, B. and Toohey, K. (2001) Changing perspectives on good language learners. *TESOL Quarterly* 35 (2), 307–322.

Norton, B. and McKinney, C. (2011) An identity approach to second language acquisition. In D. Atkinson (ed.) *Alternative Approaches to Second Language Acquisition* (pp. 73–94). London: Routledge.

Norton, B. and Pavlenko, A. (2019) Imagined communities, identity, and English language learning in a multilingual world. In X. Gao (ed.) *Second Handbook of English Language Teaching* (Vol. 2, pp. 703–718). Cham: Springer.

Norton Peirce, B. (1995) Social identity, investment, and language learning. *TESOL Quarterly* 29 (1), 9–31.

Novoa, L., Fein, D. and Obler, L.K. (1988) Talent in foreign languages: A case study. In L.K. Obler and D. Fein (eds) *The Exceptional Brain: Neuropsychology of Talent and Special Abilities* (pp. 294–302). New York: Guilford Press.

Ohara, Y. (2001) Finding one's voice in Japanese: A study of the pitch levels of L2 users. In A. Pavlenko, A. Blackledge, I. Piller and M. Teutsch-Dwyer (eds) *Multilingualism, Second Language Learning, and Gender* (pp. 231–254). Berlin/New York: De Gruyter Mouton.

Ortega, L. (2014) Ways forward for a bi/multilingual turn in SLA. In S. May (ed.) *The Multilingual Turn: Implications for SLA, TESOL and Bilingual Education* (pp. 32–53). New York/Abingdon: Routledge.

Oxford, R.L. (2022) Emotion. In T. Gregersen and S. Mercer (eds) *The Routledge Handbook of the Psychology of Language Learning and Teaching* (pp. 178–190). New York: Routledge.

Oxford, R.L. and Amerstorfer, C.M. (eds) (2018) *Language Learning Strategies and Individual Learner Characteristics: Situating Strategy Use in Diverse Contexts*. London: Bloomsbury Academic.

Paikeday, T.M. (1985) *The Native Speaker is Dead! An Informal Discussion of a Linguistic Myth with Noam Chomsky and Other Linguists, Philosophers, Psychologists, and Lexicographers*. Toronto/New York: Paikeday Publishing.

Papi, M., Bondarenko, A.V., Mansouri, S., Feng, L. and Jiang, C. (2019) Rethinking L2 motivation research: The 2 × 2 model of L2 self-guides. *Studies in Second Language Acquisition* 41 (2), 337–361.

Patel, A.D. (2007) *Music, Language, and the Brain*. Oxford: Oxford University Press.

Pavlenko, A. (2006) Bilingual selves. In A. Pavlenko (ed.) *Bilingual Minds: Emotional Experience, Expression, and Representation* (pp. 1–33). Clevedon: Multilingual Matters.

Pavlenko, A. (2007) Autobiographic narratives as data in applied linguistics. *Applied Linguistics* 28 (2), 163–188.

Pawlak, M. (ed.) (2012) *New Perspectives on Individual Differences in Language Learning and Teaching*. Berlin: Springer.

Pennington, M.C. (2021) Teaching pronunciation: The state of the art 2021. *RELC Journal* 52 (1), 3–21.

Pennington, M.C. and Rogerson-Revell, P. (2019) *English Pronunciation Teaching and Research: Contemporary Perspectives*. London: Palgrave Macmillan.

Piller, I. (2002) Passing for a native speaker: Identity and success in second language learning. *Journal of Sociolinguistics* 6 (2), 179–208.

Pimsleur, P. (1966) *The Pimsleur Language Aptitude Battery*. New York: Harcourt Brace Jovanovic.

Reiterer, S.M., Hu, X., Sumathi, T.A. and Singh, N.C. (2013) Are you a good mimic? Neuro-acoustic signatures for speech imitation ability. *Frontiers in Psychology* 4, Art. 782.

Roehr-Brackin, K. (2018) *Metalinguistic Awareness and Second Language Acquisition*. New York: Routledge.

Rubin, J. (1975) What the 'good language learner' can teach us. *TESOL Quarterly* 9 (1), 41–51.

Sáfár, A. and Kormos, J. (2008) Revisiting problems with foreign language aptitude. *IRAL – International Review of Applied Linguistics in Language Teaching* 46 (2), 113–136.

Saito, K., Tran, M., Suzukida, Y., Sun, H., Magne, V. and Ilkan, M. (2019) How do second language listeners perceive the comprehensibility of foreign-accented speech?: Roles of first language profiles, second language proficiency, age, experience, familiarity, and metacognition. *Studies in Second Language Acquisition* 41 (5), 1133–1149.

Schneiderman, E.I. and Desmarais, C. (1988) The talented language learner: Some preliminary findings. *Interlanguage Studies Bulletin (Utrecht)* 4 (2), 91–109.

Schön, D. and Morillon, B. (2019) Music and language. In M.H. Thaut and D.A. Hodges (eds) *The Oxford Handbook of Music and the Brain* (pp. 390–416). Oxford: Oxford University Press.

Schunk, D.H. and DiBenedetto, M.K. (2015) Self-efficacy: Education aspects. In J.D. Wright (ed.) *International Encyclopedia of the Social & Behavioral Sciences* (pp. 515–521). London: Elsevier.

Shintani, N., Saito, K. and Koizumi, R. (2019) The relationship between multilingual raters' language background and their perceptions of accentedness and comprehensibility of second language speech. *International Journal of Bilingual Education and Bilingualism* 22 (7), 849–869.

Simons, M. and Smits, T.F.H. (eds) (2021) *Language Education and Emotions: Research into Emotions and Language Learners, Language Teachers and Educational Processes*. London: Routledge.

Singleton, D. (2017) Language aptitude: Desirable trait or acquirable attribute? *Studies in Second Language Learning and Teaching* 7 (1), 89–103.

Singleton, D.M. and Ryan, L. (2004) *Language Acquisition: The Age Factor* (2nd edn). Clevedon: Multilingual Matters.

Skehan, P. (1998) *A Cognitive Approach to Language Learning*. Oxford: Oxford University Press.

Slavkov, N., Melo-Pfeifer, S.M. and Kerschhofer-Puhalo, N. (2021) *The Changing Face of the 'Native Speaker': Perspectives from Multilingualism and Globalization*. Berlin: De Gruyter Mouton.

Slevc, L.R. and Miyake, A. (2006) Individual differences in second-language proficiency: Does musical ability matter? *Psychological Science* 17 (8), 675–681.

Sparks, R.L., Humbach, N., Patton, J. and Ganschow, L. (2011) Subcomponents of second-language aptitude and second-language proficiency. *The Modern Language Journal* 95 (2), 253–273.

Stern, H.H. (1975) What can we learn from the good language learner? *The Canadian Modern Language Review* 31 (4), 304–319.
Swan, A., Aboshiha, P. and Holliday, A. (eds) (2015) *(En)countering Native-Speakerism: Global Perspectives*. London: Palgrave Macmillan.
Szyszka, M. (2011) Foreign language anxiety and self-perceived English pronunciation competence. *Studies in Second Language Learning and Teaching* 1 (2), 283–300.
Szyszka, M. (2017) *Pronunciation Learning Strategies and Language Anxiety: In Search of an Interplay*. Cham: Springer.
Tardy, C.M. (2012) Current conceptions of voice. In K. Hyland and C.S. Guinda (eds) *Stance and Voice in Written Academic Genres* (pp. 34–48). London: Palgrave Macmillan.
Thompson, A.S. (2017) Don't tell me what to do! The anti-ought-to self and language learning motivation. *System* 67, 38–49.
Thomson, R.I. and Derwing, T.M. (2015) The effectiveness of L2 pronunciation instruction: A narrative review. *Applied Linguistics* 36 (3), 326–344.
Trofimovich, P. (2016) Interactive alignment: A teaching-friendly view of second language pronunciation learning. *Language Teaching* 49 (3), 411–422.
Trofimovich, P., Isaacs, T., Kennedy, S., Saito, K. and Crowther, D. (2016) Flawed self-assessment: Investigating self- and other-perception of second language speech. *Bilingualism: Language and Cognition* 19 (1), 122–140.
Trudgill, P. (2000) *Sociolinguistics: An Introduction to Language and Society* (4th edn). London: Penguin.
Ushioda, E. (2009) A person-in-context relational view of emergent motivation, self and identity. In Z. Dörnyei and E. Ushioda (eds) *Motivation, Language Identity and the L2 Self* (pp. 215–228). Bristol: Multilingual Matters.
Ushioda, E. (2020) *Language Learning Motivation: An Ethical Agenda for Research*. Oxford: Oxford University Press.
Ushioda, E. and Dörnyei, Z. (2017) Beyond global English: Motivation to learn languages in a multicultural world: Introduction to the special issue. *The Modern Language Journal* 101 (3), 451–454.
Verhoeven, L. and Vermeer, A. (2002) Communicative competence and personality dimensions in first and second language learners. *Applied Psycholinguistics* 23 (3), 361–374.
Wen, Z. (Edward), Biedroń, A. and Skehan, P. (2017) Foreign language aptitude theory: Yesterday, today and tomorrow. *Language Teaching* 50 (1), 1–31.
Wen, Z. (Edward), Skehan, P., Biedroń, A., Li, S. and Sparks, R.L. (eds) (2019) *Language Aptitude: Advancing Theory, Testing, Research and Practice*. New York/Abingdon/Oxford: Routledge.
Widdowson, H.G. (1994) The ownership of English. *TESOL Quarterly* 28 (2), 377–389.
Williams, M., Mercer, S. and Ryan, S. (2015) *Exploring Psychology in Language Learning and Teaching*. Oxford: Oxford University Press.
Wilson, M. (2003) Discovery listening: Improving perceptual processing. *ELT Journal* 57 (4), 335–343.
Winke, P., Gass, S. and Myford, C. (2013) Raters' L2 background as a potential source of bias in rating oral performance. *Language Testing* 30 (2), 231–252.
Yashima, T. (2002) Willingness to communicate in a second language: The Japanese EFL context. *The Modern Language Journal* 86 (1), 54–66.
Yee, D.M., Adams, S., Beck, A. and Braver, T.S. (2019) Age-related differences in motivational integration and cognitive control. *Cognitive, Affective, & Behavioral Neuroscience* 19 (3), 692–714.
Zentner, M. and Renaud, O. (2007) Origins of adolescents' ideal self: An intergenerational perspective. *Journal of Personality and Social Psychology* 92 (3), 557–574.
Zheng, C., Saito, K. and Tierney, A. (2020) Successful second language pronunciation learning is linked to domain-general auditory processing rather than music aptitude. *Second Language Research*. Advance online publication.

Index

Abrahamsson, 8, 11
accent: discrimination, 31–32, 82, 84–85, 92–93, 95–97, 100–103; identity and, 17–19, 100–102, 103. *See also* identity; native speakerism; pronunciation; social acceptance
affect. *See* anxiety; comfort; confidence; ownership; positive emotionality; unique bond
affiliation, 155–157, 159, 161, 163, 168. *See also* identity; ownership
age effects, 9–11, 86. *See also* Critical Period Hypothesis
ambivalence, 163–168
Amelia, 23; goals, 133, 135; interest, 63–64; musicality, 74; personality, 76–77, 79–80, 138, 139–140; phonetic convergence, 72; pronunciation, 95; relationships, 119; strategic effort, 108–110
anomie. *See* ambivalence
anxiety, 39, 100–102, 103, 123, 143–148. *See also* comfort; confidence; positive emotionality
aptitude, 11–12, 51, 66–69, 83–84, 86, 171; and exceptionality, 3, 5–6, 9, 12–13; phonetic dimension of, 13–16, 93. *See also* exceptionality; musicality; phonetic talent
assimilation. *See* integration; integrativeness
attention. *See also* interest; noticing capacity
attrition, 130–131, 164–165
auditory processing, 9, 14–17. *See also* phonetic talent

Austria, 59–60, 84, 108, 122–123, 130
awareness, 12, 14, 61–65, 73, 92, 149–150. *See also* noticing; pronunciation, attention to

Baran-Łucarz, 17–18, 103–104
Baumann, 83, 135
bias. *See* native speakerism
Biedroń, 1–2, 5–7, 67, 79
Big Five. *See* personality factors
Birdsong, 8, 10–11, 19
blending in. *See* integration; integrativeness
Block, 154–155, 164, 167
bond. *See* unique bond
books. *See also* reading
Bouchard, 32–33
Braver, 86
Brazil, 38, 48, 70, 99

Canada, 56, 62, 70, 80, 82, 93, 137, 165
Canagarajah, 30, 152
Capucine, 23, 28; accent, 91, 98, 100–102, 103; effort, 133; learning process, 40–41; family influence, 48–49, 51, 117–118; identity, 157; integration, 82; ownership, 149; relationships, 120; strategies, 132, 139; success, 82–83
Carl, 23; demotivation, 84; relationships, 45, 119; Global English, 60; goals, 92; naturalistic learning, 45–46; other languages, 68; phonetic convergence, 72; strategies, 112, 132
Carroll, 13–14
childhood exposure, 44–46, 52–53. *See also* age effects; Critical Period Hypothesis

China, 38, 73, 92, 96–97
Chinese characters, 61–62, 69. *See also* Mandarin
classroom dynamics. *See* social acceptance
Clément, 151
Colin, 23; blending in, 116, 124; confidence, 75, 145; comparisons, 135–136; family influence, 51–52, 93; identity, 159, 162, 167; immersion, 58, 65; interest, 63; mimicry, 71–72, 98, 171; music, 73–74, 108; nativelikeness as phenomenon, 40–41; passing, 37; relationships, 115–120; strategies, 108, 110–11, 131
comedy. *See* humour; theatrical streak
comfort, 40–41, 99, 142–143, 146–149, 152, 156, 168, 172
communicative approach. *See* strategies, speaking
community influences, 55–57, 65, 120, 124–126, 130–131; confidence from, 144–145. *See also* family; integration; relationships; social expectations; workplace
comparisons. *See* competitiveness
competitiveness, 83–84, 117–118, 123, 128, 135–136, 141, 145
computer. *See also* internet
comprehensibility, 102–103
confidence, 40–41, 128–129, 143–149, 151–152, 161; early development of, 47, 128; identity and, 157; as personality trait, 76; from pronunciation, 19, 104; as result of feedback, 83, 123, 129; from success, 128–129, 135, 141. *See also* comfort
convergence. *See* phonetic convergence
Cook, 32–33
corrections. *See* feedback
cosmopolitan orientation, 17, 46–49, 76–79, 81, 157–159
CPH. *See also* Critical Period Hypothesis
Critical Period Hypothesis, 1, 9–11, 20. *See also* age effects
Cutler, 8
cultural products. *See also* internet, reading, television

dialects. *See also* varieties
Discord. *See also* internet
De Costa, 28–29
Denny, 23; confidence, 144–146; difficulties, 68, 107; English, 22; identity, 154, 157, 159–160, 163, 165, 168; interest, 63–64; maintaining motivation, 111, 132–133; mimicry, 71–72, 98; multiple language learning, 51; music, 74; ownership, 148–150; passing, 36; pronunciation attention, 94; role models, 99
Derwing, 18–19, 32, 102
Dewaele, 8, 32
discipline, 107–109, 112, 114. *See also* effort; habits; persistence; strategies
directed motivational currents (DMCs), 81, 83–85
discrimination. *See* native speakerism
disinterest, 51, 61, 137
Dogil, 13–15, 79
Dörnyei, 6, 8, 10–12, 21, 29, 52–53, 64–65, 67, 71, 81, 84–87, 89, 103, 125, 129–130, 140, 167, 170, 173, 178–181, 185, 188
Dutch, 47, 49, 59, 61, 161. *See also* Netherlands, the
Dweck, 139

early exposure. *See* childhood exposure
effort: conscious, 79–80, 85, 97–99, 107–109, 111, 113; as effortless, 68, 91, 112–114; sustaining, 127–129, 131; unconscious, 105–106. *See also* habits
ego boundaries, 17–18
emotions. *See* positive emotionality; unique bond
endurance. *See* persistence
English, 3, 50, 57, 63–65, 73, 166; accent, 19, 92, 95, 101–103; needing, 47, 49, 61, 123, 127–130; varieties of, 9, 39, 72. *See also* Global English
enjoyment, 71–72, 106–107, 111, 114, 116, 128, 132, 137–139; lack of, 51, 56–57, 137. *See also* positive emotionality

exams, 57, 133–134, 137–138
expertise, 155–157, 159, 162–165, 168, 173. *See also* identity
exceptionality, 1–2, 4-5, 20, 34–35; characteristics, 5-6, 11-13; Critical Period Hypothesis, 9-11; Hyltenstam and, 2–5, 10; learning process, 7; limitations, 7-9; pronunciation and, 13–20; scarcity of research on, 2, 7. *See also* nativelikeness; polyglots
expectations. *See* social expectations
extroversion, 79–81. *See also* personality factors

family influences, 46–49, 51–52, 70, 89, 125; as grounding, 165–166; parents, 45, 47–53, 59, 73, 93, 96, 117–118, 128; siblings, 44, 48–49, 51, 60, 75, 93, 117–118; unsupportive, 51–52
feedback, 83, 133–136; asking for, 109–110, 116, 121; confidence from, 96–97, 104, 129, 145, 136; negative, 95, 138–139; as progress check, 123–124; teacher, 94
films. *See also* television
Finland, 49–50, 106
first language (L1). *See* L1
foreign accent syndrome (FAS), 14
fossilisation, 19, 71, 130–131, 172
France, 19, 47–49, 100–101, 111, 136, 159
French, 56–57, 62–64, 68–69, 93, 116, 136–138, 145
friendships. *See* relationships

Gardner, 52, 60, 64, 82, 115, 125, 151
gender, 22, 59, 63
German, 41, 46, 50–51, 58, 63, 65, 68, 84–85, 107–108, 111, 116–120, 145, 157, 159, 161
Germany, 57, 82, 93, 108, 122–123, 125, 163–164
giftedness. *See* exceptionality
Global English, 44–45, 49–50, 52–53, 60–61, 150–151; resources as result of, 44–46, 53, 59, 73, 93, 160
Gnevsheva, 9, 36–37
goals, 75, 121, 130–134, 137–138, 140; energising, 108, 137; external, 111, 133–134; incremental, 128, 131, 133–134; integration, 81–83; nativelikeness, 34–35, 42, 75, 83, 99, 107, 124, 154; realistic, 128, 130–134, 144. *See also* competitiveness, directed motivational currents; vision
Granena, 10, 12
grit. *See* persistence; resilience
group membership, 9, 18, 33–34, 38–39, 42, 99–102, 103, 120, 154. *See also* identity, erasure of
Guiora, 17–18, 102

habits, 110, 112, 129, 131–132, 140–141
Hanna, 23; aptitude, 67, 134–135; Global English, 50, 53; identity, 162–163, 165; multiple language learning, 64, 137; relationships, 119–120; strategies, 106–17; variety, 37
Heidrun, 23; ambition, 130, 136; aptitude, 68; effort, 107–108, 112; identity, 82, 163; integration, 82; interest, 59–60; music, 74, 112; personality, 79; relationships, 120; role models, 100; variety, 37
Henry, A., 87, 129, 140, 167
'High-Level Proficiency in Second Language Use' programme. *See* exceptionality, Hyltenstam and; Hyltenstam
Holliday, 31, 34
Houghton, 31–33
Hungarian, 3, 64, 65, 77–79, 95, 121–122, 139, 155
humour, 71–72, 79, 100, 131, 150, 160. *See also* theatrical streak
Hyltenstam, 1, 3–4, 7–9, 11–12, 32–33, 40, 86, 170

Iceland, 34, 38, 70–71
identity, 143, 154–168, 172–173: accent and, 17–19, 101–102; erasure of, 162–165; family and, 165–166; (inter)national, 101, 157–158, 162–166; L1-associated, 126, 162–165; personal, 156–158; professional, 82, 166–167; separation of, 159–162; social, 115, 125–126. *See also* ambivalence; group membership; ownership; unique bond; vision; voice

imagined community, 124–126, 130, 154. *See also* integration; identity
immersion, 44, 46-48, 55–60, 84-85, 106–108, 131, 138–139, 143, 145, 155. *See also* school exchanges; study abroad
inheritance, 155, 159, 162. *See also* identity; ownership
instruction. *See also* pronunciation instruction; school; teachers
instrumental motivation, 60–61
integration, 73, 81–83, 89–90, 111, 115–116, 120, 124–126, 146, 162, 164–165. *See also* comfort; integrativeness
integrativeness, 77, 115, 126. *See also* integration
intelligibility, 102–103
interest, 63, 112–113, 137–138, 157–158; metalinguistic, 61–64, 109, 112; in non-linguistic activities, 44–46, 61, 108; relationships triggering, 117–118. *See also* cosmopolitan orientation; pronunciation; unique bond
international posture, 77, 89. *See also* cosmopolitan orientation
internet, 44–46, 52–53, 59, 85, 100, 111–112, 132
introversion. *See* extroversion
investment, 154, 167–168
Ira, 23, 49; accent, 94, 101; aptitude, 67; mimicry, 71, 73; Dutch vs. Global English, 49, 59, 61; goal-setting, 133; identity, 164–165; other languages, 137; relationships, 47, 120; personality, 80
Italian, 56–57, 68, 82, 122, 132, 162
Italy, 38, 56–57, 78, 93, 132

Japanese, 38, 48, 61–62, 68, 74, 81, 121
Joy, 24, 69–71; affective strategies, 80, 136–137, 139; enjoyment, 137; fossilisation, 131; integration and identity, 34, 124, 165; mimicry, 70, 99; music, 70–71, 73; other languages, 22, 137; passing, 38; relationships, 48, 100, 121; self-monitoring, 71, 74, 76
Judith, 24; aptitude, 67; early bilingualism, 48, 53; identity, 158, 167; integration, 124, 148; musicality, 74; passing, 36, 91; pronunciation, 95; strategies, 97; unique bond, 58–59

Kerry, 24; family, 52, 93; humour, 79; identity, 162; integration, 82, 94; metalinguistic awareness, 64; other languages, 68, 137; passing, 38; role models, 118, 122; strategies, 94, 132; unique bond, 55–57
Kinzler, 17, 33
Kormos, 12, 86, 88, 173
Kramsch, 39, 152, 167
Kristin, 24; classroom influences, 101; comfort, 147; new global generation, 44–45; family, 49, 51; integration, 124; progress checks, 134; role models, 100, 118; unique bond, 59, 63
Kristopher, 24; aptitude, 69; family, 51–52, 121; identity, 165, 168; music, 73–74; other languages, 69; passing, 36–38; pronunciation, 91; strategies, 80–81, 97, 109–110; unique bond, 61–62

L1, 41; accent, 14–15, 72–73, 92–93, 96, 140; comfort in, 148; comparisons with, 41, 63–65, 134; identity, 159–165, 166–168, 172–173. *See also* attrition
Lamb, 55, 65
language identity. *See* identity
languages other than English (LOTEs), 53, 64, 77. *See also* Global English
Lantolf, 87
learning resources. *See* resources
learning strategies. *See* strategies
Leaver, 5, 7, 114
legitimacy, 35, 144, 149–152, 166. *See also* ownership
Lesley, 24, 84–85; accent, 92, 93; aptitude, 67; enjoyment, 137; family, 48, 53, 93; identity, 163–164; integration, 81–82, 85, 124, 148; personality, 75, 139; relationships, 120–121; work, 122–123
Liddicoat, 39
linguistic standards. *See* standards
Lippi-Green, 32, 103
Lisa, 24; family, 49, 53; identity, 163; immersion, 131; relationships, 119;

strategies, 75–76, 134; teachers, 58, 116, 118; work, 84, 122–123
listening. *See* strategies
Livia, 24; aptitude, 68; confidence, 143–145; difficulties, 144; effort, 107, 112–113; mimicry, 71–72; music, 59–60, 93; ownership, 149, 166; passing, 36–37; progress checks, 134; pronunciation, 91; role models, 99; unique bond, 60, 65
Long, 10, 12
LOTEs. *See* languages other than English (LOTEs)
Lou, 25; family, 48–49, 51, 117–118; identity, 83, 158, 160; personality, 79–80; positive emotionality, 137–138; pronunciation difficulties, 101; unique bond, 63

MacIntyre, 60, 82, 136, 143
Mandarin, 38, 48, 51–52, 61–62, 64, 69, 73–74, 80, 91, 96–97, 109–110, 161–162. *See also* Chinese
Marjan, 25, 127–129; confidence, 143, 145; family, 48, 121; feedback, 83; music, 73–74; passing, 36; persistence, 127–129, 135; pronunciation, 94; work, 122–124; vision, 128, 130
maturational constraints. *See* age effects
memory, 5, 14, 62, 67–69, 110; strategies for, 56, 132. *See also* aptitude
Mercer, 71, 90, 136
metalinguistic awareness. *See* awareness
mimicry, 70–73, 87–89, 98–100, 103, 171. *See also* phonetic convergence
mindsets, 5, 139–141, 144; international, 22, 47, 49–50. *See also* cosmopolitan orientation; positive emotionality
mistakes, 36, 74–76, 79–80, 88–89, 109, 116, 138; noticing others', 94; pronunciation hiding, 91, 102; at work, 123, 134. *See also* self-monitoring
Modern Language Aptitude Test (MLAT), 13–14
monitoring. *See* self-monitoring
motivation–cognition interaction, 68–69, 86, 171. *See also* persistence

Moyer, 2, 4–7, 16–17, 19, 20, 33–35, 43, 54, 87, 89, 104, 113–114, 168
Muir, 82, 84–85, 99, 103, 122, 125
multicompetence, 32–33
multilingual learning. *See also* multiple language learning
multiple language learning, 51, 61–62, 116, 130, 157. *See also* Colin; Denny; Kristopher; non-nativelike second/additional languages; polyglots; Rianne
Munro, 18–19, 37, 102
music, 70–71; musicality, 16–17, 71, 76, 87–88, 170–171; musical training, 20, 73–74, 96, 108, 112, 139; pronunciation and, 93; unique bond and, 59, 63–65, 73. *See also* pitch; pronunciation

Nardo, 16, 20, 87–88
narrative approach, 27–29
national identity. *See* identity
nativelikeness: defining, 4, 22; benefits of, 158, 160–161, 164–167; as goal, 33–35, 39, 81–83, 103, 130, 154; comparisons with native speakers, 7–8; as group membership, 34, 37–38, 162–165; as phenomenon, 40–41, 148; polyglotism and, 3; as source of confidence, 146–148, 165–167; unwanted aspects of, 39, 162–165. *See also* exceptionality; passing
native speaker: as myth, 30–31; as term, 32–33; norms, 7–8; phenomenology of, 39–41
native speakerism, 31–32
naturalistic learning, 15, 44–46, 52–53, 105–107, 109–110, 127; vs. formal learning contexts, 11–12, 18, 44. *See also* New Global Generation
negative experiences, 52, 54, 62, 80, 84–85, 94–95, 100–103, 136–140
Netflix. *See also* television
Netherlands, the, 44, 46–47, 49, 53, 61, 94, 101, 103. *See also* Dutch
New Global Generation, 44–46, 52–53
non-nativelike second/additional languages. *See* other languages

Nordic countries, 53. *See also* Finland; Sweden; Norway, Iceland
Norton, 2, 114, 152, 154, 167, 173
Norway, 44–45, 58–59, 101, 124, 148
Norwegian, 97, 124, 158, 167
noticing, 65, 93–94, 96

openness to experience, 5–6, 15, 76–77. *See also* cosmopolitan orientation; personality factors
other languages, 22, 65, 68–71, 137–138
ownership, 35, 143–144, 148–153, 166, 172
Oxford, 114, 136

Paikeday, 30–31
parents. *See* family influences
passing, 8–9, 35, 91, 116, 155; appearance affecting, 38; domains of, 36; interlocutors affecting, 37; linguistic competencies, 38; pronunciation and, 13, 95; resistance to, 162–165; varieties and, 9, 116
passion. *See* interest; unique bond
passive learning. *See* naturalistic learning; New Global Generation
Pavlenko, 27, 154, 168
Pawlak, 1, 2, 5, 7, 67, 71
Peng, 25, 96–97; comfort, 147; comparisons, 136; identity, 158–159, 161–162; pronunciation attention, 73, 92, 102; noticing, 94; strategies, 74, 76, 105, 132; unique bond, 64; vision, 130
Pennington, 19–20, 102–103
perfectionism. *See* mistakes; self-monitoring
persistence, 108, 127–141; breakdown cover, 138–140. *See also* goals; habits; positive emotionality; progress checks; resilience; vision
personality factors, 5–6, 76–81, 140–141. *See also* competitiveness; extroversion; openness to experience
person-in-context approach, 27
phonetic convergence, 14–15, 72–73, 87
phonetic talent, 13–17. *See also* pronunciation
Piller, 9, 36

Pimsleur Language Aptitude Battery (PLAB), 14
pitch, 15–16, 98, 161–162
polyglots, 2–5, 12, 114, 170
Portuguese, 22, 48, 70–71
positive emotionality, 70–71, 83–84, 120–121, 129, 136–138, 140–143, 156–157, 168; pronunciation and, 19, 171–172; strategies for maintaining, 76, 103–104. *See also* enjoyment; pronunciation; unique bond
progress checks, 123, 128–129, 133–136, 140–141. *See also* competitiveness; feedback; goals
pronunciation, 13–20: attention to, 56, 63–64, 73, 91–104; family emphasis, 92–93; instruction, 19–20, 94–95, 103–104; social benefits of, 73, 95–97; as source of confidence, 19, 146, 171–172. *See also* accent; mimicry
psychological calm. *See* comfort, confidence
psychological reactance, 84–85, 139–141. *See also* resilience

radio, 59, 70, 73–74, 93, 97, 108
Ranko, 25; integration, 81–82; personality, 79; role models, 99–100; strategies, 111, 132
reading, 44–45, 49, 57–59, 63, 84–85, 108, 111, 119
reflexive thematic analysis, 28
Reiterer, 6, 15–16, 20, 79, 88
relationships, 115–126; platonic, 59–62, 99–100, 106, 116, 119–120, 122, 125, 132; romantic, 85, 117, 120–121, 131. *See also* family influences; role models
relativity, linguistic, 161
religion. *See* spirituality
resilience, 68, 79–80, 129, 138–141. *See also* persistence; psychological reactance
resources, 43–46, 89; availability of, 3, 96, 155; making use of, 54, 113–114. *See also* internet; radio; reading; television
Rianne, 25, 46–48; early confidence, 46–48, 53; confidence, 136, 145; Global English, 49; identity, 161, 166; interest, 61, 68, 81; multiple

language learning, 130; phonetic convergence, 72–73; strategies, 75; work, 84, 122–123
Rivers, 31–32
role models, 98–100, 103, 118–122, 125
routines. *See* effort; habits
Ryan, 6, 11–12, 29, 71, 86

Saito, 9, 15, 103
Samuli, 25; interest, 77; passing, 36; pronunciation, 91, 92
Sara, 25; aptitude, 67–68; confidence, 68, 146; Global English, 45–46; identity, 160–162; integration, 82–83, 124; persistence, 133–134, 139, 146; strategies, 80
Sarah, 25, 77–79; accent, 92; cosmopolitan orientation, 77–79; identity, 158; introversion, 80; mimicry, 71–72; music, 73–74; pronunciation, 95; relationships, 116, 121–122; resilience, 138–140; strategies, 80, 109, 112
Scandinavia. *See* Norway; Sweden
school, 100–103, 134: exchanges, 58–59, 116, 119, 136; as negative experience, 51, 56–57, 62, 69; as positive experience, 48–49, 82–84. *See also* teachers
self-efficacy, 48–49, 53, 83, 151–152. *See also* confidence; comfort
self-monitoring, 5, 70–76, 88–89, 111, 143–144
Sensitive Period Hypothesis. *See* Critical Period Hypothesis
shame, 19, 100–102. *See also* anxiety
Shinhye, 26; comfort/confidence, 146–148; group membership, 38; identity, 157–158, 161, 166–167; integration, 82; passing, 38; pronunciation, 95, 102; relationships, 100–101, 118; strategies, 112, 132
siblings. *See* family influences
Singleton, 11, 86
social acceptance: of language learning, 46–52; of pronunciation, 18–19, 100–103. *See also* integration; group membership; social expectations

social expectations, 49–54, 89, 115, 119, 122–123, 126. *See also* teacher expectations
social media. *See also* internet
speech convergence. *See* phonetic convergence
spirituality, 70–71, 139, 157
Sri Lanka, 50
standards, 151: linguistic, 34–35; native speaker, 2, 7–8, 13, 31. *See also* native speaker
strategies, 7, 113–115, 140–141; creative, 80, 108–112; development over time of, 111, 149–150; listening, 80–81, 97; motivational, 64–65, 133–134, 139; pronunciation, 91, 93–94, 97–100, 103–104; relaxed approach to, 105–107; speaking, 75–76, 80, 98–100, 132; vocabulary learning, 105–106, 109–112, 132; writing, 132. *See also* habits, mimicry; naturalistic learning
study abroad, 55–57, 59–60, 65, 108–109, 116–117. *See also* school, exchanges
sustaining motivation. *See* persistence
Sweden, 44–45, 60
Szyszka, 103–104

talent. *See* exceptionality
teachers, 125; expectations of, 119; intervention of, 100–103, 159; positive influence of, 116, 118–119, 159; as negative influence, 137–138; as role models, 100, 116, 118, 121–122
technology. *See also* internet; television; radio
television, 44–46, 49, 51–52, 70, 78, 82, 84–85, 94, 160
Thamarasie, 26; Global English, 50; identity, 157; musicality, 74; ownership, 150–152
thematic analysis. *See* reflexive thematic analysis
Thompson, 83, 139
theatrical streak, 79, 87, 160
Theresa, 26; aptitude, 67–68; identity, 163, 165, 168; integration, 82; naturalistic learning, 105; ownership, 150, 152; relationships, 75, 121;

speech convergence, 73; unique bond, 57–58
Timur, 26; confidence, 143; identity, 154, 163, 165–166, 168; mimicry, 98–99; ownership, 149; persistence, 140; pronunciation, 91, 94; self-monitoring, 74; strategies, 80, 98–99, 104, 112, 132; unmarkedness, 39, 82
travelling, 48, 53, 55–61, 65, 76–79, 108, 116–117, 157–158, 164. *See also* school, exchanges; study abroad
Trofimovich, 19, 92, 99, 102–103

unique bond, 64–65, 89–90, 149, 152–153, 156–157, 171–172; community, 55–58, 81; culture, 58–60; metalinguistic awareness, 61–64, 73; pragmatism, 60–61
United Kingdom, 37, 39, 59–60, 77–79, 92, 111, 120, 127, 143
United States, 46, 48, 101, 147, 157, 166
unmarkedness, 39, 82, 89–90, 146, 154. *See also* nativelikeness
Ushioda, 27, 33, 52–53, 64, 81, 89, 125, 167
Uwe, 26; comfort, 147–148; East Germany, 3; effort, 111, 113, 138; identity, 155–156, 164, 166; 'mongrel' accent, 39, 93; music, 59, 74; nativelikeness as goal, 30, 111; other languages, 65, 68; ownership, 149–150, 152; unique bond, 64

varieties, 9, 37, 39, 63, 98; first language, 73, 92, 95–96. *See also* accent; passing; Uwe, 'mongrel' accent
video games. *See also* internet
vision, 94, 128–131, 140
vocabulary, 37, 45, 118; acquiring, 85, 105, 109–113, 132; as interest, 63
voice, 142–143, 146–149, 152, 159, 172

Wattpad, 59. *See also* internet; writing
Wen, 12, 67
William, 26; competitiveness, 83, 136; internet, 45–46; other languages, 68; persistence, 138–139; pronunciation, 96, 102; relationships, 93, 99; variety, 63
workplace, 84–85, 90, 122–124, 126–128, 130, 135, 144, 166–167; mistakes, 75; pronunciation and, 95, 97, 103
writing, 160: as interest, 45, 61, 63, 143; as strategy, 59, 62, 109, 112, 118, 123, 132; proficiency, 36, 95, 111, 134, 151, 166

Yashima, 77
YouTube. *See also* internet

Zheng, 16

If you'd like to read the participants' stories in more depth you might also like the companion ebook:

STORIES FROM EXCEPTIONAL LANGUAGE LEARNERS WHO HAVE ACHIEVED NATIVELIKE PROFICIENCY

Katarina Mentzelopoulos and Zoltán Dörnyei
with Capucine Trotignon

40% DISCOUNT

~~£15 / $25 / €20~~   £9 / $15 / €12

MULTILINGUAL MATTERS

Just use the code STORIES40 on our website www.multilingual-matters.com

Prices correct at time of print

MULTILINGUAL MATTERS

For Product Safety Concerns and Information please contact our EU Authorised Representative:

Easy Access System Europe

Mustamäe tee 50

10621 Tallinn

Estonia

gpsr.requests@easproject.com